Special Issues from the *Teachers College Record*

JONAS F. SOLTIS, Series Editor

ADOLESCENCE IN THE 1990s

Risk and Opportunity

RUBY TAKANISHI
Editor

Teachers College, Columbia University
New York and London

Published by Teachers College Press, 1234 Amsterdam Avenue
New York, NY 10027

Originally published in *Teachers College Record*, v. 94, no. 3, Spring 1993.

Library of Congress Cataloging-in-Publication Data

Adolescence in the 1990s: risk and opportunity / Ruby Takanishi, editor.
p. cm.—(Special issues for the Teachers college record)
"Originally published in Teachers College Record, v. 94, no. 3, Spring 1993"—T.p. verso.
Includes bibliographical references and index.
ISBN 0-8077-3330-X (pbk. : alk. paper)
1. Adolescence. 2. Teenagers—United States. I. Takanishi, Ruby. II. Series.
HQ796.A33258 1993
305.23'5—dc20 93-36058

ISBN 0-8077-3330-X

Printed on acid-free paper

Manufactured in the United States of America

99 98 97 96 95 94 93 7 6 5 4 3 2 1

Erratum (p. i):

Ellen Condliffe Lagemann is both the editor of the *Teachers College Record* and the series editor of Special Issues from the *Teachers College Record*

Contents

Foreword

ELLEN CONDLIFFE LAGEMANN
Teachers College, Columbia University

Long before G. Stanley Hall popularized the term *adolescence* at the start of this century, the years between childhood and adulthood were of concern to parents, teachers, ministers, and public authorities. As early as 1649, the "uncivil carriage" of Massachusetts youth and their escape from parental "government" were noted in Middlesex County court records; and in the 1680s, the Puritan divine Cotton Mather called for the formation of "Associations of Young Folks" to direct the energy of youth into positive channels.[1] However expressed—as worry about the health, education, or behavior of young people or as hope for positive growth and achievement—discussion of adolescence has been a constant refrain in the United States. The stage of life that romantics from Rousseau to Hall have described as a second birth seems always to have stirred the full range of aspirations and anxieties associated with generational change.

That said, there is cause today for renewed concern about youth. Much is amiss in the world in which we ask young people to grow up. Horrifying violence greets too many of them at their front doors. Too often, illegal drugs and the other accoutrements of peer-sanctioned dangerous activity are more readily available than adults willing and available to talk, take a walk, or otherwise simply spend time with young people. Even leaving aside the extremes of teen stress, the problems facing young people are myriad.

It is noteworthy, for example, that a significant proportion of teens today are what might be described as "overengaged." Some years ago, Dale Mann, professor of education at Teachers College, Columbia University, described people in this group as "super youth"—while enrolled in school full time, they also work, after school or at night, and, in some instances, they also carry family responsibilities and pursue extracurricular activities.[2] Not only are such overengaged students vulnerable to physical exhaustion, they have little chance for the seemingly aimless musing and daydreaming that enable one to ponder who one wants to be and where one wants to go in life. Beyond that, teens often work in dead-end, age-segregated, routine jobs such as those at McDonald's. The wages they earn may be sufficient to buy the expensive jeans and sneakers that are the style in our consumerist economy, but the cost in terms of time *not* spent on schoolwork or other more enduringly generative activities is high. That employment among school-going youth is more prevalent in the United States than in Canada, Sweden, or Japan is not irrelevant to comparative measures of school achievement.[3]

Equally worrisome in a different way are data gathered by two University of Chicago psychologists, Mihaly Csikszentmihalyi and Reed Larson, for their study *Being Adolescent: Conflict and Growth in the Teenage Years*. By using an ingenious beeper system that enabled them to track teens throughout the day, wherever they were and whatever they were doing, Csikszentmihalyi and Larson were able to identify when and under what circumstances adolescents experienced "flow"—a state of self-transcendence in which people feel "harmony between dimensions of consciousness: between goals, thoughts, emotions, and activations."[4]

Sadly but not surprisingly, Csikszentmihalyi and Larson found that flow was more commonly associated with leisure activities than with time spent in school. They also discovered that regardless of a student's ability, performance was best in classes that were enjoyable. "Educators might stop worrying about how to transmit information," they suggested, "and concentrate instead on how to make learning enjoyable, because only when going to school becomes a flow activity will students be motivated to learn on their own, and grow in the process. Otherwise, education becomes just another alienating experience."[5]

Equally important, they observed, adolescents need help learning how to transform challenges that are not initially enjoyable into experiences that can evoke concentration, active engagement, and the other characteristics of flow. To do this, Csikszentmihalyi and Larson maintain, adult role models are necessary to provide "examples of how to choose among goals, how to persevere, how to have patience, how to recognize the challenges of life and enjoy meeting them. We can help adolescents by letting them share our own hard-won habits of skill and discipline," they insist.[6]

Unfortunately, however, there are woefully few opportunities for learning by observing and doing with a skilled, caring adult guide. Schools are not organized to allow teachers to model learning as a process of engagement and problem solving, and adults in other settings, including the family, are often themselves under far too much personal, financial, or job-related stress to serve as models of personal command, equanimity, and concentration. Sadly, Csikszentmihalyi and Larson's study, which is consistent with many others, leads one to conclude that we are not offering young people the human resources and the possibilities for pleasure in learning that they need and deserve.

Clearly, then, there are many negatives prompting a renewal of concern about youth, but compelling positive considerations are also involved. For several reasons, the time is right for reconsidering what we know about adolescence and how that knowledge can be put to use. As Ruby Takanishi, executive director of the Carnegie Council on Adolescent Development, explains in *Adolescence in the 1990s: Risk and Opportunity*, more than ever before there is a widespread consensus today concerning the needs of *all* American youth. It is widely agreed that young people must "experience secure relationships with a few human beings," she writes. Each individual needs "to be a valued member of groups that provide mutual aid and caring relationships, to become a competent individual who can cope with the exigencies of everyday life, and to believe in a promising future in work, family, and citizenship." Each individual needs the care and challenge that comes from belonging to a community, whether that community takes the form of a family, a school, an after-school program, a religious organization, or a neighborhood. Apart from such associations, one cannot experience the shelter and acceptance combined with expectations and responsibilities that are now understood as essential ingredients in the transition to adulthood.

The new consensus of which Ruby Takanishi writes derives from new developments in the world of research. Increasingly, throughout the university, scholars are moving beyond the disciplinary boundaries that have shaped their questions and conceptions of method throughout this century in order to center their work in problem-based, cross-disciplinary conceptions of knowledge. This reconfiguration of knowledge has had striking and important effects on the study of adolescence. Biologically based views of adolescence are no longer seen as distinct from views that are primarily grounded in the social sciences. Instead, as S. Shirley Feldman and Glen R. Elliott have noted in their introduction to *At the Threshold: The Developing Adolescent*, the challenge is determining how "biological drives and social prescriptions *combine* to define adolescence in the United States today."[7] This new emphasis on investigating interactions between biology and society is auspicious because it promises a lessening of the determinism that has too often characterized studies of human behavior. We should now be able to avoid both the overly pessimistic, sometimes almost Darwinist determinism associated with exclusively biological conceptions and the overly optimistic, naively perfectionist social determinism associated with a total faith in social engineering.

If current views of adolescence reflect new possibilities for collaboration within the academy, they also stem from growing appreciation of the need for collaboration among all the professions involved in actually providing health, education, and social services to youth. Today, professionals in fields other than education are becoming increasingly interested in schools and schooling because they are recognizing the primacy of schools as a site for youth intervention. As H. Craig Heller, chairman of the program in human biology at Stanford, explains to us in this collection, health professionals and social policy analysts now understand that "any campaign to improve adolescent health must involve the schools to be successful. . . . We have the broadest access to young people in the schools. . . . Through the schools we have the best chance to present useful knowledge to adolescents to help them make meaningful and wise life decisions."

Cross-professional interest in education holds great promise for the comprehensive policies and multifaceted programs adolescents need. Not surprisingly, however, some educators will regard the strategic interest in schools that Heller and others have expressed with suspicion. They are keenly aware that, too often in the past, professionals from outside of education as well as concerned citizens' groups have sought to pursue their agendas through the schools without first establishing genuine, equal collaboration with teachers, principals, and other school administrators. In the past, this has undermined whatever benefit reform initiatives might otherwise have had since new curricula or technologies were quickly set aside when their primary sponsors left the schools.

History aside, we live at a time when negative criticisms of education have tended to obscure the daily successes and the continuing effectiveness of many schools. Achievement levels that are too low are featured in the press without accompanying data to suggest the extraordinary difficulties involved in educating. This has resulted in justifiable resentment among many educators, and outsiders eager to work with them will have to proceed with respect and an eager ear if the promise of the present moment is to be actualized. Teachers and administrators want help in meeting the enormous challenges involved in educating children and they will welcome outsiders who can bring new resources, new perspectives, and a new commitment to genuine collaboration in behalf of youth. To the extent, then, that there is a willingness on the part of external professionals to explore possibilities for establishing and sustaining real partnerships with educators, to improve curricula, deliver health and social services, increase the holding power of schools, and do much else besides, broadening and merging definitions of professional service domains promise considerable benefit to adolescents.

Finally, one might note that consensus concerning the importance of community membership for adolescents reflects and should advance a recognition that there is a community of need among people of all age groups. This means, first and most obviously, that the needs of young people are not essentially different from those of other humans, younger and older. Although age-related developmental challenges should not be forgotten, recent research indicates that adolescence is neither as stormy nor as difficult to survive as was once generally believed. Growing up does, of course, involve physical, emotional, intellectual, and social challenge. There are always tensions associated with growth. But if adolescents were once the James Dean-style rebels we imagined, or the "Angry and Beat" young men of Paul Goodman's *Growing Up Absurd*, they are not seen that way today. Eager for connections with other people, younger and older, adolescents may need "space," but, like the rest of us, they also need opportunities for conversations and for a great variety of formal and informal apprenticeships.

Beyond that, new views of adolescents should support a more generous view of human need, generally. More often than not, the well-being of any discrete group within a society is dependent on the well-being of all the other groups and an individual's competence in one setting is related to his or her experience in other settings. Adolescents cannot thrive in our society if adults are under stress; and, rhetoric notwithstanding, problems at work cannot be left at the shop door.

In the need for reciprocal interchange evident among today's youth, then, there is an opportunity for bold social thinking. Significant interchange between young people and adults requires commitments of time and caring on the part of both, and this, in turn, requires supportive social structures—to begin, schools that count time for informal conversation as part of a teacher's regular workload; public libraries and recreation facilities that have ample staff, well trained as educators or youth workers; and, most important of all, work places that provide flextime, family leave, and opportunities to involve young people (for example, the children of employees) in their daily operations. It is not necessary to elaborate the very long chain of interconnected needs that can and should be seen as instrumental to the well-being of youth to make this one essential point: To better understand and guide adolescents, we will have to rethink and rebuild the social supports that will allow the caring and commitment needed and wanted by everyone.

Adolescence in the 1990s: Risk and Opportunity should be helpful in doing that. It presents chapters written by some of the most thoughtful and effective people currently studying and working with adolescents. It grew out of the work of the Carnegie Council on Adolescent Development, which, over the last few years, has been an important catalyst for new thinking about adolescence. It was planned by Ruby Takanishi with characteristically keen insight, knowledge, and energy. This collection should offer encouragement to anyone who cares about young people and who worries about creating the kinds of communities in which adolescents, and all the rest of us, can thrive.

Notes

1 Roger Thompson, "Adolescent Culture in Colonial Massachusetts," *Journal of Family History* 9 (Summer 1984): 127–44.

2 Dale Mann, *Chasing the American Dream: Jobs, Schools, and Employment Training Programs in New York State* (New York: Community Service Society, 1980), pp. 16–31.

3 Ellen Greenberger and Laurence Steinberg, *When Teen-agers Work: The Psychological and Social Costs of Adolescent Employment* (New York: Basic Books, 1986), p. 23.

4 Mihaly Csikszentmihalyi and Reed Larson, *Being Adolescent: Conflict and Growth in the Teenage Years* (New York: Basic Books, 1984), p. 261.

5 Ibid., p. 259.

6 Ibid., p. 284.

7 S. Shirley Feldman and Glen R. Elliott, "Introduction," in *At the Threshold: The Developing Adolescent*, ed. S. Shirley Feldman and Glen R. Elliott (Cambridge: Harvard University Press, 1990), p. 2 (emphasis added).

Changing Views of Adolescence in Contemporary Society

RUBY TAKANISHI
Carnegie Council on Adolescent Development,
Carnegie Corporation of New York

A major paradigm shift in our conception of adolescence in contemporary America may be occurring. Originating from two traditionally isolated parts of our highly specialized society— professionals who have direct contact with adolescents and researchers who study their development from separate disciplines—this shift reflects a growing consensus about the universal and essential requirements for healthy development during the second decade of life.[1]

This consensus can be simply stated. All adolescents, regardless of economic background, race and ethnicity, gender, and geographical region or country, have basic needs that must be satisfied: to experience secure relationships with a few human beings, to be a valued member of groups that provide mutual aid and caring relationships, to become a competent individual who can cope with the exigencies of everyday life, and to believe in a promising future in work, family, and citizenship.

To meet these needs, all societies, including our own, must provide adolescents with an education, broadly conceived, that provides a basis for making informed and wise decisions about their futures. This learning must occur in caring communities, whether in schools or in other community organizations, where well-prepared individuals are respectful of and sensitive to adolescents' developmental needs. Above all, social and economic policies must be coordinated to stimulate and to enhance the development of vital human resources or human capital.[2]

This growing consensus acknowledges that adolescents in American society grow up in diverse racial and ethnic communities with different resources and values, and that their daily experiences may differ widely.[3] It also takes into account significant changes in the national economy and in the nature of family and community life, especially in the period from World War II to the present. The consensus holds that while these social transformations seriously threaten adolescents' capacities to grow up well educated and healthy, the essential requirements of development during adolescence have remained virtually unchanged.[4] What have been slow to adapt to the new conditions are our pivotal institutions such as schools and community organizations, particularly those serving young people, and businesses and other work places.

If I am correct in my assessment, this convergence of views has enormous implications for our search to better educate and guide students during the adolescent period, to promote their healthy development, and to prepare them for adult responsibilities. Some of these views, it must be noted, are not entirely new. Earlier attempts to incorporate them into educational practice are not encouraging.[5] What is new is that the views are not isolated within the research community or the educational sector, but that more and more of those concerned with adolescents, whether in professional practice or in policymaking arenas, are recognizing the power of these ideas to reverse the ways in which we think about adolescents and, therefore, how we structure environments and form policies to prepare them for adult life.[6]

BUILDING BLOCKS OF A CONSENSUS

Given the many troublesome problems faced by more and more youth today, we have tended to characterize adolescence as an inherently turbulent period. The very word *adolescence* has a negative valence, and implies a life state that should be dismissed or not taken seriously.

ADOLESCENCE: FROM A PERIOD OF GREAT RISK TO GREAT OPPORTUNITIES

Adolescents may well be the most maligned and misunderstood age group in our culture. Physicians, teachers, and parents alike groan at the prospect of having to deal with adolescents. Leading writers refer to the period as the "nightmare years." Adolescents are supposed to be rebellious, defiant of adult authority, moody, unmanageable, high risk-takers with no thought of the future, alienated, and so on. It is no wonder that adults are, at best, ambivalent about adolescents, and that adult reactions range from wanting to control adolescents entirely to having nothing to do with them at all.

In the last twenty years, research on adolescents has had a remarkable renaissance.[7] In contrast with that of an earlier period, the focus of this research has shifted from almost entirely clinical and problem populations to adolescents growing up in diverse communities. What we now have is a more diverse picture of American adolescents, including those who live in rather adverse circumstances.[8]

One aspect of the paradigm shift is a move away from a view of adolescents as solely risk-ridden to one constituting great opportunities, with attention to the preventing of problems and to engaging youth themselves in the constructive solution of problems. Whether under the rubric "youth development" or "youth as resources," the shift is clearly from viewing adolescents as liabilities to seeing them as assets.[9]

There is now widespread societal consensus about the critical importance of the early childhood years, achieved after several decades of solid research, program development and evaluation, and visible advocacy.[10] For the adolescent years, in contrast, there is growing awareness, not yet widespread, that another critical period occurs in the lives of young people today that was not so critical in our own adolescence: early adolescence, the period roughly from nine to fourteen years. As several authors state, most notably David Hamburg, early adolescence is unmatched in the juxtaposition of simultaneous changes—cognitive, biological, social, and emotional—by any other period in the life span. Early adolescence is now recognized as a "crucially formative period," a time not only of great risks, but of great opportunities.[11]

ADOLESCENCE: FROM ALIENATED TO CONNECTED YOUTH

Another major shift is from viewing adolescents as inherently alienated from adults to seeing their need to be intimately connected with caring adults. Contrary to popular opinion, most adolescents are not alienated from their parents, families, and other adults. If there is a recurring lament that is shared by adolescents from all backgrounds, it is the lack of available adults who listen, hear, understand, and guide them.[12]

Most people believe that adolescents fight with their parents all the time, and that conflict is endemic during the adolescent years. Adolescents, it is often said, want to be free of their parents; parents no longer count and should stand gracefully aside. To the contrary, as James P. Comer says, "They don't want you to disappear; they want you to be just around the corner when they need you."[13]

The overwhelming majority of American adolescents continue to look to their parents for guidance and direction in their lives regarding important decisions involving moral values and career choices. Peers are important sources for style and taste in fleeting fashion and entertainment, but not for enduring values. Adolescents complain that there is no one to talk to about their concerns and feelings, especially about the future. And it is to their parents over peers, teachers, religious counselors, if their parents were available, that they would turn first about the really important issues.[14]

The evidence is so strong, so counter to what prevailing wisdom is, that it requires us to rethink how parents and families can be brought back constructively into adolescents' lives.[15] Much of professional thinking in therapeutic interventions, even to the present, focuses on the adolescent in isolation from his or her family. While the family support and resource movement is very strong for the early childhood years, little of this energy has thus far been directed toward families of adolescents. An untapped potential is the opportunity to provide anticipatory or preventive guidance in the critical transition from childhood to adolescence that can assist in the necessary renegotiations of parent-adolescent relationships.[16]

I hope that in the future there will be more attention given to the ways in which parents, families, and guardians can be more fully engaged in the lives of their adolescents. There is no question that teenagers would welcome this engagement on new terms and find it desirable. There is no question that attachments to family members and other caring adults will ease the erosion of social and emotional support that all adolescents lament. As so many of the authors of the chapters in this book attest, there is simply no question that the development of strong, resilient young people depends on the availability of caring adults in families and in communities.

Professional practice, including the education of teachers, must attend to ways of reaching and working with parents of adolescents.[17] Together, parents and schools can form mutual-aid agencies in support of the education and healthy development of adolescents.[18]

FROM A FOCUS ON THE INDIVIDUAL TO THE CRITICALITY OF SETTINGS

Perhaps the most significant of the changing views about adolescence is that adolescent behavior, especially behavior considered to be problematic, is profoundly shaped by how we as adults have organized adolescents' educational and other social experiences.[19]

It is not inevitable that adolescents lose self-esteem and interest in learning as they move from small elementary schools to much larger junior highs or middle schools.[20] It is not inevitable that parents and adolescents experience intense conflict, especially over daily matters,[21] and it is not inevitable that non-college young adults are not prepared adequately for the work place.[22] If school, family, and work-place environments, norms, and expectations are altered to be more in tune with adolescents' needs and changed economic and social conditions, then adolescents will not necessarily behave in the dreaded, stereotypical ways associated with this period.

Thus the onus of responsibility for problems is shifted from the individual adolescent to shared responsibilities with adults and institutions in the community. The communities of influence in which adolescents grow up—schools, families, media, community and youth organizations, religious groups, and others—and the congruence among these key social organizations can make a significant difference in the life experiences and future well-being of adolescents.[23]

The call for "comprehensive, integrated services" for children and adolescents has achieved the status of a virtual mantra in policy circles.[24] By whatever label, there is currently a broader perspective on addressing adolescent development than a singular focus on changing adolescent behavior itself.

The contributions of pivotal institutions such as schools and families and their collaboration to sound developmental outcomes have led to programmatic approaches that recreate naturally occurring social support networks and are adapted to new social conditions.[25]

Yet in many of our communities, these are the very institutions under siege, undervalued, and functioning in isolation from one another. Since we have created various institutional arrangements, we can conceivably alter them to have more beneficial outcomes for adolescents. That possibility and the approaches and solutions described in these chapters give me great cause for hope.

TRANSLATING THE CONSENSUS INTO ACTION

Whether these changing views of adolescence will make a difference in how adult society responds to youth and provides opportunities for their optimal development remains to be seen. The central ideas to guide action, whether at the program or institutional level or on state and national policy agendas, are now available. Adolescence is a period that offers opportunities to prevent damaging outcomes and to assist young people toward a promising future.[26] Adolescents themselves seek the caring guidance of adults, and this guidance is essential for them to negotiate the pathways to healthy adulthood. The ways in which we organize adolescents' experiences in schools and elsewhere to match their developmental needs can be extremely powerful in shaping desirable outcomes.[27]

Today, we know much more about how to educate healthy adolescents than we are willing to put into practice. The unconscionable result is that we have lost and continue to lose large numbers of our future prime work force and adult citizens as we enter the twenty-first century.[28] The search for solutions has been engaged in by economists and business people, by our national leaders and those in local organizations. Enough of the answers are now at hand to proceed with confidence.

In this collection, the authors speak with deep conviction and from broad experience. Together they attest to an emerging consensus about adolescents, their needs, and how we can guide them toward productive and meaningful adulthood. For the sake of all our futures, especially those of young people, we must pay serious attention to the accumulated wisdom and shared reflections represented in these articles. If we continue on our present course, we risk compromising our own futures and severely diminishing those of all our children.

Ellen Condliffe Lagemann deserves full credit for initiating this book. Her advice and support throughout a two-year process of organizing these chapters were crucial during an especially health-challenging period of my life. As in all intellectual enterprises, the insights of pro bono reviewers only strengthen the ultimate content. I thank the reviewers for this book: Paul Barton, John Bishop, Claire Brindis, Gloria Primm Brown, Samuel Halperin, Anthony Jackson, Julia Graham Lear, Dorothy Rich, Diana Scott-Jones, and Judith Senderowitz. In successfully completing this book, Linda Schoff was, and continues to be, an indispensable associate in so many ways. To all my colleagues, I express my deep appreciation.

Notes

1 See David A. Hamburg, "The Opportunities of Early Adolescence," *Teachers College Record* 94 (Spring 1993): 466–71; and idem, *Today's Children* (New York: Times Books, 1992).

2 See Robert W. Glover and Ray Marshall, "Improving the School-to-Work Transition of American Adolescents," *Teachers College Record* 94 (Spring 1993): 588–610.

3 Francis A. J. Ianni, *The Search for Structure* (New York: The Free Press, 1990).

4 Hamburg, "The Opportunities of Early Adolescence."

5 Fred M. Hechinger, "Schools for Teenagers: A Historic Dilemma," *Teachers College Record* 94 (Spring 1993): 522–39.

6 Richard H. Price, Madalyn Cioci, Wendy Penner and Barbara Trautlein, "Webs of Influence: School and Community Programs that Enhance Adolescent Health and Education," *Teachers College Record* 94 (Spring 1993): 487–521; and Jacquelynne S. Eccles and Rena D. Harold, "Parent-School Involvement during the Early Adolescent Years," *Teachers College Record* 94 (Spring 1993): 568–79.

7 S. Shirley Feldman and Glen R. Elliott, eds., *At the Threshold: The Developing Adolescent* (Cambridge: Harvard University Press, 1990), pp. 1–12.

8 Ianni, *The Search for Structure.*

9 See Elena O. Nightingale and Lisa Wolverton, "Adolescent Rolelessness in Modern Society," *Teachers College Record* 94 (Spring 1993): 472–86.

10 Ruby Takanishi, "An Agenda for the Integration of Research and Policy during Early Adolescence," in *Early Adolescence: Perspectives on Research, Policy, and Intervention*, ed. R. Lerner (Hillsdale, N.J.: Lawrence Erlbaum & Associates, in press).

11 Hamburg, "The Opportunities of Early Adolescence."

12 Girl Scouts of the United States of America, *Girl Scouts Survey on the Beliefs and Moral Values of America's Children* (New York: Girl Scouts of the United States of America, 1989), p. 39.

13 See James P. Comer, "At the Crossroads: Voices from the Carnegie Conference on Adolescent Health—The Potential Effects of Community Organizations on the Future of Our Youth," *Teachers College Record* 94 (Spring 1993): 658–61.

14 Girl Scouts of the United States of America, *Girl Scouts Survey*, p. 7.

15 Stephen A. Small, "Preventive Programs That Support Families with Adolescents," (A working paper commissioned by the Carnegie Council on Adolescent Development ([Washington, D.C.: Carnegie Council on Adolescent Development, 1990]).

16 Myrna Cohen and Charles E. Irwin, Jr., "Parent-time: A Psycho-Educational Workshop for Parents," *Health and Social Work* 8 (1983): 196–202.

17 Eccles and Harold, "Parent-School Involvement during the Early Adolescent Years"; and Deborah Meier, "At the Crossroads: Voices from the Carnegie Conference on Adolescent Health—Transforming Schools into Powerful Communities," *Teachers College Record* 94 (Spring 1993): 654–57.

18 Eccles and Harold, "Parent-School Involvement during the Early Adolescent Years"; Feldman and Elliott, *At the Threshold*; and Price et al., "Webs of Influence."

19 Eccles and Harold, "Parent-School Involvement during the Early Adolescent Years."

20 Ibid.; and Anne C. Petersen, Klaus Hurrelmann, and Nancy Leffert, "Adolescence and Schooling in Germany and the United States: A Comparison of Peer Socialization to Adulthood," *Teachers College Recrod* 94 (Spring 1993): 611–628.

21 Small, "Preventive Programs That Support Families with Adolescents," p. 12; and Laurence Steinberg, "Autonomy, Conflict, and Harmony in the Family Relationship," in Feldman and Elliott, eds., *At the Threshold*, pp. 255–76.

22 Petersen, Hurrelmann, and Leffert, "Adolescence and Schooling in Germany"; and Glover and Marshall, "Improving the School-to-Work Transition."

23 Price et al., "Webs of Influence."

24 Joy G. Dryfoos, *Adolescents at Risk* (New York: Oxford University Press, 1990), pp. 251–55; and idem, "Schools as a Place for Health, Mental Health, and Social Services," *Teachers College Record* 94 (Spring 1993): 540–67.

25 Price et al., "Webs of Influence."

26 Hamburg, "The Opportunities of Early Adolescence."

27 Eccles and Harold, "Parent-Student Involvement during the Adolescent Years"; Price et al., "Webs of Influence"; and Petersen, Hurrelmann, and Leffert, "Adolescence and Schooling in Germany and the United States."

28 H. Craig Heller, "At the Crossroads: Voices from the Carnegie Conference on Adolescent Health—The Need for a Core, Interdisciplinary Life-Sciences Curriculum in the Middle Grades," *Teachers College Record* 94 (Spring 1993): 645–52.

The Opportunities of Early Adolescence

DAVID A. HAMBURG
Carnegie Corporation of New York

The United States is truly a great nation, now admired around the world as our ideas, values, and institutions are catching on. Yet for all that authentic greatness, we are inadvertently doing immense damage to our children and adolescents. Now there is a powerful opportunity to prevent most of that damage.

In our unique society, probably the most technically advanced, the most affluent, the most democratic the world has ever known, the crucial years of childhood and adolescence have become battlefields, literally as well as figuratively. Our schools as well as our hospitals and our streets are littered with avoidable casualties. The time has come to stop the killing, stop the maiming, and stop the enormous waste of talent and loss of human potential.

ADOLESCENCE: PREVENTING DAMAGE FOR A LIFETIME

Adolescence, in particular, is a time of great risks and great opportunities. Its onset is a crucially formative phase of development beginning with puberty, about as dramatic a biological upheaval as occurs in a lifetime. That upheaval coincides approximately with drastic changes in the social life of adolescents, particularly the move from elementary to junior high or middle school.

These are stressful times for adolescents and their families, rich and poor alike, whether they live in inner cities, suburbs, or rural areas. The early adolescent years specifically, ten to fifteen years of age, are open to the formation of behavioral patterns that have lifelong consequences for the educational performance and health status of adolescents. These dangerous patterns are only beginning to get the public attention they deserve.

Becoming alienated from school and later dropping out; starting to smoke cigarettes, drink alcohol, and use other drugs; starting to drive automobiles and motorcyles in high-risk ways; not eating an appropriate diet or exercising enough; and risking early pregnancy and sexually transmitted diseases are all dangerous activities. Initially, adolescents explore these new behaviors in a tentative way. Before damaging patterns are firmly established, we have a major opportunity for intervention to prevent later casualties in education and in health. The formation of healthy life-styles during early adolescence can have a positive effect on the entire life course.

What are the essential requirements for healthy adolescent development? In my view, it is essential that we help young adolescents to acquire constructive knowledge and skills, inquiring habits of mind, dependable human relationships, a reliable basis for earning respect, a sense of belonging in a valued group, and a way of being useful to their communities. These are the fundamental underpinnings of healthy development during adolescence for all young people, in our society and throughout the world.

Adolescents look for constructive expressions of their inherent curiosity and their enormous exploratory energy. They need a basis for making informed, deliberate decisions rather than ignorant, impulsive ones about matters that have large, lifelong consequences for their health, education, parental and family roles, and contributions to their communities.

THE CHANGED CIRCUMSTANCES OF ADOLESCENT DEVELOPMENT

The crucial transition from childhood to adulthood is now very different than it was in the past. Throughout most of human history, for millennia, the transition was steady, gradual, cumulative, and well ordered. Children could see what their parents did for a living. They could observe what the dangers and opportunities were. They were given tasks from an early age that bore some discernible resemblance to adult responsibilities. These tasks traditionally grew more complex and broader in scope as the children grew older. By the time they reached adolescence, they were quite familiar with what would be required of them, and what their adult roles would be.

In the twentieth century, however, the ground rules changed, and the rate of change has accelerated in the past few decades. Young adolescents now have less and less opportunity for direct participation in the adult world. It is less clear how to be useful, less clear how to earn respect in one's community. The time between childhood and adulthood has grown longer, and the outcomes are less clear. The requirements, risks, and opportunities of this period are now highly ambiguous for most adolescents.

The adolescent period is complicated by the very easy, the very attractive availability of activities or substances that constitute a high risk while at the same time appearing to be terrific, recreational, tension-relieving, and gratifying. Adolescents have ready access now in our affluent society to deadly poison in the guise of casual experience and fun—drugs, vehicles, weapons, and, indeed, the many ways in which they may use their bodies dangerously.

The social context of adolescence is very different from that of even three decades ago. Statistics document the drastic changes from 1960 to 1990 in

American families. We are much more likely now than we were three decades ago to bypass marriage altogether, to live alone, to end marriage by divorce or to have revolving marriages, to have both parents work outside the home when the children are young and throughout childhood, to live in single-parent families, typically with the mother present but no adult male, and very often no other adult person.

These are difficult conditions for child-rearing—by no means impossible but, on the average, rather stressful. Also in the past three decades, the change in regular contacts between children and their adult relatives is remarkable. Not only are their mothers home much less than they were two or three decades ago, but there is very little evidence nationwide of increased time spent by fathers at home to compensate. The general picture across the country is one of mother gone, father gone, and grandparents not there either. The Norman Rockwell family of breadwinner father, mother working at home, and two children now constitutes just 6 percent of all American families. Only about 5 percent of American children now see a grandparent regularly.

Taken together, such changes tend to erode the support and guidance functions that were provided by available, cohesive families in relatively small, stable communities that characterize most of human history over these millennia. These support and guidance functions are essential to healthy adolescent development. They have historically come mainly from the family, but they can come from other sources as well—from responsible, caring adults in schools, in community and youth organizations, in religious organizations, and many more.

THE NATURE OF OUR PRESENT CHALLENGE

The erosion of social supports cuts across our entire society. Even in affluent communities and certainly in poor ones, we are all searching for ways to adapt to new circumstances. How can we compensate for the erosion of family functions? How can we find adequate conditions for optimal development so that our young people can emerge from the crucial transition to adulthood in good shape for a lifetime, healthy and vigorous, inquiring and problem solving, decent and constructive?

To address these questions, we have drawn on the initiatives stimulated by the Carnegie Council on Adolescent Development, other activities of the Carnegie Corporation, and those of related foundations and governmental organizations. The cross-cutting themes of these efforts include identifying elements of effective and promising approaches to promoting educational achievement and healthy development during adolescence. Another theme is how a range of pivotal institutions, from schools, health-care systems, families, peers, media, and community and youth organizations, can, working together, meet the developmental needs of young adolescents. Most important, a singular message is that there are now available constructive approaches to address directly the changed circumstances in which adolescents grow up today.

A DEVELOPMENTAL APPROACH TO PREVENTING DAMAGE

Our approach aims to foster fundamental developmental attributes. We are talking about the whole person, rather than about this disease and that disability. We are talking about what it takes to grow up as a whole person: intact, vigorous, healthy, problem-solving, decent, and constructive. We are saying that if a young person acquires knowledge and skills, an openness to inquiry, strong human relationships, and membership in a valued group, and contributes to his or her community, that individual acquires a considerable degree of protection against a lot of rotten outcomes. Such a person is less likely to get syphilis, gonorrhea, and AIDS, less likely to have an unwanted pregnancy, and less likely to break bones—those of others or one's own. The individual is less likely to become alienated from school and end up without the skills necessary to participate in the mainstream economy.

Effective and promising approaches to sound development during adolescence include three vital components: information, skill building, and motivation, all supported by mutually reinforcing social institutions. As children become adolescents, they emerge into a period in which they feel they should quickly become adults. They ask, in effect, How should I use my body? Any responsible education must answer that basic question with a substantial life-sciences curriculum integrating the biological and the behavioral sciences and broad enough to be personally meaningful to adolescents.[1]

Important as information is, indeed vital as it is, information alone is not enough. The question that arises is how to be able to make good use of accurate and personally meaningful information about one's own development and that of other living organisms. Here we add life-skills training, which can become a vital part of education in schools, community and youth organizations, and elsewhere. Through this approach, adolescents will learn how to make informed, deliberate, and constructive decisions about things that matter.

Such life-skills training can also enhance people skills, which are important for every aspect of life from parental competence to work to friendship—and especially during adolescence. I mean ways of relating decently, especially in unpleasant experiences. Conflicts need to be resolved without violence. Skills are needed to establish dependable friendships and ways to participate in supportive groups that address problems jointly. People also need to weather the inevitable difficulties of growing up, the stresses and disappointments of education, and the turbulent search for ways to protect your own health and the health of those you care about. To the extent that contemporary families are unable to meet those needs, specially designed social-support interventions can be exceedingly helpful.[2]

Thus there is a necessary and practical conjunction of a life-sciences curriculum linked with life-skills training and social-support interventions. Even this is not enough. There has to be support for and reinforcement of the motivations to maintain one's health. Thus deliberately designed social-support interventions that connect adolescents with a responsible, caring adult in the family or outside of it are essential to enhance the adolescents' motivation to invest in their own education and health for the life span.

Our institutions, including families but extending beyond them to schools, health organizations, community organizations, and the media, can provide the vital information, skills, and motivation necessary to meet the essential requirements of healthy development during the adolescent years. However, in many places these institutions must be challenged to adapt to new needs and circumstances.

THE MIDDLE-GRADE SCHOOL AS A PIVOTAL INSTITUTION

The middle-grade schools—called junior high, intermediate, and middle schools—are pivotal institutions in the lives of young adolescents. The 1989 publication *Turning Points*, the Carnegie Council on Adolescent Development's report addressing the reform of middle-grades education, provided some guiding principles: developmentally appropriate education drawing on research on adolescent development; teaching of life sciences as an organizing principle for the curriculum; schools of small units created on a human scale; a mutual-aid ethic among teachers exemplified by interdisciplinary team teaching; sustained individual attention in the context of a supportive group; learning for cooperation in future human relationships and for the work place; and service to the community.[3] A cross-cutting theme is one of partnerships, with the school as part of a network of cooperating organizations that integrate education, health, and the development of young adolescents.

True, we are asking schools to do more than they have ever done, and we must. True, schools and people who work in them have been greatly depreciated. But there is no practical alternative. This means that the powerful sectors of the society, from the business community to scientific organizations, from higher education to community-based organizations, are going to have to become more involved than they have ever been. This might take the form of direct contributions, but raising the status and resources of the schools through advocacy and political support for education is absolutely necessary.

OUR PROSPECTS

I believe we have a very high degree of consensus that we can prevent much damage to children and adolescents, and that that effort involves very modest expenditures up front for very large savings and very large benefits for the nation over the long term. In our pluralistic society, leadership is crucial at all levels. We must not be paralyzed by the realization of the challenges before us. We can all contribute to a well-informed national movement on children and youth by building interest and making the issues of healthy adolescent development salient, and by creating mutual aid among organizations and institutions in communities across our nation.

I express my deep appreciation to Ruby Takanishi for her superb collaboration in every phase of the work of the Carnegie Council on Adolescent Development.

Notes

1 For further discussion of this approach, see H. Craig Heller, "At the Crossroads: Voices from the Carnegie Conference on Adolescent Health—The Need for a Core, Interdisciplinary Life-Sciences Curriculum in the Middle Grades," *Teachers College Record* 94 (Spring 1993): 645-52.

2 See Richard H. Price, Madalyn Cioci, Wendy Penner, and Barbara Trautlein, "Webs of Influence: School and Community Programs That Enhance Adolescent Health and Education," *Teachers College Record* 94 (Spring 1993): 487-521.

3 Task Force on Education of Young Adolescents, *Turning Points: Preparing American Youth for the 21st Century* (Washington, D.C.: Carnegie Council on Adolescent Development, 1989).

Adolescent Rolelessness in Modern Society

ELENA O. NIGHTINGALE
Carnegie Corporation of New York

LISA WOLVERTON
Prague, Czechoslovakia

> The young are in character prone to desire and ready to carry any desire they may have formed into action. Of bodily desires it is the sexual to which they are most disposed to give way, and in regard to sexual desire they exercise no self-restraint. They are changeful too, and fickle in their desires, which are as transitory as they are vehement; for their wishes are keen without being permanent, like a sick man's fits of hunger and thirst.
>
> —Aristotle

As this quotation from Aristotle illustrates, some of our views of adolescents have changed little over the centuries. The word *adolescent* is representative of the problems this age group faces. In addition to having a negative connotation, "adolescent" is defined largely by what it is *not*—neither child nor adult—legally, in status, role, or function. Adolescents have no prepared place in society that is appreciated or approved; nonetheless they must tackle two major tasks, usually on their own: identity formation and development of self-worth and self-efficacy. The current social environment of adolescents makes both tasks very difficult.

For these reasons, adolescents today are said to be suffering from "rolelessness." Of course, they are not truly roleless because society in general, parents, and schools do set certain roles for them, though these roles are not as meaningful and productive as they could be. Adolescents also have other roles, most often determined by their peers, which are perceived by adults as undesirable. Thus, when we speak of "rolelessness" what we decry is that adolescents do not have contributing, active, productive roles that are consistent with and valued by adult society. Since current adolescent roles arose by default, much can be done to restructure these roles in positive ways.

The onset of adolescence is a critical period of biological and psychological change for every child. These changes are not often synchronized and individual variation is vast. For many in our society, adolescence involves dramatic changes in the social environment as well. For example, the transition from elementary to middle or junior high school or the easy access to potentially life-threatening substances and activities can make adolescence a particularly difficult time.

In the past ten to twenty years, rapid erosion of traditional family and social-support networks has added to the difficulties. Despite the biological, social, and technological changes impinging on adolescent development, especially in this century, there appear to be fundamental human needs that are enduring and crucial to healthy development and survival. These fundamental needs include the need to find a place in a valued group that provides a sense of belonging and the need to feel a sense of worth as a person.[1] It is a challenging but not impossible task to find ways to fill these needs. Otherwise, the long period—10 to 15 years out of a life expectancy of 71.8 years for males and 78.5 years for females[2]—of biological maturity combined with social dependence and rolelessness can only contribute to the familiar litany of disenchantment with learning, drug abuse, early unplanned pregnancy, violence, injury, and other damaging behaviors.

ABOUT WHOM ARE WE TALKING?

Adolescents are a diminishing and precious resource. The population of adolescents between the ages of 12 and 17 in the United States has fluctuated between 18 and 24 million in the past 30 years, and is projected to remain approximately steady through the year 2000. In 1989, the population of 0–17-year-olds was 64 million[3] with 2.5 million homeless.[4] The ratio of Hispanic and/or nonwhite children age 0–17 to the total youth population was 26 percent in 1989 and is expected to increase to 33 percent in 2000 and to 45 percent by the year 2080[5] (see Figure 1).

In the last 100 years, however, both the population and the ratio of young people to adults have changed a great deal (see Figure 2). In 1890, youth 14–24 years of age numbered only 14.1 million while the ratio to the population aged 25–64 was 57 percent. By 1950, the population of young people had increased to 24.2 million but the ratio to the mature population segment had dropped to 32 percent.[6] In 1989, the ratio remained steady at 32 percent, but the population aged 14–24 reached 40.1 million. By comparison, the ratio of persons over 65 to adults 25–64 rose from 16 percent, in 1950, to 24 percent in 1989.[7] Therefore, while the number of adolescents has continued to increase, their proportion of the population as a whole has been almost cut in half since 1890—a change that took place primarily before 1950—while the proportion of elderly has increased. We should systematically consider how to enlist older and still vigorous people in helping the young.

For at least the last century, adolescence has been viewed as a distinct stage in human development. Previously, older children were termed "youths" and adolescence "the formative years" (for adult life) and children

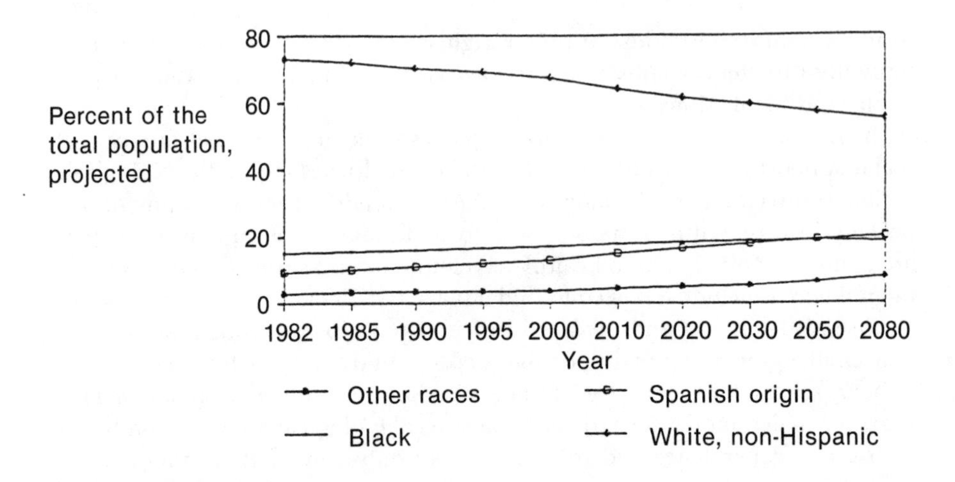

Figure 1. Projected Changes in the Racial and Ethnic Makeup of the U.S. Population under Age 18, 1982 to 2080

Source: U.S. Department of Commerce, Bureau of the Census, *Projections of the Hispanic Population: 1983 to 2080*, Current Population Reports, Population Estimates and Projections, Series P-25, No. 995 (Washington, D.C.: Government Printing Office, January 1986). Reprinted from U.S. Congress, Office of Technology Assessment, *Adolescent Health-Volume I: Summary and Policy Options* OTA-H-468 (Washington, D.C.: Government Printing Office, April 1991), p. 122.

generally could more easily make the transition from childhood to adulthood. In earlier times, youths were likely to move into adult roles that were familiar—accepting adult tasks and responsibilities progressively as they grew up. The extended family and other adults were mirrors of what the young would become. Responsibilities increased with maturity, but there was little doubt about what was expected.

In the nineteenth century, urban youth, at age twelve or thirteen, both male and female, often went directly from school to work in order to contribute to the support of the family. Their assistance was needed by the family for survival and often children suffered from having to work under harsh conditions. Rural youth similarly contributed by working side by side with adults on the family farm from an early age. Particularly in the rural areas, children performed the same tasks as their parents, enjoyed the same types of entertainment, and had the same expectations of life.[8] Adolescents were often aware early on that their role within the family and society would be similar to that of their parents, and their parents and other adults provided an abundance of role models. Moreover, the acceptance of adult responsibility occurred at, or even before, the time of the biological changes of puberty.

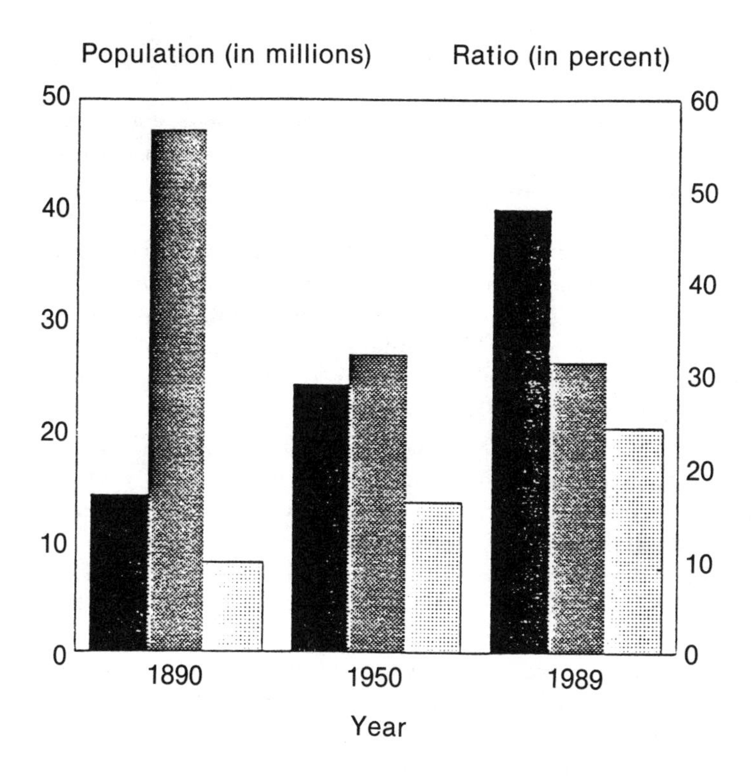

Figure 2. Ratio of Youth (14–24) to the Adult (25–64) and Elderly (65 +) Population

Source: U.S. Department of Commerce, Bureau of the Census, *Historical Statistics of the United States: Colonial Times to 1970*, Series A 160-171 (Washington, D.C.: Government Printing Office, September 1975), and *Statistical Abstract of the United States: 1991*, No. 13 (Washington, D.C.: Government Printing Office).

By 1900, most young people were less often needed to support the family. Stricter child labor laws were enacted and school years were extended. Now out of the work place and sequestered in school, youths were separated from adults for most of the day and had fewer adult responsibilities. Opportunities for interaction with adults decreased, as did communication between generations.

Due primarily to the control of many infectious diseases and better nutrition and hygiene, children over the past two centuries have been reaching puberty at younger ages. In the United States, 150 years ago, the average age of menarche was sixteen; today it is twelve and may still be dropping. The trend for boys is similar but more difficult to document. At the same time, the social changes described have postponed the end of adolescence—and of dependence—until much later, sometimes until age twenty-five (for example, for those who study for a profession). This phenomenon of a ten- to fifteen-year period of physical maturity combined with social dependence—and rolelessness—is relatively new.

Not too surprisingly, a study reported in *Being Adolescent* (like most other studies, largely involving white working- and middle-class youth) showed that the adolescents whose activities were followed spent 40 percent of their time on leisure activities and 27 percent alone. They averaged eighteen hours a week at menial jobs. Thirty-eight hours a week were spent in school (in contrast, children in Japan spend fifty-nine hours a week in school and have sixty-nine more days in the school year). They spent only 4.8 percent of their time with their parents and 2 percent with adults who were not their parents—for a total of only 7 percent of waking hours spent with adults. Half of the adolescents' waking hours were spent with their peers, and they clearly lacked meaningful contact with caring adults. They worried most about school, their looks, and being liked. Except for school—an important exception—these worries may indicate a lack of concern about the adolescent's role in the family and community.[9] According to another study, the majority of adolescents do not consult or communicate with their parents on topics of importance, such as school, sex, or drugs (see Table 1).[10] It seems that adolescence may have become a "waiting period" of enforced leisure, with few responsibilities and little meaningful contact with adults.

The relative isolation of adolescents from adults contributes to the view of adolescence as an alien subculture with no meaningful role in society. According to a 1986 Harris poll, 52 percent of adults see drug abuse as the most serious problem among youth. Less than half of adults polled believe that young people have a good education or are basically happy, or feel that parents in general do a good job, especially regarding values and discipline, or that the schools are doing a good job. And 75 percent of adults polled feel that the government is not taking proper responsibility for youth. There seems to be concern that something is wrong, and a willingness to look outside the family for help. However, despite these negative perceptions of youth, the majority of adolescents in the United States *do* become productive citizens.

Table 1. Problems about which Adolescents Ask Their Parents' Advice

JOB	45%
COLLEGE	39%
SCHOOL PROBLEMS	39%
SIBLING PROBLEMS	29%
HEALTH/DIET	23%
DRINKING	20%
SEX	17%
TROUBLE WITH OTHER ADOLESCENTS	16%
DRUGS	16%

Source: J. Norman & M. W. Harris, *The Private Life of the American Teenager* (New York: Rawson, Wade, 1981).

TRANSITION TO ADULT ROLES

Inconsistency and ambiguity in defining adult responsibility are pervasive. Driving, one of the accepted rites of passage, may begin as early as age fourteen or as late as eighteen, depending on the state. In some states, execution is legal for crimes committed prior to age eighteen. But military service and voting remain set at eighteen. It is understandable that young people are confused and frustrated by inconsistencies in being allowed to assume adult responsibility for diverse actions of personal significance.

But the difficulties of transition to adulthood vary depending on the conditions in which adolescents find themselves. Relatively affluent youth are generally expected to go to college and their outlook is better, though not trouble free. In 1989, 40 percent of high school graduates were enrolled in college.[11] The group that does not attend college encounters a variety of problems in making the transition to adulthood that college-bound youth do not share. Minority and inner-city youth in areas of concentrated poverty encounter the most obstacles to remaining in school. In 1989, only 23 percent of black male and 18 percent of Hispanic male high school graduates attended college.[12]

The transition to adulthood is probably easiest for college-bound youth because their adolescence, although lengthened by continued dependency on parents, is structured by years of study, athletics, and other activities, and because their parents have the energy and resources to create and access opportunities for them. Higher skill levels also make satisfying employment easier to obtain. College-bound students often consciously postpone other aspects of adulthood, such as marriage and childbearing, until school is completed and they are working and settled. They are future-oriented and not truly roleless, but the chosen roles may not be in line with adult desires. Too often adolescents—even those who are college bound—have become "takers" rather than "givers" in both family and society.[13] In fact, even many adolescents who do work during high school and college do so in food-service or sales—not in career-related posts—to have money for personal items or entertainment to the detriment of their studies and other activities.[14] In this way, work may even become dysfunctional to maturity.

Noncollege youth have a rockier road. According to a report from The William T. Grant Foundation on noncollege youth in America, many of this group's problems stem from the inability to find work at all or at a meaningful level and wage.[15] Even while they are in school, and employment is badly needed, jobs are difficult to find. From 1960 to 1985, the unemployment rate among youths in school (age sixteen to seventeen) almost doubled, although it has declined somewhat between 1986 and 1989 (see Table 2). The unemployment rate among blacks is especially high—for black males it is 27 percent.

Table 2. Unemployment Rate* among 16- to 17-Year Olds Enrolled in School

	1960	1970	1975	1980	1985	1989
All Ethnic Groups						
Males	11.0	16.5	17.4	19.8	20.8	16.7
Females	9.5	16.0	19.2	16.8	19.0	10.7
White						
Males	—	15.1	16.9	17.4	18.7	15.1
Females	—	14.9	17.9	15.3	15.6	9.3
Black						
Males	—	33.3	25.7	43.3	41.2	27.0
Females	—	32.1	36.1	39.6	50.8	22.5

*The unemployment rate is the proportion of those in the labor force who are not working and are seeking employment.

Source: Data from U.S. Department of Labor, Bureau of Labor Statistics, *Special Labor Force Reports*, nos. 16 and 68; *Handbook of Labor Statistics*, Bulletin 2217 (Washington, D.C.: Government Printing Office, June 1985); and unpublished data. Table from U.S. Department of Education, Office of Educational Research and Improvement, *Youth Indicators 1991: Trends in the Well-Being of American Youth* (Washington, D.C.: Government Printing Office, April 1991).

The problem continues after graduation from high school. In 1986, only 48.9 percent of males and 41.9 percent of females were employed full-time, a decrease from 72.7 and 57 percent, respectively, in 1968 (see Table 3). One

Table 3. Employment to Population Ratios and Full-Time Employment to Population Ratios of High School Graduates Not Enrolled in College, 1968–1986

	Males		*Females*	
	Employment to Population Ratio	*Full-Time Employment to Population Ratio*	*Employment to Population Ratio*	*Full-Time Employment to Population Ratio*
March 1968	86.5	72.7	68.9	57.0
March 1974	85.6	69.6	69.1	47.6
March 1986	75.2	48.9	71.9	41.9

Source: The William T. Grant Foundation, Commission on Work, Family and Citizenship, *The Forgotten Half: Non-College Youth in America* (Washington, D.C.: The William T. Grant Foundation, 1988), p. 23.

important factor in the employment problem is that many corporations will not hire high school graduates, especially for career-track positions, until they are in their mid-twenties. Many employers think that recent high school graduates are irresponsible, unqualified, or simply inappropriate for many jobs. This leaves young people floundering and roleless for several years or working at menial and dead-end jobs. The jobs young people can obtain usually pay extremely low wages—too low to allow settling down or supporting a family. In 1985, only 42 percent of all males earned a real annual income at or above the three-person poverty line (see Table 4). The percentages were lower for black and Hispanic young men—24.9 and 35.4 percent respectively.[16]

William Julius Wilson cites the example of a twenty-nine-year-old black man who works as a dishwasher in Chicago. Still living at home, he has never been on welfare and has worked as a dishwasher for three years, making $4.85 an hour. Because his employer said he could easily be replaced, he has never called in sick. On the day Wilson's assistants interviewed him, he had just had a tooth pulled and was in great pain. Having borrowed money from friends to pay for the extraction, he could not afford any painkillers. In spite of the pain, he went to work that night and washed dishes.[17]

As Wilson's example illustrates, the situation among truly disadvantaged minority youth is much worse than that of most American youth. These youths have an even greater difficulty finding jobs. In fact, the *adults* in their

Table 4. Percent of 20–24-Year-Old Males (All Educational Groups) with Real Annual Earnings at or above the Three-Person Poverty Line, by Race/Ethnic Group: 1973–1985

	1973	1979	1985
All Males	59.4%	57.5%	43.7%
White, non-Hispanic	60.4%	60.4%	48.5%
Black, non-Hispanic	55.2%	41.2%	24.9%
Hispanic	61.1%	54.1%	35.4%

Source: Data from U.S. Bureau of Census, CPS Public Use Tapes, March 1974, March 1980, and March 1986; tabulations by Center for Labor Market Studies, Northeastern University. Table from The William T. Grant Foundation Commission on Work, Family and Citizenship, *The Forgotten Half: Non-College Youth in America* (Washington, D.C.: The William T. Grant Foundation, 1988), p. 22.

community are likely to be unemployed, working for poverty-level wages, or on welfare. These adolescents "may not know a single adult whose stable employment supports an even modest standard of family life."[18]

Wilson's book *The Truly Disadvantaged* depicts how urban centers of concentrated poverty developed.[19] Those who succeeded in attaining a solid standard of living often moved away from the city to the suburbs, further depriving young people of role models. Such young people have no experience working or living among people with mid-level or different kinds of jobs and their choices are often limited to poorly paying and unrewarding jobs or quick money from drug running or other criminal activities. Often the only role models available in areas of concentrated poverty are gang members or drug dealers, who appear to have what adolescents desperately want, respect and money.

In these neighborhoods, many adult women were adolescent mothers themselves. Their daughters, in turn, may see a child of their own as the only hope for affection and respect, and perhaps even stability. However, the babies quickly become demanding toddlers. Usually the fathers of these children do not marry the mothers or provide family support. Too early childbearing can have disastrous consequences for both mother and child, including dropping out of school and long-term unemployment for the mother and low birth weight and other health problems for the child.

Although the situation of disadvantaged youth is particularly precarious, among youth of any background, frustration over the inability to get a job, to take control of one's own life, to assume adult responsibilities, or to be valued and needed can contribute to drug and alcohol abuse, unnecessary risk-taking, and violence directed at one self or others.

Those adolescents who are already disconnected from family, school, work, or community may look for support elsewhere. What adults may term "deviant" behavior may be one way for adolescents to increase self-esteem and obtain a sense of belonging to a valued group. For example, a gang member stated that he became involved in a robbery because "I resented that my father was not involved. Now I don't care but I wouldn't have gotten involved in a gang if he had a job and if he had a relationship with me. The only adult male in my life is an uncle who retired from working for the city."[20]

A serious though not life-threatening aspect of rolelessness among all youth is the lack of civic responsibility. Sixty-seven percent of eighteen- to twenty-year-olds and 62 percent of twenty-one- to twenty-four-year-olds did not vote in the presidential election of 1988, apparently feeling that they had no stake in the future of their country or that voting was not the avenue to express their stake.[21] This civic apathy may be an expression of perceived rolelessness among older adolescents—that what they do makes no difference to anyone.

WHAT CAN WE DO?

A 1942 study of young men who served in the Civilian Conservation Corps (CCC) showed that their main reason for joining was to help their families (see Table 5).[22] However, over 50 percent joined either primarily or to some extent because they were tired of having nothing to do. When given the opportunity to be of use, many welcomed it.

In the 1980s, several different plans for involving adolescents in youth service were proposed, ranging from mandatory national service to optional service programs for credit in schools. Whatever the plan, the goals were essentially similar: to give youth a sense of self-worth and accomplishment; to bring them in contact with adults who could serve as mentors and role models, thus increasing the 2 percent of time spent in contact with unrelated adults;[23] to provide service to those in need; and to teach responsibility and behaviors appropriate to holding a job and performing well.

Promoters of mandatory national service also see it as a rite of passage marking and perhaps easing the transition to adulthood. Some think that adolescents' "insulation from the real business of life produces 'the more subtle, subjective states such as apathy, self-hatred, boredom, acute feelings of frustration, loneliness, and meaningless-ness,' " and that youth service can be used to combat these feelings.[24] Others believe that youth service can promote a commitment to others and thus shape the communitarian values of society in the future. By addressing the frustration of youth and providing them with constructive values, youth service can help to combat the risky behaviors that often result from a lack of meaningful contributing roles. Other proposals include monitored work experience; school volunteer service as part of the curriculum, graduation requirements, or extracurricular activi-

Table 5. Reasons Given by Interviewed Enrollees for Enrolling in the CCC

	Percentage of the boys who gave a specific reason	
Type of Motivation	*As the chief reason*	*Among all reasons*
Boy desired to help family	62.4	77.5
Boy was tired of having nothing to do	18.5	52.3
Boy wanted to get away from home	3.1	15.0
Family wanted boy to go	2.2	15.0
Relief agency wanted boy to go	2.0	8.3
Boy's friends were going	1.7	20.1
Other reasons	10.1	15.2
Number of boys	356	374

Source: Kenneth Holland and Frank Ernest Hill, *Youth in the CCC* (Washington, D.C.: American Council on Education, 1942).

ties; and job corps and other options for out-of-school and out-of-job youth.[25] Voter registration drives with adolescent participation or political activities through organizations such as the League of Women Voters or the Youth Policy Institute may serve to foster civic responsibility.

Another promising possibility is linking adolescents with retired persons. For example, in the Partners Program developed by Joan Schine (bringing adolescents and the elderly together), young adolescents develop new and meaningful relationships with adults outside their immediate family or school.[26] The elderly, in turn, are able to reach out to a new and very different population, at a time when their own circle of friends or contacts may be shrinking. Interviews with middle-school students who regularly visited a nursing home revealed that the students aimed to make friends with the elders, whom they viewed as bored and lonely. These adolescents worked hard to be liked by their elderly companions. Simple events such as giving the partner a snack or going with him to his room helped to individualize relationships. The students interviewed believed that friendship is healing, that it makes both the older person and the youth feel good about themselves.

It seems clear that all youth need to develop strong one-on-one relationships with adults in their communities, schools, and work environments.[27] For minority youth in poverty, who are at greatest need and greatest risk, youth-service programs are even more important because they provide an opportunity to succeed outside of school tasks. Although many scattered programs exist, a more intense and systematic commitment is required to provide each young person with at least one human anchor.[28] A key to the success of service programs is "examined experience"—the service opportunity is "examined" with the mentor, and the young person learns from reviewing the experience and trying again. Programs that link school and community also serve the purpose of giving the school experience more meaning.

Beyond community service, there is also a need to help non-college-bound youth to secure stable employment at an earlier age. This may be done through school programs, on-the-job training programs, or programs that aid the job search and teach how to work. Robert W. Glover and Ray Marshall discuss this more thoroughly in "Improving the School-to-Work Transition of American Adolescents" in this issue.

For many young people, schools, as they are structured, have proved dysfunctional and do not provide the necessary preparation for the responsibilities that lie beyond graduation. Schools need to be restructured and their curricula improved and made more meaningful by incorporating health education, human biology, community service, marketable technical skills, and career information.

Businesses should be more flexible about hiring high school graduates. More businesses could develop responsible positions and job-training programs for young people, offer reasonable salaries, and allow opportunities for advancement, rather than a job with no opportunities and at minimum wage. From a business view, this is an investment in the quality of the work force.

Procedures for registering to vote need to be simplified and young people recruited to vote, for example by programs to contact youths on their eighteenth birthdays and registration when applying for driver's licenses, or on election day. This is one aspect of civic responsibility that can mold a sense of personal worth and stimulate social participation.[29]

The health professions—including but not limited to physicians—have a particular responsibility to be sensitive to early signs of trouble in adolescents and to follow through on appropriate referrals. The participation of health professionals in school-linked centers can have positive effects, especially on mental health and reproductive services. A study of the first two school-linked clinics in high schools in St. Paul, Minnesota, showed that child-bearing among participating female students decreased by more than 50 percent within three years.[30]

The role of religious institutions in increasing the life chances of adolescents is also important but often given too little attention. In the *National Education Longitudinal Study of 1988*, a profile of eighth-graders revealed that 34 percent participated in religious youth groups.[31] A number of studies show a correlation between religious belief and/or practice and lower frequency of some high-risk behaviors.[32] Religious institutions, of course, have traditionally provided support for youth, but their role can and should be adapted to current circumstances—for example, in reaching out to rootless youth. The black churches in particular can be strong forces to help youth in their communities.

Youth organizations—such as the Scouts, 4-H Clubs, Camp Fire Girls and Boys—sprang up in the first half of the twentieth century to stress skills, character building, and service to others. They were organized to take advantage of the new leisure time of youths who were not working. Now these organizations need to adjust to the changing needs of adolescents, and to increase the commitment of adults. They have the capacity to make dependable connections with many lonely and isolated young people.[33]

CONCLUSION

Although there is reason to be concerned about the problems of youth, adolescents *must* be claimed as assets to society.[34] We must change the view that many people hold of *all* youth as troubled and harmful to the rest of society. We particularly need a social commitment to providing opportunities for meaningful roles for young people who will not have many years of formal education.

Self-esteem from secure loving relationships and success at tasks are important to the development of any individual. Fortunately, the developmental process continues throughout life. The span of years of adolescence is long and offers opportunities for not one but many turning points in looking toward potentially productive later years. How can we redefine roles and tasks for adolescents, particularly those at high risk, so that they are more adaptive?

This redirection—or creation of constructive, rewarding roles for all adolescents, including those at high risk—can include supplying universal prenatal care with simultaneous enriched educational opportunities for pregnant girls; providing alternatives to premature assuming of adult roles with regard to sexual activity and buying power, before appropriate maturational steps have taken place; drawing on the commitment of elders and the innovative ideas of youth—linking of generations, communities, and youth through mentoring; linking of schools to communities so schools become a more desirable and relevant part of all adolescent experience; capitalizing on the growing empathy and affinity for humanitarian causes displayed by youth (for example, in the past several years hundreds of groups of Amnesty International have been formed in high schools); providing social supports, which, with opportunities to enhance self-efficacy, provide buffers for coping in times of stress; and encouraging multidisciplinary research on adolescents of different cultures, ethnic background, socioeconomic status, geographic areas, and gender. Different groups have different vulnerabilities and we cannot generalize from research on middle-class white youth. For all groups except white middle-class youth, so far, we have barely begun to count the casualties; we do not yet understand how they happen or how to prevent them. Rolelessness *is* a problem, but there is much that we can do to add purpose to the years of adolescence.

There are at least two major reasons for these efforts: making adolescents' experience *as adolescents* as rewarding and productive as possible is the right and humane thing to do; and we all depend on them for our future.

This chapter is revised and updated from a 1988 working paper prepared for the Carnegie Council on Adolescent Development. This chapter reflects the views of the authors and not of the Council or the Carnegie Corporation of New York.

Notes

1 David A. Hamburg, *Today's Children: Creating a Future for a Generation in Crisis* (New York: Times Books/Random House, 1992).

2 U.S. Department of Commerce, Bureau of the Census, *Statistical Abstract of the United States: 1991* (111th ed.) (Washington, D.C.: Government Printing Office, 1991), No. 105.

3 U.S. Department of Commerce, Bureau of the Census, *U.S. Population Estimates, by Age, Sex, Race, and Hispanic Origin: 1989* (Washington, D.C.: Government Printing Office, March 1990), Series P-25, No. 1057.

4 Fred M. Hechinger, *Fateful Choices: Healthy Youth for the 21st Century* (New York: Hill and Wang, 1992), p. 30.

5 U.S. Congress, Office of Technology Assessment, *Adolescent Health – Volume I: Summary and Policy Options*, OTA-H-468 (Washington, D.C.: Government Printing Office, April 1991), p. 122.

6 U.S. Department of Commerce, Bureau of the Census, *Historical Statistics of the United States: Colonial Times to 1970* (Washington, D.C.: Government Printing Office, September 1975), Series A 160-171.

7 U.S. Department of Commerce, Bureau of the Census, *Statistical Abstract of the United States: 1991*, No. 13.

8 John Demos and Virginia Demos, "Adolescence in Historical Perspective," *Journal of Marriage and the Family*, November 1969, pp. 632–38.

9 Mihaly Csikszentmihalyi and Reed Larson, *Being Adolescent: Conflict and Growth in the Teenage Years* (New York: Basic Books, 1984).

10 J. Norman and M. W. Harris, *The Private Life of the American Teenager* (New York: Rawson, Wade, 1981).

11 U.S. Department of Commerce, Bureau of the Census, *Statistical Abstract of the United States: 1991*, No. 258.

12 Ibid.

13 Charles H. Harrison, "Student Service: The New Carnegie Unit" (Washington, D.C.: Carnegie Forum on Education and the Economy, 1987).

14 Ellen Greenberger and Laurence Steinberg, *When Teenagers Work: The Psychological and Social Costs of Adolescent Employment* (New York: Basic Books, 1986).

15 The William T. Grant Foundation, Commission on Work, Family and Citizenship, *The Forgotten Half: Non-College Youth in America* (Washington, D.C.: The William T. Grant Foundation, 1988).

16 The William T. Grant Foundation, Commission on Work, Family and Citizenship, *The Forgotten Half: Pathways to Success for America's Youth and Young Families* (Washington, D.C.: The William T. Grant Foundation, 1988), p. 24.

17 Reported in *Boston Globe*, April 27, 1988.

18 The William T. Grant Foundation, *The Forgotten Half: Non-College Youth in America*, p. 25.

19 William J. Wilson, *The Truly Disadvantaged: The Inner City, the Underclass, and Public Policy* (Chicago: University of Chicago Press, 1987).

20 Testimony of gang member before House Select Committee on Children, Youth, and Families, March 1988.

21 U.S. Department of Commerce, Bureau of the Census, *Statistical Abstract of the United States: 1991*, No. 450.

22 Kenneth Holland and Frank Ernest Hill, *Youth in the CCC* (Washington, D.C.: American Council on Education, 1942).

23 Csikszentmihalyi and Larson, *Being Adolescent*.

24 Richard Danzig and Peter Szanton, *National Service: What Would It Mean*? (Lexington, Mass.: D.C. Heath, 1987), p. 58.

25 The William T. Grant Foundation, *The Forgotten Half: Non-College Youth in America*.

26 Joan Schine, "Community Service for Young Adolescents: A Background Paper" (Washington, D.C.: Working paper for the Carnegie Council on Adolescent Development, June 1989).

27 Ellen Hoffman, "What Confronts Today's Youth," *Junior League Review*, Fall 1987, pp. 8-10.

28 Columbia University's Department of Psychology and Carnegie Corporation of New York, [Summary] Conference on Adolescent Violence: Research and Public Policy, New York, February 1987.

29 Judith Torney-Purta, "Youth in Relation to Social Institutions," in *At the Threshold: The Developing Adolescent*, ed. S. Shirley Feldman and Glen R. Elliott (Cambridge: Harvard University Press, 1990), pp. 457–78.

30 U.S. Congress, Office of Technology Assessment, *Healthy Children: Investing in the Future*, (Washington, D.C.: Government Printing Office, February 1988), p. 259.

31 National Center for Education Statistics, *A Profile of the American Eighth Grader: National Educational Longitudinal Study of 1988* (Washington, D.C.: U.S. Department of Education, Office of Educational Research and Improvement, 1988), pp. 54–56.

32 Kenda Creasy Dean, "A Synthesis of the Research on, and a Descriptive Overview of Protestant, Catholic, and Jewish Religious Youth Programs in the United States" (Report prepared for the Task Force on Youth Development and Community Programs, Carnegie Council on Adolescent Development, for presentation at meeting, March 1991).

33 Carnegie Council on Adolescent Development's Task Force on Youth Development and Community Programs, *A Matter of Time: Risk and Opportunity in the Non-School Hours* (New York: Carnegie Corporation of New York, 1992).

34 The William T. Grant Foundation, *The Forgotten Half: Non-College Youth in America*.

Webs of Influence: School and Community Programs That Enhance Adolescent Health and Education

RICHARD H. PRICE, MADALYN CIOCI,
WENDY PENNER, AND BARBARA TRAUTLEIN
University of Michigan, Ann Arbor

Consider how black inner-city eighth graders sense their future. More than half of the class will never graduate from high school, and if the usual statistics hold true, more of the boys in this class will be in jail than in college by the time they reach the age for college. Where will they find encouragement to believe that one day they might go to college? In some classrooms there is a group of "Dreamers"—students with mentors to guide their efforts, sharpen their academic skills, and promise them that if they do graduate from high school, their college expenses will be paid.

In another adolescent world, a fifteen-year-old girl has found she is pregnant. As the oldest girl in a single-parent family, she is confronted with a series of agonizing choices and few places to turn. Should she quit school or get a job? Who will help her learn about taking care of herself now that she is pregnant? Who will help her prepare for the abrupt transition from being a child to being a parent? Most girls in her situation may have few places to turn. However, in some places visiting nurses are helping such girls gain access to maternal health clinics and are providing prenatal instruction on nutrition, child care, and parenting skills. These nurses seem to know that more than medical issues are at stake. They have talked to carefully selected members of the girl's friendship network and extended family and have enlisted people willing to help if difficult circumstances arise.

Adolescents in each of these cases face a transition where health and educational opportunities are in jeopardy. Intentionally and thoughtfully provided social support can make a critical difference in reducing the risk of poor health and diminished educational attainment. How we can mobilize that support for young adolescents facing a range of challenges and risks is the subject of this chapter.

THE RISKS OF TRANSITIONS DURING ADOLESCENCE

Adolescence is a time of dramatic transition that involves multiple developmental changes, each with its own risks and challenges.[1] Physical changes in growth and sexual maturity are accompanied by changes in self-concept and future prospects. Challenges of achievement in school are accompanied by increases in autonomy and expectations of independence. Personal and social values become more differentiated and decisions about health, substance use, and achievement all are shaped during this critical period.

At the same time, sexual development and sexuality are accompanied by changes in intimate relationships and personal commitment. For some adolescents, the transition to adulthood may involve encounters with the criminal justice system, which may indelibly alter the course of future prospects and well-being. For others, the transition to adult status may be unexpectedly sudden, as when pregnancy and child-bearing occur in early adolescence. The risk of school failure and encounters with drugs are also commonplace experiences at this crucial period of development.

The lives of adolescents are sometimes further complicated by the erosion of familial and social supports as reflected, for example, in the rise of single-parent families, "especially those involving very young, poor, or socially isolated mothers, and in scattering the entire family, leaving many adolescents lonely, isolated, depressed, with a feeling of having no control over their destiny."[2]

While families are changing, becoming smaller and encompassing fewer generations, other social and community institutions vital to the successful development of adolescents are also facing major challenges. New demands are being placed on schools to strengthen their core educational mission, while at the same time they are expected to meet a variety of social needs. These critical societal institutions, the school and the family, also need strengthening so they can provide the support that adolescents so urgently need as they negotiate the transition to adulthood.

SOCIAL SUPPORT FOR ADOLESCENTS

What kinds of social support are needed by adolescents and how can we strengthen those institutions whose role it is to nurture and guide adolescent development? Social support has generally been defined as the provision of *aid, affirmation,* and *affect.*[3] Supportive aid refers to practical services and material benefits. Affirmation refers to feedback that raises self-esteem and strengthens identity. Affect refers to the provision of affection, caring, and nurturance. More recently, Heller and his colleagues have suggested that social support should also refer to social structures such as the school or family and to caring relationships that can foster the development of competence, esteem, and belonging.[4]

To understand the role of social support more clearly, its structural and relational aspects should be detailed. We need to better understand the nature of networks of social support and how such networks can be strengthened through programmatic efforts that aid in the transition to productive and satisfying adult roles. We will concern ourselves primarily with three arenas of the adolescent social environment: the family, the school, and various community organizations as shown in Figure 1. In most cases, families include one or two parents, siblings, and extended family members, but a wide variety of different family relationships may exist for adolescents, sometimes providing adequate levels of support, unfortunately in other cases failing to do so.

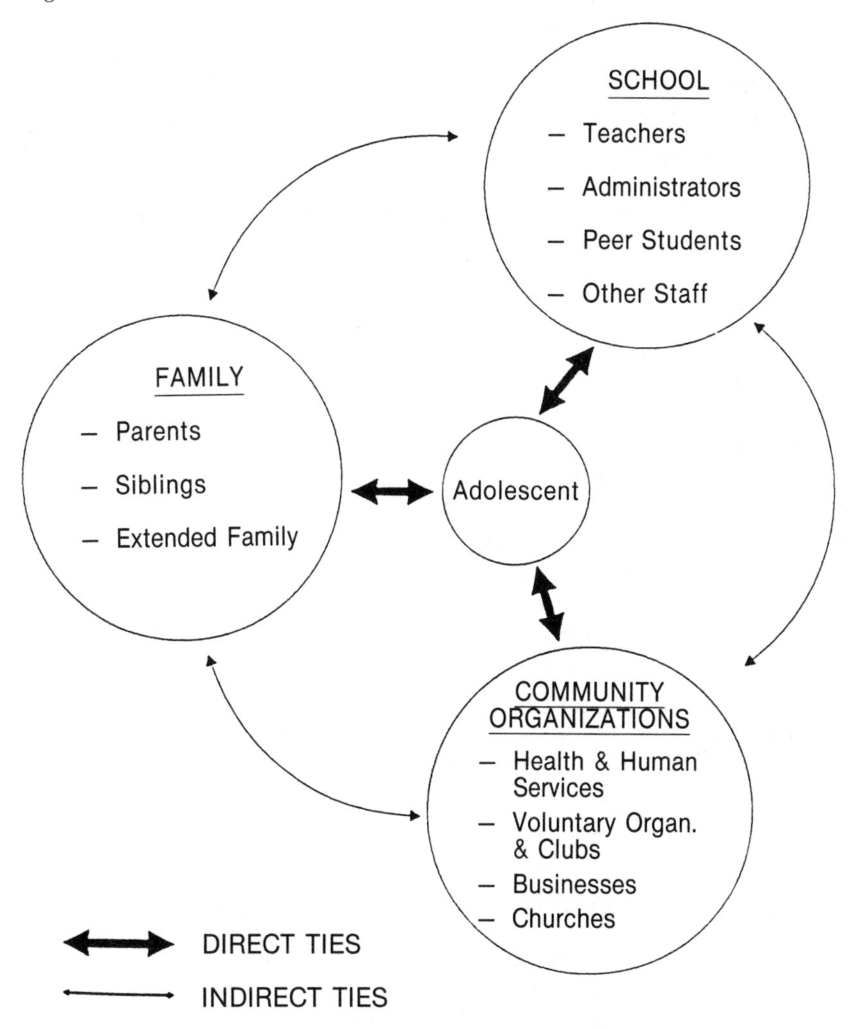

Figure 1. Arenas of the Adolescent Social Environment

For most young adolescents, school represents a major arena of involvement. For the fortunate few, the school and its teachers, student friends, counselors, and other staff members represent a community of commitment and support where academic and social challenges can be presented at developmentally appropriate times. All too often, however, schools represent a very different kind of social environment, one in which close ties to teachers are never established, where enduring relationships with peers are difficult to maintain, and where the school represents a setting for failure rather than success.

Finally, community organizations represent another potential arena of involvement for young adolescents, one in which involvement may be either substantial or almost nonexistent. This arena represents a portion of the adult world in which young adolescents will become increasingly involved as they grow older. Community and youth organizations, including clubs and other voluntary organizations, health and human service agencies, businesses and churches, all may exert supportive or alienating influences on young adolescents. Some organizations such as the juvenile courts are, by their very nature, focused on deviant rather than prosocial behavior. Others, such as business, may have a great but unrealized capacity for the support of adolescents in the developmental transition to adulthood.

Figure 1 illustrates an often unrecognized aspect of the social environment of adolescents. The heavy arrows represent *direct ties* between the adolescent and various aspects of the social environment. These direct ties represent major channels through which social support resources may flow. However, equally important are the *indirect ties* between arenas in the social environment. The ties between family and school, school and community, and family and community represent critical relationships that, depending on their nature and strength, can have important influences on adolescent development. For example, the adolescent whose social environment includes strong cooperative relationships between teacher and parent is likely to have a very different experience when dealing with problems of academic achievement from that of a young person whose parent-teacher relationship is hostile and conflict-ridden or almost nonexistent. These indirect ties in the social lives of adolescents constitute important avenues for influence and support, but are frequently ignored when we try to understand the social environment of adolescents.

SOCIAL-SUPPORT NETWORKS OF ADOLESCENTS

Figures 2A and 2B illustrate the social-support network during early adolescence in two different ways. Here we have portrayed existing relationships in the lives of an adolescent in more detail. The links between the actors and the social network of the young adolescent represent the channels through which information, influence, and messages of affirmation may flow. They represent direct and indirect relationships of potential support for adolescents as they cope with the transition to adulthood. Of course, not all individuals in such a support network are necessarily connected, and it is likely that not all of the relationships are equally strong or equally positive.

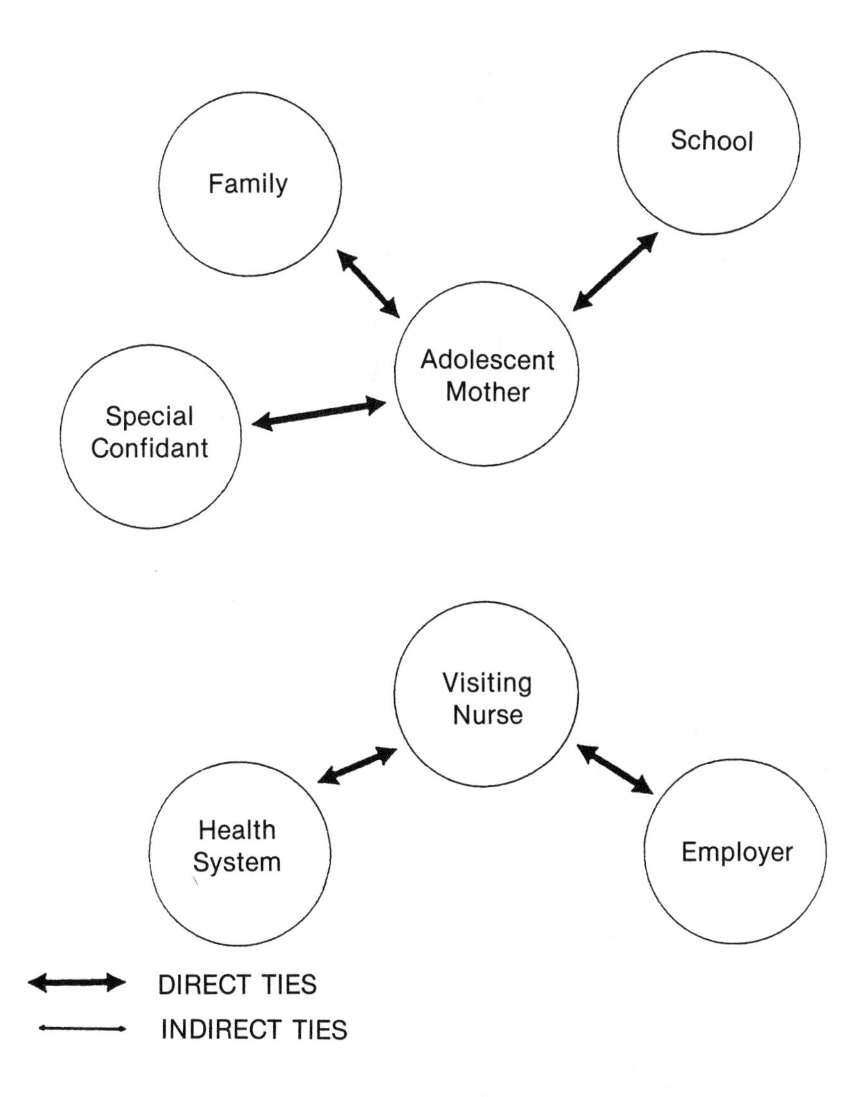

Figure 2A. Social-Support Network of Pregnant Adolescent before Support Intervention

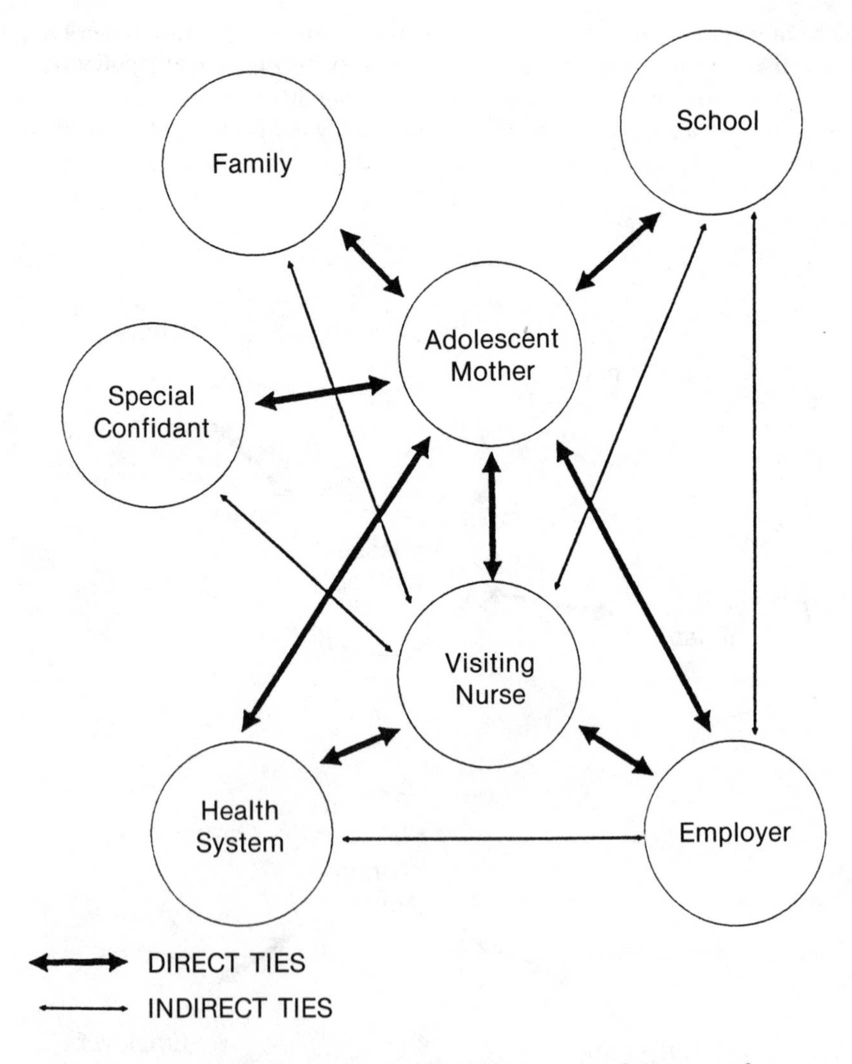

Figure 2B. Social-Support Network of Pregnant Adolescent after Support Intervention

Nevertheless, social-support networks of the kind illustrated have important implications for the prevention of social and developmental problems encountered in early adolescence. A richly connected network of positive relationships, reaching across several arenas of the social environment, can provide multiple sources of information, caring, and commitment as well as alternative points of view and access to still other additional resources. In contrast, a support network that is impoverished and has only a few weak connections or one that is filled with conflictual relations provides access to only inadequate or inappropriate resources, which can place an adolescent at risk for major developmental and social problems.

Consider Figure 2A again, this time assuming that the person at the center is a young adolescent girl who is pregnant. Faced with such a major and abrupt transition to an adult role, the adolescent in this network (and her future child) is faced with major needs and challenges, including the need to obtain adequate health care, prenatal education and nutrition, and emotional and social support from family and friends; the decision to remain in or drop out of school; and the need for eventual paid employment. Whether the abrupt transition to motherhood and adult responsibilities will be successful for both mother and child critically depends on whether supportive relationships can be drawn on or created to aid with the transition.

Figure 2B shows how such relationships might have developed if this girl had been a participant in the prenatal-infancy support project developed by David Olds.[5] The heavy lines depict the new or strengthened supportive ties in the adolescent's relationships. This support program uses public-health nurses to reach out to socially isolated pregnant adolescents and their families to provide support and counseling on prenatal and postnatal care, medical referrals to community health organizations, continuing relationships to school where appropriate, and relationships to potential employers when needed. The program also mobilizes the support of family members or peers on whom the young mother feels she can count in times of difficulty.

Our portrayal of the social-support networks of adolescents involves relationships of the adolescent both to primary groups such as family and friends and to more formal organizations such as schools and human-service agencies. As Litwak and Messeri have observed, it is the combination of relationships both to primary groups and to formal organizations that provides a supportive network that has both the commitment and effective ties characteristic of family and friend groups and the access to resources and influence characteristic of formal organizations.[6]

We see then that a social-support program designed for preventive impact can be thought of as an *intentional organizational effort to alter the availability of supportive relationships and resources to adolescents as they experience the transition to adulthood.* When such supportive relationships are not available, the likelihood of a successful transition will be lower, even though some adolescents and their families may succeed in identifying and mobilizing the supports they need for a successful transition. However, when critical supportive resources are lacking, the developmental trajectory of many young adolescents is likely to be less than optimal. In the most unfortunate cases, the result may be poor school achievement and dropout, substance abuse, school-age pregnancy, involvement with the juvenile justice system, welfare dependency, and neglect.

Preventive health and education efforts that support adolescents in the transition to adulthood have great potential. We will identify critical elements of these supportive prevention approaches as well as innovative programs, and we will identify lines of inquiry that need further exploration. In our review of supportive programs where evidence of success is apparent we have noted it. Where only promising but not yet proven programs exist, we have tried to qualify our description of programmatic effects. In addition, we have attempted to identify the characteristics of successful programs. We now turn to a summary of those characteristics followed by a review of a number of innovative support programs for young adolescents.

INGREDIENTS OF SUCCESSFUL SOCIAL-SUPPORT PROGRAMS FOR ADOLESCENTS

While systematic field experiments to identify features of programs that maximize supportiveness and preventive impact for adolescents are yet to be conducted, our survey of existing programs permits some preliminary conclusions. Table 1 summarizes key ingredients of successful social-support programs for adolescents. We now turn to a more detailed discussion of each of these characteristics, drawing on examples from supportive programs described later in this article.

EMPATHY WITH ADOLESCENT GOALS AND ASPIRATIONS

Erickson, Gottlieb, and others have observed that if a program is not seen by adolescents as relevant to their needs and aspirations, the likelihood of participation will be low.[7] Perhaps the clearest example of a supportive program designed to respond to adolescent aspirations and to provide immediate incentives is Eugene Lange's "I Have a Dream" program. The promise of a college scholarship for students successfully completing their high school education makes the incentive for participation real. Furthermore, in this particular approach, Lange and his colleagues have provided a well-conceived, strong, supportive mentoring program to demonstrate a personal interest in the child and to aid with the concrete tasks of improving academic achievement in high school.

Several other writers have sounded a slightly different theme. Erickson and Hedin have both noted that programs that readily acknowledge a partnership with youth are much more likely to be effective than those that offer support primarily aimed at the control of behavior.[8] Such a partnership orientation is more likely to communicate a sense of positive reward and minimize the message that adolescent behavior is inevitably a problem or that young people cannot make important positive contributions.

Table 1. Ingredients of Successful Social-Support Programs for Adolescents

EMPATHY

Programs are sensitive to adolescents' own goals, values, and aspirations.

INSIGHT

Programs recognize the interrelatedness of adolescent needs and problems.

OPPORTUNITIES FOR GROWTH AND MASTERY

Programs provide roles and activities that:

- encourage active participation
- provide opportunities to learn new skills, and
- provide clear expectations and a predictable environment.

RESPONSIVENESS TO ADOLESCENT DEVELOPMENT

Programs are designed to:

- be sensitive to the timing of potential risks and developmental changes, and
- provide continuity over time.

ORGANIZATIONAL SUPPORT

Programs are organized to:

- forge relationships among potential supporters of adolescents, and
- provide flexibility and willingness to commit resources.

INSIGHT INTO INTERRELATED PROBLEMS AND NEEDS

Jessor summarizes longitudinal studies of problem behavior in adolescence by concluding that many adolescent problems do not occur in isolation, but instead tend to occur together.[9] The clustering of problems may reflect the fact that two or more different problems such as drug use and school failure are likely to occur together in a single individual or that problems may be causally interrelated—for example, when alcohol and tobacco use complicates pregnancy and places an infant at risk. School-linked health clinics, for example, recognize that a broad spectrum of health issues must be addressed for adolescents.[10] Similarly, programs aimed at reducing school failure or resisting substance use are also frequently directed at the development of adolescent social skills, identity, and self-esteem.

OPPORTUNITIES FOR GROWTH AND MASTERY: PARTICIPATION, ROLES WITH SKILL OPPORTUNITIES, AND CLEAR EXPECTATIONS

A number of strategies exist for enhancing participation, including the rotation of leadership in group activities and use of small groups.[11] Heller et al. have argued that suppportive relationships that allow opportunities for adolescents to give as well as receive may be particularly beneficial.[12] Indeed, the lack of opportunities for active participation may undercut the potential effectiveness of programs. Mueller and Higgins make the related observation that programs that employ experiential learning techniques are more successful than those that require only passive listening and learning.[13] Our survey of preventive programs has identified a number of such programs, including the Youth Action Program, which supports active involvement by youth in improving their own community.[14]

Nightingale and Wolverton note that the concept of adolescence is largely defined in terms of what it is not: neither child nor adult.[15] They argue that adolescents lack roles in society that are appreciated and approved. At the same time, adolescents must take on two major developmental tasks—identity formation and development of the sense of self-efficacy and self-worth. The transition to adult roles is probably easiest for young people going to college because adolescence is lengthened by continued dependency on parents and structured by years of study, athletics, and other activities, and because the parents of college-bound young people frequently have the resources and energy to create opportunities for their children. On the other hand, non-college-bound youth frequently find it difficult to obtain work or productive activity that is meaningful and provides adequate wages.[16]

Several strategies exist for increasing meaningful roles for adolescents, including the possibility of a youth corps, linking adolescents to retired persons, and the provision of opportunities to succeed outside of school. Schine and Campbell's program for school helpers and Olds's program to teach parenting roles to pregnant adolescents, designed to move young people out of the downward trajectory of delinquency and into meaningful jobs, are examples of programs that provide such roles.[17]

During early adolescence, the demands of the social environment shift dramatically. Among the programs reviewed is the School Transition Environment Program (STEP), which provides a school setting in which the transition from junior high to high school is supported by a more predictable environment featuring a committed homeroom teacher and a single group of peers who meet academic challenges as a group.[18] In this more stable and supportive environment, there is an opportunity for peer support to develop while students face the increased academic and social demands of secondary school.

In many cases, the predictable environment and clear norms of successful programs are produced by well-trained professional or nonprofessional staff.[19] Sensitive and well-prepared staff recognize the balance that must be struck between a clear and predictable social environment on the one hand, and the need for a setting that supports spontaneity and initiative from adolescents on the other.

RESPONSIVENESS TO ADOLESCENT DEVELOPMENT: TIMING AND CONTINUITY

Effective prevention programs take information about the developmental characteristics of adolescents into account. Programs designed to prevent teenage pregnancy need to anticipate the probable point at which sexual fertility and activity may begin and substance abuse prevention programs must reach young children before many of them are actively using tobacco, drugs, or alcohol. While some choice points for the timing of supportive interventions may seem obvious, such as before sexual activity or before substance use is commonplace, the choices may not always be so clear-cut. For example, in some cases, programs supporting more effective parent-child relationships may need to begin earlier to prevent the disintegration of parent-child relationships during adolescence itself.[20] Clearly, this is a question about which more reliable information is needed.

One-shot programs of brief duration are not likely to provide the expected benefits of programs of longer duration and continuity that provide support before and during adolescent development. Zabin et al. noted that teenagers were more likely to return to a school health clinic to see a staff member with whom they had already established a trusting relationship.[21] Programs of longer duration have the dual advantage of establishing long-term relationships and providing support over a larger portion of the course of adolescent development. Lange's "Dreamer" program provides an excellent example.[22] Designed to occur over the course of six years from the end of sixth grade through high school graduation, the program retains a group of aspiring students in a continuing relationship, and provides a stable staff coordinator whose job is to help clarify academic and career goals and to provide the needed support to attain those goals.

ORGANIZATIONAL SUPPORT: LINKING SUPPORTERS AND COMMITTING RESOURCES

Programs that foster relationships between the various supporters of adolescents are likely to be effective. Programs aimed at preventing school failure that involve both parent and teacher appear to be more effective than programs that involve only one member of the role set.[23] Similarly, programs for pregnant teenagers that involve both a visiting nurse and a friend provide an example of this special quality.[24] We referred to this earlier as the existence of secondary ties in the support network of adolescents. It may be that programs that intentionally encourage secondary ties have particular advantages since they involve and mobilize broader or wider aspects/parts of the social world of the adolescent.

Price and Lorion and D'Aunno have noted that the receptivity of the host organization, such as a school or health center, is a critical but frequently overlooked factor in the development and implementation of effective preventive programs.[25] D'Aunno describes the complexity of factors in the host organization as "organizational readiness." These factors include the beliefs of critical authorities that a problem actually exists, as well as the attitudes and beliefs of leaders in the host organization itself. While problem recognition and the beliefs of people both within and outside the organization are critical factors in organizational readiness, so is the availability of resources to engage in an innovative activity. Organizational mechanisms that provide flexibility and support for innovation are critical ingredients of readiness. For example, the degree to which a program is structured so that integration and collaboration occur across community services may be critical to its success.

There is a professional consensus that providing supportive aid, affirmation, and affect—the core attributes of social support—is necessary but not sufficient to produce effective support programs for adolescents. Additional ingredients are critical for the implementation of successful programs. Having described these ingredients, we now review some innovative support programs for adolescents in school and community settings, summarized in Table 2. Reviewing these programs serves both to illustrate the generalizations we have drawn and to suggest models of support programs for the future.

SUPPORTIVE INTERVENTIONS FOR ADOLESCENTS IN THE SCHOOLS

In school, the young adolescent encounters challenges perhaps never before experienced, including pressures to achieve academically, to follow regimented schedules, and to adhere to strict behavioral guidelines. The transition from elementary school to junior high or high school places new demands on the student, including challenges to navigate a new and often overwhelming environment.

Schools are particularly important social arenas for adolescents, because of their potential impact on cognitive and social development. They are also social organizations that often contain ready-made channels for preventive interventions. Schools are, after all, places in which young adolescents spend a large portion of each waking day and are potent sources for both reward and punishment. At their best, schools can be organizations in which the benefits of group participation can be reaped, where transitions to adult responsibilities and challenges can be negotiated, where peer support can be encouraged, and where organizational connections to needed health care can be made available. We now examine several supportive interventions that capitalize on the potential advantages of the school for supporting adolescent development.

ENHANCING STUDENT AND FAMILY PARTICIPATION

Two studies demonstrate the value of increasing the positive participation of peers, family, and teachers in the learning and developmental tasks of young adolescents.[26] When involvement and participation of the members of the support network of adolescents are increased, more opportunities for exchange of valuable resources, ideas, and indications of commitment and concern are possible. This research suggests that even small reorganizations of the school can have beneficial effects, particularly for adolescents whose current levels of achievement and social support require improvement.

ENHANCED CLASSROOM PARTICIPATION

The creation of small student groups in schools can be particularly beneficial in mobilizing support for adolescents. Benefits that derive from small groups include greater opportunity for participation, access to multiple roles, and access to valued resources. For example, small-group participation can provide increased interaction with teachers and more opportunities to build friendships, as well as a greater chance to exercise interpersonal skills. Small groups, as opposed to large classrooms, afford adolescents these advantages because the small groups are "undermanned settings."[27] That is, small-group settings allow students to occupy more roles and have more successful experiences, which may lead to a sense of task completion, self-efficacy, and self-esteem, whereas in larger settings, only a few students can actively try out new roles and practice new skills.

Richter and Tjosvold describe a field experiment that investigated the effects of enhanced classroom participation. When participation was encouraged, students decided on the topic and major learning activities they would engage in with the teacher. Results obtained through students' self-reports and observations made by independent observers showed that students who

Table 2. Social-Support Programs for Early Adolescents That Promote Positive Health and Education Outcomes

School Support Programs

PROGRAM	MECHANISM AND OUTCOMES
Enhanced Classroom Participation (Richter & Tjosvold, 1980)	Enhanced classroom participation produced favorable attitudes toward school, independence, internal commitment to learning.
Mobilizing Parent and Teacher Support (Bein & Bry, 1980)	Conferences, group meetings increased parental contact, improved school achievement, and reduced discipline problems.
Peer Leadership in Smoking Prevention (Klepp et al., 1986)	Peer leaders serve as models, teach skills to resist peer pressure to smoke, and identify health-enhancing alternatives.
School Transition Environment Program (Felner & Adan, 1988)	Reorganizes school environment to produce a stable peer group and a supportive home room teacher and aid the transition to high school. Produces higher school achievement, lower dropout, higher self-esteem. Examples include Boys and Girls Clubs in public housing projects.
School Linked Health Clinics (Zabin et al., 1986a, b)	Makes access to health clinic available through the schools. Reduced pregnancy and childbirth rates, later onset of sexual activity.

Table 2. Social-Support Programs for Early Adolescents That Promote Positive Health and Education Outcomes (Continued)

Community Support Programs

PROGRAM	MECHANISM AND OUTCOMES
Youth Organizations (Erickson, 1982)	Students who join are more likely to participate in community activities in later life, show higher self-esteem.
Youth Action Program (Stoneman, 1988)	Active student participation and governance of community projects encourages self-esteem, commitment.
Early Adolescent Child Care Helper Program (Schine & Campbell, 1987)	Early adolescents care for younger children, learn caring skills and responsibility, and help with child-care burden.
"I Have a Dream" (Lange, 1986)	With the promise of a college scholarship, poor students commit to high school graduation and receive support in developing academic skills. Results are higher graduation rates and academic achievement.
Las Madrinas (Stanton, 1988)	Young, high-achieving Hispanic "godmothers" serve as mentors to Hispanic junior high school girls to discuss relationship, achievement, future career concerns.
Prenatal/Early Infancy Project (Olds, 1988)	Visiting public-health nurses link pregnant adolescents to health care and provide parenting skills and information. Result is lower rates of second pregnancy, less child abuse and neglect, higher birth weight, higher levels of maternal employment.
Project Spirit (Crawford, 1988)	Black churches provide special classes for black children with school problems, support parents, and provide tutoring.

participated in classroom decisions developed more favorable attitudes toward school and subject matter, related more positively with peers, worked more consistently without supervision, and learned more than students whose teachers made all the decisions.[28]

Richter and Tjosvold assert that "participation in making decisions may integrate students into school life and develop their commitment to learning."[29] The study outcomes, including positive attitudes, internalized commitment, and positive peer relationships, all contribute to high levels of learning. When students are permitted to participate in decision making, "they feel recognized as capable of contributing to classroom management and gain satisfaction through influencing decisions."[30] In addition, the researchers observed that "students generally opted for active, innovative learning experience," and concluded that "results of this study suggest that a major outcome of participation is more positive peer groups."[31] Enhanced participation can increase the amount of supportive aid, positive affect, and personal affirmation available, not only for those who might naturally elicit it, but also for those who might remain isolated in less participatory classroom environments.

MOBILIZING PARENT AND TEACHER SUPPORT

Bein and Bry developed an intervention strategy in the school to mobilize both family support and small-group support in the school. This intervention focused on a group of seventh-grade students, selected because of low academic motivation, family problems, and records of disciplinary referrals to the vice-principal's office.[32]

The successful intervention had three components: (1) teacher conferences, (2) group meetings, and (3) parental contacts. The teacher conference component was a biweekly meeting between program staff and individual teachers. In these conferences the teachers were presented with the idea that the students were in the program because of their potential to achieve. The group-meeting component consisted of biweekly student group meetings. The parent-contact component included two parent meetings held during the school year. Furthermore, during the intervals between the meetings, group leaders contacted parents by notes, phone calls, and personal visits. A crucial aspect of the intervention was that program staff emphasized to both teachers and parents that the students could do better in school, and that this was why they were chosen for the program. Stressing to both teachers and parents that the adolescent has the ability to succeed may create a "self-fulfilling prophecy" for the students: Students are expected to succeed, and they often will.

Bein and Bry speculated about how the contact with parents may have contributed to program success: "Since the school has largely been an arena of negative experience for them, these young people are probably less open to influence during school hours than other young people."[33] Thus, we need to learn more about the ways in which adolescents' perceptions of the school are important in determining the success of preventive interventions in schools.

SUPPORTING HEALTH BEHAVIOR THROUGH PEER LEADERSHIP

Peer influence has long been recognized as a powerful force in the lives of adolescents. As their social world expands beyond the immediate family, peer attitudes and behavior take on a new salience and become potentially influential in shaping health-related behavior. A number of programs have attempted to mobilize peer influence to shape health norms and behavior, to sustain healthy behavior, and to provide social support to resist pressures to smoke.

Klepp et al. have reviewed programs using a peer-leadership intervention strategy, and concluded that "results from school-based, peer-led psychosocial smoking prevention programs suggest that this approach is effective in reducing smoking onset rates."[34] Peer leaders serve as potential role models, demonstrate and create a norm of nonuse, and provide alternatives to drug use. Peer leaders reinforce the importance of social responsibility and of health. At the behavioral level, peer leaders teach social skills to resist pressures to use drugs and to help students identify and practice health-enhancing alternatives to drug use.

Peer leaders provide normative information rather than merely providing facts. Research has shown that while teachers have more credibility regarding factual information, peers have more credibility relaying information about norms for social encounters.[35] This finding suggests the importance of understanding what specific meaning offers of social support may hold for specific subgroups of adolescents.[36]

Although little is known about how these programs affect the onset of smoking, Klepp et al. report a process evaluation conducted on four programs. Results indicated that (1) students would have selected the same peer leaders again; (2) peer leaders felt and were perceived as adequately trained; (3) being a peer leader is a positive experience; (4) students felt positive about having peer-led programs; and (5) drug-use outcomes may depend on how supportive teachers are in these programs.[37]

Klepp et al. further note that training peer leaders works best when conducted during regular school hours. Program implementers "need to persuade teachers that peer-led learning is special."[38] When designing training programs for teachers, one must create an engaging environment, allow for a thorough review of the curriculum, and provide hands-on experience. Peer-led programs need institutional support from teachers and staff to be successful.

REDESIGNING THE ORGANIZATION OF SCHOOLS TO ENHANCE SUPPORT

Bronfenbrenner observes that students changing levels of schools are confronting a major "ecological transition" that involves adapting to both new roles and settings.[39] Because the ecological transition between elementary and junior high school is likely to occur for most adolescents, and may lead to stress and maladaption, the school transition is an ideal point for a preventive intervention. Felner and his colleagues have studied the transitional tasks accompanying the transition from junior high and to high school and argue that the difficulty experienced in attempting to master new tasks reflects both the social context and the individual's history and current coping abilities.[40]

THE SCHOOL TRANSITION ENVIRONMENT PROGRAM (STEP)

Felner and Adan have initiated a supportive prevention program called the School Transition Environment Program (STEP).[41] STEP seeks to modify those aspects of the environment that hinder students' successful mastery of transitional tasks. STEP modifies the "two critical features of the school setting that affect the difficulty students have in mastering the essential transitional tasks . . . [specifically] the complexity of the school environment and the setting's capacity to respond to students' needs."[42]

STEP employs two strategies to alter the school ecology to ease these transitions for students: (1) reorganizing the regularities of the school environment to reduce the degree of flux and complexity of the social and physical settings that the student confronts, and (2) restructuring the roles of homeroom teachers and guidance personnel to provide more personal contact, caring, and support.

Reorganizing the school environment is intended to reduce the degree of confusion the student confronts on entering the new school, to facilitate reestablishment of a stable peer-support system, and to establish a stable teacher-support program. It is also intended to enhance the students' sense of belonging in the school and to foster perceptions of the school as "a stable, well-organized, understandable and cohesive place."[43]

Restructuring the homeroom teachers' roles is intended (1) "to increase the instrumental and affective social support students perceive as being available from school-based sources; (2) to reduce the difficulties students have in obtaining important information about school rules, expectations, and regularities, thus facilitating their efforts to deal with the transitional task of reorganizing their own daily school-related routines; (3) to increase students' feelings of accountability and decrease their sense of anonymity; and (4) to increase teachers' familiarity with students, and decrease the time it takes for such familiarity to develop."[44]

Felner and Adan report that STEP students did not show the same decreases in academic performance and self-concept scores and increases in absenteeism that controls did.[45] Process evaluation results indicated that "compared to controls, STEP students perceived the school environment as more stable, understandable, well organized, involving, and supportive. Students also saw teachers and other school personnel as providing higher levels of support, especially by the end of the school year."[46] Further, the dropout and failure rates for STEP students were less than half that for controls.

SUPPORT FROM SCHOOL-LINKED HEALTH CENTERS

The use of school-linked centers to support adolescents' health-care needs is increasing.[47] Medical schools or local health departments have been the major sponsors of adolescent health centers, although the schools are often responsible for providing space, maintenance, security, and access to the student population.[48] Because of this, the school-linked health clinic can constitute a supportive link between the school and the health-care system.

As Millstein notes,

> The school system and its personnel play a crucial role in the acceptance of school-linked centers by students, parents and the community. Health education has traditionally been the responsibility of the schools, who may or may not have the resources to provide well-developed, appropriate curriculum in this area. With the presence of school-linked health centers, schools have the potential to strengthen their health education programs.[49]

THE ADOLESCENT PREGNANCY PREVENTION PROGRAM

This school-based health program based much of its design on research findings about adolescent needs and practices.[50] The "Adolescent Pregnancy-Prevention Program" was developed and evaluated by a group of researchers at Johns Hopkins University and was implemented in clinics near the targeted schools.

The development of the clinic incorporated several prior research findings. First, Zabin et al. found that young people will rarely return to a site for education if they have already received the medical services they need.[51] Therefore, education and counseling need to be provided at the same time as medical services. Second, teenagers need continuity of support over time. This allows the building of trust and an opportunity to reflect on what they have learned with a trusted adult.[52] Third, the researchers found that adolescents have a much higher risk for pregnancy in their first months of sexual exposure and when coitus is initiated in early adolescence. Teenagers tend to delay visiting clinics for contraceptives for more than a year after initiating intercourse and often visit only if pregnancy is suspected. Treatment and facilities need to be located near where adolescents spend their time, and clinic services need to be confidential if students are to be reached soon after the first sexual exposure.

As a result of these findings, a program was developed targeting the predominantly black, lower-socioeconomic-level students from an urban high school and junior high school in Baltimore. The major intervention strategy was to have the clinic staffed by social workers and nurse practitioners who were available both through the clinic and the school. For the students, this meant there was some assurance of consistency of both caregivers and information across settings.

Education, counseling, and medical services, including the dispensing of contraceptives, were available confidentially during one visit to the clinic, and repeat care was offered by the same caregiver as often as possible. The clinics were located near both of the participating schools, but not on school grounds. Thus the school, though it supplied support and students for the program and allowed the education to occur in the classroom at times, did not place itself in jeopardy in the eyes of more conservative members of the community. The clinic operated only during the hours after school, making it convenient for students without interfering with classes.

This was one of the few programs of its kind designed for evaluation from the outset. Questionnaires were administered to all the students of the two schools before and after the development of the program. The program resulted in increased contraceptive use for all who used the clinic compared with those who did not. Knowledge of contraceptives and of the risks for pregnancy went up 13 percent. This is an expected result because of the educational component of the program. However, health-related behaviors were also significantly affected: "Rates of pregnancy and childbirth were reduced in a period when rates went up in the comparison schools. In less than three years of the program's operation, the proportion of sexually active ninth to twelfth grade girls who had babies went down 25 percent."[53] In addition, girls became sexually active at a later age after being exposed to the program. The average age at first intercourse rose seven months: from fifteen years and seven months to sixteen years and two months.[54]

It is clear that schools can provide a range of opportunities for programs to support adolescents in the critical years when educational attainment and health behaviors are being shaped. Programs to encourage peer, parent, and teacher support can have positive effects on school achievement and self-esteem, as well as school discipline and dropout problems. Peer and school-support programs that help adolescents to resist pressure to smoke and provide access to health care can have preventive impacts on adolescent health. As indicated in the report *Turning Points*, schools can become sources of support and caring rather than institutions that are indifferent to the educational, health, and emotional needs of young adolescents.[55] The programs reviewed here suggest some of the ways in which social support can be mobilized in schools to enhance adolescent health and education.

COMMUNITY SUPPORTS FOR ADOLESCENTS

Some commentators have suggested that a community can provide a variety of supports and resources for adolescents.[56] A community—whether defined in terms of geographical space, a political unit, or a network of associations—remains a critical locus in which the developmental tasks of adolescents are represented in the activities of everyday life.

In assessing the capacity of communities to support adolescent development, Wynn et al. developed a typology of community supports. They argue that community supports include: (1) "opportunities to participate in organized groups, (2) avenues for contributing to the well being of others, (3) sources of personal support, and (4) access to and use of community facilities and events."[57] While this typology is not intended to suggest mutually exclusive categories, it does provide a useful organizing schema for our review.

A community provides the adolescent an arena between the institutions of family and school on the one hand and those of the wider world on the other. It is an arena in which adolescents can have an opportunity to learn and practice the skills useful in the wider world and to practice adult roles, including those of worker, parent, and citizen. Each of these sources of support in the community can also call on a wide range of skills and may increase the likelihood of and opportunity for supportive adolescent-adult relationships. We now turn to a survey of each of these types of community supports, briefly noting concrete examples, research findings, and emerging themes.

YOUTH ORGANIZATIONS THAT CONTRIBUTE TO COMMUNITY WELFARE

Youth organizations represent a major community resource in which adolescents can participate. Over 300 national youth organizations currently operate with chapters of varying size and membership throughout the United States.[58] These organizations include career exploration groups, such as Junior Achievement; groups aimed at character building, such as the Scouts; political groups, such as Young Democrats and Republicans; and ethnic groups, such as Indian Youth of America. It is estimated that approximately 71 percent of all eighth-graders participate in one or more outside-school groups.[59]

Survey data indicate that youths who join such groups are more likely to participate in community activities in adulthood and tend to display higher self-esteem, are better educated, and come from families with somewhat higher incomes.[60] These data do not allow us to assert unequivocally that joining such groups will automatically enhance self-esteem, but they do suggest that opportunities for participation in youth groups may provide resources that could be made more broadly available, especially to less affluent adolescents. In general, participation in youth organizations offers the adolescent experience in and the opportunity for learning both interpersonal and organizational skills vital to being an adult.

The value of caring for and contributing to the welfare of others may well be underemphasized in our society. Erickson suggests that the metaphors of competition and justice may have dominated research on adolescent development, rather than those of caring and concern.[61] Even so, scholars are now recognizing the importance of caring as a major orientation.[62] Caring for others often sets the stage for both giving and receiving social support. Heller et al. note the importance of reciprocity in social-support relationships.[63] Contributing to the welfare of others can also elicit affirming and supportive relationships.

Our communities are replete with numerous opportunities to contribute to the welfare of others. Adolescents can help their peers through activities such as mentorship, tutoring, and counseling. They can work with the elderly in nursing homes or with younger children in schools, day care centers, or hospitals. They can become engaged in identifying and solving community problems and can provide help to human service agencies.

Boys and Girls Clubs in Public Housing Projects

Currently, Boys and Girls Clubs are being established in places where young adolescents are at highest risk for school dropout, delinquency, and substance abuse problems—public housing projects. Clubs are being established in fifteen housing projects in a representative sample of American cities. The effort is being evaluated over a three-year period and will compare projects where no clubs are available, where standard club chapters are established, and where special substance-abuse prevention programs are established as well.[64] The Club Programs are designed to provide individual, small-group, and drop-in supportive activities in larger groups to enhance educational and personal development.

Preliminary results of the housing project experiment indicate that establishing the clubs helps reduce vandalism, public substance abuse, and delinquent behavior. These are encouraging results, and further research should clarify the impact of clubs on adolescent youth.

The Youth Action Program

Participating in activities that contribute to the welfare of others can have powerful energizing effects on adolescents. A compelling example is the

Youth Action Program.[65] The program is a youth-run community service organization developed by Dorothy Stoneman, a former teacher in East Harlem, New York City. The Youth Action Program involves several different projects, including a young peoples' block association that has transformed a vacant lot into a park and garden and a youth patrol that makes its rounds in housing projects to cut down on crime. Another project, the "Home Away From Home Network," finds places for teenagers who have family problems.

The following material from a Youth Action Program publication communicates how this program provides support for teenagers, and, at the same time, provides opportunities for both giving and receiving support and an appreciation of the strengths of teenagers.

> The basic premise of the Youth Action Program is that young people can be a strong force for good in their communities. They have a clear perception of what is wrong in the world and vivid ideas for constructive change; they lack only the confidence and skills needed to carry them out. The role of YAP's adult staff is to draw out the young people's ideas and to give the personal support and technical assistance necessary to realize them.
>
> The process of youth government is central to our concept. Each project is governed by a core group of leaders, while the overall program is governed by a policy committee consisting primarily of young people. Critical decisions about staffing, program policy, budget, and community action are in the hands of the policy committee."[66]

While this program has not been subjected to a rigorous evaluation, the teenagers themselves believe they have acquired significant skills and a sense of self-esteem. In the words of one of the participants: "Working in YAP, we learned from the meetings and discussions the decisions we had to make. We learned group dynamics, how to deal with people and problems. We were empowered because the program was based on our ideas. We got a sense of pride, of importance, something teenagers in East Harlem don't get anywhere else."[67]

Adolescents in low-income communities, in particular, may gain from participation in projects such as the Youth Action Program a sense that they can indeed make a difference in their own community.

The Early Adolescent Child Care Helper Program

The Center for Advanced Study and Education of the City University of New York has developed the Early Adolescent Child Care Helper Program to involve young people ages eleven to fourteen working as interns in local day care and Head Start centers.[68] The internship experiences are supplemented by weekly seminars conducted by junior high school staff. The goal of the program is to motivate students before they reach high school to stay in school, to provide structured settings for children who otherwise might be unsupervised, and to help them learn first-hand about the world of work and the roles of citizens, workers, and parents. In addition, the program provides extra help for community service agencies where overworked staff welcome the enthusiasm and energy of young volunteers.

Studies of the Early Adolescent Child Care Helper Program suggest that helpers in day care settings provided additional opportunities for children to talk with an older person and encouraged language development in younger children. Research results indicate that the program could benefit from being better integrated into the school setting and from more communication between program seminar leaders and teachers. Nevertheless, students who were involved in the Early Adolescent Child Care Helper Program reported that they enjoyed being a good influence on those younger than themselves, and that they learned patience and reliability in interacting with small children.[69]

PERSONAL SUPPORT THROUGH MENTORING

Stephen Hamilton and Nancy Darling describe the mentor role: "The word mentor evokes the image of a wise counselor—someone who is at the same time nurturing, challenging and experienced. At a more concrete level, the mentor relationship connotes a special bond between an inexperienced or naive student and someone more skilled than him or herself who is willing to act as a guide in a new or unfamiliar situation."[70] Clearly, the mentor role is one that can convey all three aspects of the supportive relationship: material aid, a sense of affirmation, and positive affect and emotional support. We describe two examples of supportive mentoring programs.

"I Have a Dream"

How to help students to become high academic achievers and to stay in high school is the focus of the "I Have a Dream" project.[71] The program prompts students to come together in small groups, receiving tutoring and encouragement from a full-time coordinator throughout their junior high school and high school careers. Students are promised a scholarship for college if they successfully complete high school and enter college.

The program was conceived by Eugene M. Lange as he addressed the sixth-grade graduating class of Public School 121 of East Harlem in 1981. As he encouraged the children to work hard in school and aim for college, he realized that 75 percent of these students were likely to drop out even before they completed high school. During the speech, he was inspired to make the promise of a college scholarship for each student who graduated from high school. Afterward, with Youth Action Program Director Dorothy Stoneman, Lange developed the "I Have a Dream" project to provide the organizational underpinnings for his inspiration.

The "I Have a Dream" project shares many elements with other preventive support interventions. The program creates small peer groups through which students can support each other. "I Have a Dream" offers students access to an information-rich and powerful resource, a full-time coordinator. The environment of the school and the project sponsors are supportive of individual student achievement and personal growth. The monetary incentive may be viewed not only as a tangible goal to strive for, but also as evidence that each student's "dream" is believed in by powerful people in their environment. This intervention is particularly important because it attempts to reach and support minority adolescents living in poverty areas.

Five years later, fifty of the fifty-one original students who heard Lange's speech were in school and nearly all were expected to earn high school diplomas. Approximately half of this sixth-grade class planned to take up Lange's offer and go to college. The "I Have a Dream" project has now been duplicated in over 125 projects operating in 25 cities. Local sponsors have been found who are willing to contribute scholarship money and contribute to the support of the local program.

While formal evaluations of the "I Have a Dream" project have not been conducted, the program is straightforward in conception and apparently effective in improving school achievement and preventing dropout among young people who would otherwise be at high risk for school failure. The program also illustrates the importance of incentives for participation in supportive programs for youth.

Las Madrinas

Another example of a community-based mentoring support program, called Las Madrinas, promotes leadership and school retention among young Hispanic women.[72] Las Madrinas means "godmothers" in Spanish, and the girls are described as Ahijadas, "goddaughters." The Madrinas are young professional Hispanic women who are high achievers and are willing to return to their own communities to share their talents and experiences.

The program combines the development of intense personal bonds with structured group activities. It begins with orientation sessions to teach Madrinas what can be done with young girls. Both Ahijadas and Madrinas fill out intake forms describing their interests and backgrounds as well as their individual needs and aspirations. A pairing of godmothers and goddaughters then occurs and godmothers commit to the program for a minimum of two hours every two weeks for thirty weeks.

Program activities include seminars, field trips, and informal contacts of a variety of kinds. In addition, girls learn social skills in role-playing activities, giving and receiving feedback, and analyzing case studies describing problems that girls might encounter as they grow up. The case studies are discussed so that alternative solutions to problems can be better understood.

PERSONAL SUPPORT THROUGH OUTREACH

Support for teenage mothers often involves home visits by health-care professionals and coordination of community services.[73] These programs are focused on pregnant adolescents and, to some extent, on the partners of these adolescents. Program goals include the prevention of school dropout, child abuse, and unemployment.

Such support programs make a special effort to smooth the transition to motherhood and work by creating social-support networks through the health-care worker and through family or friends and community services. The home-visit intervention is usually accomplished by having a female nurse, social-worker, or volunteer visit the new adolescent mother in her home and provide medical advice, parenting instruction, and support for the mother in her new role. The Prenatal/Early Infancy Project has been strikingly successful and differs from other programs in the clarity of its rationale for various components of the program.[74]

Prenatal/Early Infancy Project

Olds developed the Prenatal/Early Infancy Project to mobilize social support for pregnant teenagers based on the fact that too early parenthood without adequate social support may lead a mother to school dropout, poverty, and having a low-birth-weight baby who is likely to grow up in an unstable home environment.[75] The program focuses heavily on teaching pregnant teens parenting skills and health care, recruiting informal support from boyfriends and family friends, and using nurses to link pregnant teens to health and social service agencies.

The intervention involves a substantial parent and health-education component and was designed to recruit informal support of boyfriends, family, and other friends. The teenager was asked to name persons she could "count on" for help. These friends and relatives in her social network were encouraged by intervention staff to offer her both emotional and material support for maintaining health behaviors such as weight reduction and quitting smoking.

Still other aspects of the pregnant teenager's existing support system had to be taken into account in designing the supportive intervention. The young women lived in a semi-rural area where health services were not especially responsive to isolated pregnant teenagers. Visiting nurses were seen as ideal staff for the program because they had the appropriate credentials, training, commitment, and resources to intervene.

The support intervention used nurses in a proactive outreach fashion, and the home-visit strategy became the cornerstone of the intervention. Because they were nurses, creating links to the health and social service system for teenagers was a natural part of their professional roles. Olds specifically recruited professional nurses who were also parents for his intervention staff. He suggests that the parental experience of the nurses both increased the nurses' empathy for the circumstances of the pregnant teens and increased the legitimacy of the nurses in the eyes of both teenagers and other agency staff, who initially were skeptical about the visiting-nurse program. Olds also formed a local steering committee to promote cooperation among health and human service agencies and to provide legitimacy for the social-support intervention.

Evaluations indicate that the program was highly successful. The adolescent mothers experienced greater informal social support, improved their diets more, and smoked less than a control group. During the first four years of the children's lives, "the nurse-visited, poor, unmarried woman worked 82% longer than their [control group] counterparts."[76] In addition, the women in the program had 22 percent fewer subsequent births than did young women who were not part of the program.

SUPPORT THROUGH EXISTING COMMUNITY ORGANIZATIONS: BLACK CHURCHES

While specially designed organizations for adolescents can have supportive effects, existing community organizations should not be overlooked. The connections to family and to ethnic and cultural traditions that often exist in community organizations can offer a reservoir of caring and commitment that both offers aid and affirms ethnic identity. The black church is a prime example.

Project Spirit

The role of black churches in supporting parents who want to improve the academic performance and self-esteem of their children is growing. Project Spirit, launched in 1986 as a program of the Congress of National Black Churches, is working cooperatively with parents and schoolchildren in several urban sites to provide morale building, academic tutoring, and instruction in living skills for children while enrolling parents in a related parent-education program.[77]

Project Spirit seeks underachievers who may have discipline problems and low grades. More than half of the referrals come from schools that have almost given up on these children. Vanella Crawford, director of Project Spirit, observes that "the Black church is one of the few institutions owned and operated by Blacks within the Black community that can effectively assist large numbers of Black adults in enhancing their capacities as parents."[78]

Project Spirit has an after-school tutorial program and a six-hour per week program for parents. It also has a pastoral counseling program that enables participating ministers to become more helpful in dealing with a range of family problems. Retired and active public school teachers participate as tutors in the program. Skits, songs, games, and role playing real-life experiences are a big part of the program. The black churches are taking a wider role in the community, and are overcoming a traditional reluctance to grapple with problems of sexuality, contraception, and drugs, issues that affect many in the black community.[79] Church officials were uneasy at first with the subject matter of some of the programs, but they soon discovered that centers for teenage parents in churches that involve tutoring, child care, and classes on sexuality came to be accepted once they were begun.

In New Orleans, adolescent boys have joined in a black manhood training program as part of the Greater Liberty Baptist Church and hold discussions on spirituality, health, the importance of education, and issues of sexuality as they affect black men. The program seems to be filling a need. As one fourteen-year-old participant who lives with his grandmother and his aunt states, "I like it here, because there is some things you get from a man that you can't get from a woman. And my grandmother is not so worried now because she knows where I am every day, and I'm not on the streets.[80]

FUTURE DIRECTIONS

While these programs to support young adolescents facing major life challenges under adverse circumstances are encouraging, we know far too little about how and why supportive efforts work. Needed research will involve both methodological rigor and a willingness to challenge our own ideas and assumptions. Several other directions for future research deserve explicit mention. We will discuss each of them briefly and consider some of the questions these topics raise.

THE ROLE OF ETHNICITY IN THE DEVELOPMENT OF EFFECTIVE PROGRAMS FOR ADOLESCENTS

For young people who are members of ethnic and minority groups, ethnicity is a critical factor in the development of identity and self-esteem.[81] While some research has been done on the relationship between patterns of social support and ethnic identity,[82] we know far too little about the relationship between patterns of support, coping, and ethnic identity. Furthermore, many supportive programs for adolescents have been developed and tested primarily with middle-class white young people The degree to which such programs are generalizable and appropriate for ethnic minorities and disadvantaged young people is unclear. A few programs, such as Las Madrinas, have been specifically developed to provide a mentoring relationship consistent with Latino family and cultural traditions. Such programs may help young people reflect on their own cultural traditions and both the dilemmas and supports that may emerge in bicultural and bilingual contexts.

Nevertheless, the vast majority of such culturally responsive programs exist only as demonstration projects. While we should adapt programs developed with middle-class white adolescents to low-income and ethnic populations, such a proposal does not go far enough. We need to understand the social meanings of ethnicity and the identity development of minority adolescents. Such research may help us to understand how strengthening ties to ethnic traditions may optimize adolescent competence and well-being. This knowledge is essential if we are to respond supportively to the rapidly growing numbers of ethnic and minority young people in our society.

THE ROLE OF GENDER IN THE DEVELOPMENT OF SUPPORTIVE PROGRAMS FOR ADOLESCENTS

Just as ethnicity is critical in understanding identity and self-esteem in adolescents, so is the role of gender and gender identity.[83] Early adolescence is a time when the salience of gender becomes greater both for the adolescent and for those in his or her family and community. Developmental tasks at this age differ to some degree for men and women in part because of cultural and in part because of biological differences. Maccoby has observed that early adolescence is a time during which young men and women come together in a variety of settings after a substantial previous period of age segregation.[84] She goes on to observe that how young adolescents learn to collaborate and make decisions in mixed-sex groups and whether the essential style of decision making is dominated by one gender or another may foreshadow the style of relationship and problem solving between men and women that occurs much later in the work setting.

Heller et al. point out that different combinations of cross-sex support may not be equally effective.[85] For example, male-male support relationships have a very different character from relationships in which women provide a supportive role for men or vice versa. In some cases, traditional cultural roles that cast women into the helping role may account for some of these differences and, indeed, account for the higher level of burden to provide support that women frequently report.[86] Nevertheless, questions about the value of support provided by same-sex or different-sex persons serving as models or mentors have not been answered and more research both in the intervention mode and in more traditional field research is clearly in order.

SYSTEMATIC EVALUATION OF PROGRAM IMPACT

Our survey of published reports on supportive programs for adolescents in schools and communities convinced us that systematic evaluations were the exception rather than the rule. Most often innovative programs report descriptive information and less frequently report outcome data comparing program impact with that of comparable groups or programs. Where systematic research has been conducted, findings on the impact of supportive programs has been encouraging. However, systematic evaluation of innovative programs remains a major challenge. Program developers and sponsors need to appreciate that providing resources to evaluate program effectiveness is as important as providing resources for the program itself.

SUPPORT FROM WHOSE POINT OF VIEW?

Erickson raises another perspective that cannot be overlooked in setting a research agenda to better understand the role of social support in adolescent development, observing that the idea of adolescence itself sets this age group apart from other groups in society.[87] Thus, we often characterize adolescence with descriptions and metaphors that may express the desires of adults more effectively than the perceptions of adolescents themselves.

Erickson[88] notes that sociologists have suggested that these symbolic environments in which individuals are socialized can be thought of as "symbol spheres."[89] These spheres of symbols may influence not only the way we view groups in society such as adolescents, but also the way in which we structure the social institutions designed to socialize and support them. At the heart of the question, Erickson believes, is whether the symbols and metaphors we use to describe adolescence actually match the reality of adolescents as they experience it. She asks,

> Are the supports that a community believes it is providing youth perceived by the youth to be supportive? What do adolescents believe to be the real functions that youth serving systems have been designed to perform? Upon what metaphors might programs be built if they are to be perceived as supportive by youth? Do different types of programs require different metaphorical foundations? How does a community wean itself from the possibly dysfunctional metaphors of control over youth to those of partnership with youth from symbolizing adolescence as an abstract hope for the future to considering them as a genuine resource for today?"[90]

ADOLESCENCE IN SOCIETAL PERSPECTIVE

We should remember that contemporary economic and social institutions as well as the professions have shaped our images of adolescence. These images can have a powerful influence on our ideas about the intensity and kind of social support we see as appropriate and needed by adolescents. In particular, the mental health professions, until recently, have portrayed adolescence as a time of major turmoil and disruption.[91] New research is providing a different picture in which turmoil and conflict represent the exception rather than the rule.

Modell and Goodman provide a searching historical perspective on the emergence of adolescence as a relatively recent social category in modern Europe and America. They argue that the dominant political economy in an era helps define adolescence, both as a descriptive and a prescriptive notion.[92]

If we are to understand adolescence and the role of social support in adolescent development, we cannot do so outside of the historical institutions or contexts that shape our perceptions of adolescent problems. We should recognize that we as social actors shape the actions of institutions such as the school, the juvenile justice system, and the work place just as these institutions shape our perceptions of adolescents and adolescents' perceptions of themselves. An understanding of the metaphors and images of adolescence and the ways those images shape supportive organizational arrangements is a research agenda only now coming into focus.[93]

CONCLUSION

We need to build, through all of our efforts, networks of social support and integration. We have to recognize the fragmentation and lack of support that exist in the adolescent's world, selves, families, and communities. With that recognition, we can build the webs of influence that can enhance the educational and health prospects of all our young people.

Notes

1 See David A. Hamburg, "Personal Correspondence" (New York: Carnegie Corporation of New York, 1986); idem and Ruby Takanishi, "Preparing for Life" *American Psychologist*, May 1989, pp. 825-827; and Anne C. Peterson, "Adolescent Development," *Annual Review of Psychology* 39 (1989): 583-607.

2 Hamburg, "Personal Correspondence."

3 J. S. House and R. L. Kahn, "Measures and Concepts of Social Support in Community and Clinical Intervention," in *Social Support and Health* (New York: Academic Press, 1985), pp. 83-108.

4 K. Heller et al., "The Role of Social Support in Community and Clinical Interventions," in *Social Support: An Interactional View*, ed. B. R. Sarason et al. (New York: John Wiley, 1990), pp. 482-507.

5 D. Olds, "The Prenatal/Early Infancy Project," in *Fourteen Ounces of Prevention: A Casebook for Practitioners*, ed. R. H. Price et al. (Washington, D.C.: American Psychological Association, 1988), pp. 9-23.

6 E. Litwak and P. Messeri, "Organizational Theory, Social Supports and Mortality Rates," *American Sociological Review* 54 (1989): 49-67.

7 See J. B. Erickson, "A Commentary on 'Communities and Adolescents: An Exploration of Reciprocal Supports,' " in *Youth and America's Future* (New York: The William T. Grant Foundation, 1988), pp. 77-87. For a general overview see B. H. Gottlieb, "Supporting Interventions: A Typology and Agenda for Research," in *Handbook of Personal Relationships*, ed. S. W. Duck (New York: John Wiley, 1988).

8 Erickson, "A Commentary on 'Communities and Adolescents," pp. 77-87; and D. Hedin, "A Commentary on 'Communities and Adolescents: An Exploration of Reciprocal Supports,' " in *Youth and America's Future*, pp. 69-76.

9 See R. Jessor, "Critical Issues in Research on Adolescent Health Promotion," in *Promoting Adolescent Health: A Dialog on Research and Practice* (New York: Academic Press, 1982); and idem, "Bridging Etiology and Prevention in Drug Abuse Research," in *Etiology of Drug Abuse: Implications for Prevention*, NIDA Research Monograph 56, DHHS Publication No. (ADM) 85-1335 (Washington, D.C.: US Government Printing Office, 1985).

10 See Joy G. Dryfoos, "Schools as Places for Health, Mental Health and Social Services," *Teachers College Record* 94 (Spring 1993): 540-67.

11 R. H. Price, "Behavior Setting Theory and Research," in *The Human Context*, ed. Rudolph H. Moos (New York: John Wiley, 1976), pp. 213-47.

12 Heller et al., "The Role of Social Support in Community and Clinical Interventions," pp. 482-507.

13 For a general overview, see D. P. Mueller and P. S. Higgins, *Funders' Guide Manual* (St. Paul, Minn.: Amherst H. Wilder Foundation, 1988).

14 D. Stoneman, in *Youth Action Program: Press Highlights* (New York: East Harlem Block, Nursery, Inc., 1988).

15 Elena O. Nightingale and Lisa Wolverton, "Adolescent Rolelessness in Modern Society," *Teachers College Record* 94 (Spring 1993): 472-86.

16 The William T. Grant Foundation Commission on Work, Family and Citizenship, *The Forgotten Half: Non-College Youth in America* (Washington, D.C.: The William T. Grant Foundation, 1988), p. 19.

17 For a general overview, see J. Schine and P. B. Campbell, "Helping to Success: Early Adolescents and Young Children" (Report to the Bruner Foundation, CASE: Early Adolescent Helpers Program, Graduate Center, City University of New York, New York, October 1987); and Olds, "The Prenatal/Early Infancy Project," pp. 9-23.

18 R. D. Felner and A. M. Adan, "The School Transition Environment Project: An Ecological Intervention and Evaluation," in *Fourteen Ounces of Prevention*, pp. 111-22.

19 See Mueller and Higgins, *Funders' Guide Manual*.

20 J. F. Alexander and B. V. Parson, "Short-term Behavioral Intervention with Delinquent Families," *Journal of Abnormal Psychology* 81 (1973): 219-25; and for a general overview, see L. Steinberg, "Interdependency in the Family: Autonomy, Conflict and Harmony in the Parent-Adolescent Relationship" (Ph.D. diss., University of Wisconsin, 1988).

21 L. Zabin et al., "Adolescent Pregnancy-Prevention Program: A Model for Research and Evaluation," *Journal of Adolescent Health Care*, 1986, pp. 77-87.

22 E. M. Lange, "Reference Documents and Personal Correspondence from the I Have A Dream Foundation" (New York, 1986).

23 B. H. Bry, "Reducing the Incidence of Adolescent Problems through Preventive Intervention: One- and Five-Year Follow-Up," *American Journal of Community Psychology* 10 (1982): 265-76.

24 Olds, "The Prenatal/Early Infancy Project," pp. 9-23.

25 R. H. Price and R. P. Lorion, "Prevention Programming as Organizational Reinvention: From Research to Implementation," in *Prevention of Mental Disorders, Alcohol and Drug Use in Children and Adolescents*, ed. D. Shaffer et al. (Rockville, Md.: Office of Substance Abuse Prevention and American Academy of Child and Adolescent Psychiatry, Prevention Monograph #2, 1989), pp. 97-123; and T. D'Aunno, "AIDS Prevention among Intravenous Drug Users: Organizational Factors" (Grant proposal submitted to National Institute on Drug Abuse [unfunded]).

26 N. Z. Bein and B. H. Bry, "An Experimentally Designed Comparison of Four Intensities of School-Based Prevention Programs for Adolescents with Adjustment Problems," *Journal of Community Psychology*, 1980, pp. 110-16; and R. D. Richter and Tjosvold, "Effects of Student

Participation in Classroom Decision Making on Attitudes, Peer Interaction, Motivation and Learning," *Journal of Applied Psychology* 65 (1980): 74–80.

27 K. R. G. Barker, "Ecology and Motivation," in *Nebraska Symposium on Motivation*, ed. M. R. Jones (Lincoln: University of Nebraska Press, 1960), pp. 1-49.

28 Richter and Tjosvold, "Effects of Student Participation in Classroom Decision Making," pp. 74–80.

29 Ibid., p. 74.

30 Ibid., p. 75.

31 Ibid., p. 79.

32 Bein and Bry, "An Experimentally Designed Comparison," pp. 110–16.

33 Ibid., p. 115.

34 K. Klepp et al., "The Efficacy of Peer Leaders in Drug Abuse Prevention," *Journal of School Health* 56 (1986): 407–11.

35 Ibid.

36 See Gottlieb, "Supporting Interventions."

37 Klepp et al., "The Efficacy of Peer Leaders in Drug Abuse Prevention," pp. 407–11.

38 Ibid., p. 409.

39 For a general overview, see Urie Bronfenbrenner, *The Ecology of Human Development: Experiments by Nature and by Design* (Cambridge: Harvard University Press, 1979).

40 R. D. Felner et al., "Primary Prevention during School Transitions: Social Support and Environment Structure," *American Journal of Community Psychology* 10 (1982): 277–90.

41 Felner and Adan, "The School Transition Environment Project," pp. 111–22.

42 Ibid., p. 113.

43 Ibid., p. 114.

44 Ibid., p. 116.

45 Ibid., pp. 111–22.

46 Ibid., p. 117.

47 Dryfoos, "Schools as Places for Health, Mental Health, and Social Service Centers."

48 S. Millstein, "The Potential of School-Linked Centers to Support Adolescent Health and Development" (Working paper prepared for the meeting of the Carnegie Council on Adolescent Development, Washington, D.C., February 1988).

49 Ibid., pp. 23–24.

50 Zabin et al., "Adolescent Pregnancy-Prevention Program," pp. 77–87; and idem, "Evaluation of the Pregnancy Program for Urban Teenagers," *Famiy Planning Perspectives* 18 (1986): 119–26.

51 Zabin et al., "Adolescent Pregnancy-Prevention Program," pp. 77–87.

52 Ibid.

53 L. Schorr, *Within Our Reach* (New York: Doubleday, 1988), p. 53.

54 Zabin et al., "Evaluation of the Pregnancy Program for Urban Teenagers," pp. 119–26.

55 See Task Force on Education of Young Adolescents, *Turning Points: Preparing American Youth for the 21st Century* (Washington, D.C.: Carnegie Council on Adolescent Development, 1989).

56 See R. Rubinstein et al., "The Interdisciplinary Background of Community Psychology: The Early Roots of an Ecological Perspective," *American Psychological Association, Division of Community Psychology Newsletter* 18 (1984): 10–14; and for a general overview, see J. G. Kelly, *The High School: Students and Social Context in Two Midwestern Communities* (New York: Behavioral Publications, 1977).

57 J. Wynn et al., "Communities and Adolescents: An Exploration of Reciprocal Supports" (Paper prepared for Youth and America's Future: The William T. Grant Foundation Commission on Work, Family and Citizenship, 1988), p. 11.

58 For a general overview, see J. B. Erickson, *Directory of American Youth Organizations*, (Boys Town, Neb.: Father Flanagan's Boys Home, 1983).

59 National Center for Education Statistics, *National Education Longitudinal Study of 1988: A Profile of the American Eighth Grader* (Washington, D.C.: Government Printing Office, 1990).

60 For a general overview, see J. B. Erickson, *A Profile of Community Youth Organization Members, 1980* (Boys Town, Neb.: Boys Town Center for the Study of Youth Development, 1982).

61 Erickson, "A Commentary on 'Communities and Adolescents,' " pp. 77–87.

62 Carol Gilligan, *In a Different Voice: Psychological Theory and Women's Development* (Cambridge: Harvard University Press, 1982).

63 Heller et al., "The Role of Social Support in Community and Clinical Interventions," pp. 482–507.

64 See Boys and Girls Clubs of America, "Boys and Girls Clubs in Public Housing Projects: Interim Report" (Minneapolis, Minn.: Boys and Girls Clubs of America, May 12, 1989).

65 For a general overview, see D. Stoneman *Youth Action Program: Press Highlights* (New York: 1988).

66 Ibid.

67 Ibid.

68 Schine and Campbell, "Helping to Success."

69 Ibid.

70 S. F. Hamilton and N. Darling, "Mentors in Adolescents' Lives," in *The Social World of Adolescents: International Perspectives*, ed. K. Hurrelmann (Berlin: Walter deGryter, in press), p. 1.

71 Lange, Reference documents and personal correspondence from the I Have A Dream Foundation.

72 See N. Stanton, "Las Madrinas Program" (New York: Hispanic Women's Center, 1988).

73 See Olds, "The Prenatal/Early Infancy Project," pp. 9–23; J. Osofsky, "Perspectives on Infant Mental Health," in *A Decade of Progress in Primary Prevention*, ed. M. Kessler and S. Goldston (Hanover, Vt.: University Press of New England, 1986); and Schorr, *Within Our Reach*, p. 53.

74 Olds, "The Prenatal/Early Infancy Project," pp. 9–23.

75 Ibid., pp. 9–23.

76 Ibid., p. 12.

77 Carnegie Corporation of New York, "Black Churches: Can They Strengthen the Black Family?" *Carnegie Quarterly* 33 (1988): 1–9.

78 Ibid., p. 7.

79 T. Lewin, "Black Churches: New Mission of Family," *New York Times*, August 24, 1988, pp. 1, 9.

80 Ibid., p. 9.

81 S. Harter, "Self and Identity Development," in *At the Threshold: The Developing Adolescent*, S. S. Feldman and G. R. Elliott (Cambridge: Harvard University Press, 1990), pp. 352–87.

82 A. M. Cauce, "Social Networks and Social Competence: Exploring the Effects of Service Activities on Adolescent Alienation," *Adolescent*, 1986, pp. 675–87.

83 Heller et al., "The Role of Social Support in Community and Clinical Interventions," pp. 482–507.

84 E. E. Maccoby, "Personal Communication" (Washington, D.C.: Carnegie Corporation on Adolescent Development, 1988).

85 Heller et al., "The Role of Social Support in Community and Clinical Interventions," pp. 482–507.

86 T. LaBelle, "An Introduction to the Nonformal Education of Children and Youth," *Comparative Education Review* 25 (October 1981): 313–29.

87 Erickson, "A Commentary on 'Communities and Adolescents,' " pp. 77–87.

88 Ibid.

89 H. Gerth and C. W. Mills, *Character and Social Structure: The Psychology of Social Institutions* (New York: Harcourt, Brace & World, 1953), p. 274.

90 Erickson, "A Commentary on 'Communities and Adolescents,'" pp. 83–84.

91 For a general overview, see L. Steinberg, "Interdependency in the Family: Autonomy, Conflict and Harmony in the Parent-Adolescent Relationship" (Madison: University of Wisconsin, 1988).

92 J. Modell and M. Goodman, "Historical Perspectives on Adolescence and Adolescents" (Pittsburgh: Carnegie Mellon University, July 25, 1988).

93 W. R. Scott, "The Adolescence of Institutional Theory," *Administrative Science Quarterly* 32 (1987): 493–511.

Schools for Teenagers: A Historic Dilemma

FRED M. HECHINGER
Carnegie Corporation of New York

The inherent and continuing dilemma of schools for teenagers is described by Nancie Atwell, a gifted teacher:

> In general, what our adolescent students get from us by way of schooling isn't very good. Our main concern as teachers seems to be to skirt all the messiness—and exuberance—of these years, mostly by regimenting our kids' behavior: tracked groupings, busy work and seat work, few opportunities for students to initiate activity or work together. . . . Our policies tell junior high kids that their active participation is too risky an enterprise.[1]

The invention of the junior high school in the first decade of the twentieth century was perhaps the earliest acknowledgement by the American education establishment that adolescence calls for a special educational response. Up to that point, the elementary school had dealt with what had been considered children, typically from ages five or six to fourteen. After that, the four-year high school took over, at least for the relatively small number of adolescents who continued their education.

As educators and psychologists began to pay greater attention to the development of children and adolescents, they discovered what most parents had long known: Young adolescents, roughly between the ages of ten and fifteen, are different from children. Puberty, among other changes, affects their bodies and minds, the ways they think and behave. Their interests and reactions undergo substantial revision. They seek greater independence from adults; they test the limits of adult authority; they explore; they argue; they challenge rules.

Unless adults understand those changes, they move on a collision course with young adolescents. In school, this can lead to either open or passive hostility between students and their teachers. Instead of seizing new opportunities to engage the young adolescents' curiosity and restless energy, teachers who are accustomed to dealing with more docile children may react to adolescents' challenges with frustration and anger.

Creating a new segment within the American school, attuned to young adolescents' needs and behavior, seemed a sensible answer. In theory, at least, the junior high school seemed to provide that answer.

Americans pride themselves on believing in progress, but their institutions often resist change. Schools are no different. When change does come to American education, it is usually driven by outside forces rather than by insiders' expert planning. Education reforms tend to be introduced as a response to only indirectly school-related or poorly understood crises: changing needs of the labor market, the civil rights movement, the launching of Sputnik, international economic competition. When facing such external pressures, education's leaders understandably try to justify their response by cloaking the reforms in educational, often psychological, terms. And so it was with the creation of the junior high school.

The pressure for a new way of dealing with the education of young adolescents did not come entirely from within the education establishment. Great numbers of these youngsters were, for a variety of reasons, dropping out of school. In the past, this had not been considered a matter of national concern: There were plenty of jobs that required little education. In fact, the term *dropout* had not yet been invented. But the economy was changing, and early in the twentieth century too many youngsters without adequate schooling began to be an economic concern. Under such conditions, it would make sense to look for a reorganization of the schools in a way that promised to prevent young adolescents from dropping out.

Pragmatism has been the major engine of the way American schools are run and occasionally reorganized. It is the exceptional policymaker or philosopher who looks at the school as something more than an organization intended to serve the needs of the adult society. Benjamin Franklin, who himself had no formal schooling, wrote that school could be "delightful."[2] John Dewey pictured schools as the instrument that would create a "more worthy, lovely, and harmonious" society. School reform to Dewey did not mean an occasional updating or reorganizing but a dedication to continual change—not to adjust to society but to improve it.[3]

And so it is not surprising that the junior high school was born of a mix of pragmatism, idealism, and new developmental theories. It was a response to a variety of pressures: of the progressive views of a new class of educational philosophers, of an immigration-driven changing student population, of the needs of modern industrial society. It was also a response to the critical view of the existing common school by the dominant elite, the higher education leadership.

CALLS FOR CHANGE

In 1893, the Committee of Ten, which reviewed the state of the secondary schools under the chairmanship of president Charles W. Eliot of Harvard, decided that the existing system was inadequate to prepare the college-bound elite.[4] The committee called for shortening the elementary school years and proposed instead a system of six years of elementary and six years of high school. It stated bluntly: "It is impossible to make a satisfactory secondary school program limited to a period of four years and founded on the present elementary school subjects and methods."[5] It recommended a shorter but academically tougher elementary school, with the inclusion of Latin and algebra, and an extended secondary school—thus, an initial push for the first major school reorganization.

The college-oriented Committee of Ten was not alone in arguing for a change in the existing school structure. By the turn of the century it had become evident that Horace Mann was overly optimistic in his fervent belief that once the schools were opened to all, children would want nothing more than to devote themselves to learning. History soon proved such idealistic expectations wrong. Masses of students dropped out without completing the eight elementary school years. Psychologist E. L. Thorndike studied the trend and concluded that "not more than half of the youth who entered the common school completed eighth grade."[6] The crucial years during which youngsters gave up were the seventh and eighth grades.

At the same time, the labor market had begun to change. Such expert studies as that of the Massachusetts Commission on Industrial and Technical Education found educators and researchers in agreement that adolescents, between the ages of twelve and sixteen, belonged in school rather than in the labor force.[7] Poorly educated, these youngsters would become victims of exploiting employers. They could be forced into undesirable, unskilled jobs—dead ends that closed off prospects for future advancement.

While some of these youngsters, mainly children of poor immigrants, left school because they had to add their meager wages to the family income, the majority of those who dropped out did so not because they had to work but rather because they disliked school. The changes proposed by the Committee of Ten may have helped the small college-bound elite; they did nothing to improve the education of the great majority whose futures were too complicated and unpredictable to be served by a clearly mapped out course of higher education.

The junior high school—a new institution with wide-open possibilities for a different curriculum and an as yet undefined pedagogy—would be the answer. In 1910, Frank Bunker, the superintendent of the Berkeley, California, schools, opened the first junior high school, McKinley School, actually known as the Introductory High School. Located in its own building, it turned the seventh, eighth, and ninth grades into a separate institutional entity. (Several other communities, it should be noted, also claim to have been first to establish a junior high school around the same time, and the model was replicated in many places.)

Berkeley's school administrators—particularly Bunker and C. L. Biedenbach, principal of McKinley Grammar School—deserve much credit for this daring step. In fact, they had already experimented with a number of unconventional ideas, including the introduction of academic departments in the upper grades of the elementary school; but their desire to create an entirely new school organization might well have come to nothing had there not been too many bodies to fit into the local high school's ninth grade. It was lack of space that made it possible for Bunker to commandeer an elementary school as the site for a reorganized seventh-, eighth-, and ninth-grade school. At least in part, America's first junior high school was born of an inexpensive solution to an overcrowded high school. The 6-3-3 plan became the reformers' preferred organizational plan.[8]

In 1913, the Committee on the Economy of Time in Education,[9] borrowing heavily from earlier proposals by the National Education Association, endorsed the 6-3-3 plan, in large part because of the feeling that youngsters at age twelve are already concerned about training for future jobs. Five years later, the committee outlined an even stronger rationale for the concept of the junior high school by urging educators to respond to changes in the society, changes in the composition of the secondary school population, and changes in the understanding of adolescent growth and development.

The report, known as *Cardinal Principles of Secondary Education*,[10] criticized the eight-year elementary school: "The last two years . . . in particular have not been well adapted to the needs of the adolescent." Therefore, the report continued, many pupils lose interest and drop out. It recommended that the junior high school gradually introduce departmental instruction, offer some electives and prevocational courses, and stress the development of a "sense of personal responsibility."[11]

THE FACTORY MODEL

From its beginning, the idea of the new junior high school clashed with the earlier concept of the American common school whose democratic ideal was to be reflected in a system that provided the same education for all children. In fact, public school leaders in the late nineteenth and early twentieth century were obsessed with the search for "the one best way"—the professionally approved solution. The antidote to chaos in politics seemed to the new breed of education managers the "scientific" approach to the schools, testing everything with the aim of arriving at one standard way that would fit all. In what was almost a parody of that approach, John Philbrick, who was Boston's school superintendent from 1856 to 1878, put it in simple terms: "The best is the best everywhere. If America devised the best school desk, it must go to the ends of the civilized world."[12]

The American ideal at the time was the factory, which guaranteed the best and most economically designed product. Why not apply it to the schools? In 1874, William T. Harris, superintendent of schools in St. Louis and subsequently U.S. Commissioner of Education, explained the new system's purpose and attraction: "Great stress is laid on (1) punctuality, (2) regularity, (3) attention, and (4) silence, as habits that are necessary in an industrial and commercial civilization."[13] It was hardly surprising that restless young adolescents left such schools.

The creators of the new junior high school sensed that changing social and economic conditions and an increasingly diverse population made the one best way intensely undemocratic. Children differ. The idea of the right education for every child clashes head-on with the effort at creating a standard education in which the one best way fits all. Moreover, economic changes also called for what came to be known as "differentiation," separating children according to their talents and, perhaps more important, their future place in the economy.

Elwood P. Cubberley, professor of education at Stanford University, rationalized those changing economic conditions by calling on the schools to "give up the exceedingly democratic idea that all are equal, and that our society is devoid of classes." In a differentiated junior high school, future workers would be prepared for modern social and industrial life and for the growing specialization of labor, while also having instilled in them "social and political consciousness that will lead to unity amid diversity." He saw the schools as "factories in which the raw products [children] are to be shaped into products to meet the various demands of life."[14]

New philosophers of education brought to the schools a different view of childhood and learning. John Dewey was less concerned with scientific theories of schooling than with the political and social developments in society. If conditions of life have changed, he said, then the educational response must also change.

It would be misleading to suggest that the new junior high schools were dedicated to Dewey's progressive views of childhood, but his departure from "the one best way" helped to free them from the rigid existing rules of school organization and curriculum. Leonard Koos, professor of education in Minnesota, wrote in *The Junior High School* in 1927 that "it is now a truism that equalization of educational opportunity cannot be achieved without adjustment to individual differences."[15]

In a way, the original junior high school became something of a sorting agency, preparing the academic elite for the universities and others for opportunities in the marketplace, thus creating academic and vocational or commercial tracks.

Much of the tracking was based on questionable grounds and methods. Theories had begun to circulate among educators about innate differences between certain ethnic groups and about the meaning of certain physical characteristics. Head shapes were often thought to be indications of mental ability, and such pseudo-scientific theories usually favored youngsters of Anglo-Saxon and Northern European descent. Southern Europeans and Eastern European Jews were thought to be of inferior intellect. Children of such heritage were often treated by teachers condescendingly or with undisguised contempt. Undoubtedly, such stereotyping played a significant part in early tracking.[16]

Concerned about such bias-driven sorting of youngsters, educators looked for less subjective ways of judging students' potential and assigning them to specific programs on the basis of more scientific data. They sought the answer in the newly developed instrument of standardized intelligence tests. The approach had strong appeal, partly because the subjective yardsticks had led to so much abuse and partly because of Americans' simplistic faith in anything that appeared to be scientific.

As happens so often in American policymaking, the pendulum swung from one extreme to another. Instead of leaving to the teacher the assessment of youngsters' talents and capacities, the task was assigned to the newly developed tests. While it was true that teachers had often misjudged and misassigned students, usually in belief that they were serving the cause of instant Americanization, excessive reliance on tests invited new abuses. Dewey's concern about individual children was increasingly lost in test-dominated tracking. Children became stuck in tracks without much hope of moving into paths more appropriate to their talents. Since the junior high schools were thought to be the ideal place for such sorting, they assigned students according to what were viewed as scientific teaching instruments in the hands of school bureaucracies.

By the early 1930s, support for the separate junior high school faded. Although progressive reformers originally intended the new schools to respond to the developmental needs of young adolescents—to encourage them to explore, and to build on their special talents—the junior high schools had essentially become prep schools for high school. Many rural districts fell back on the 6-6 organization.

In 1933, Chicago became the first major city to eliminate its junior highs, largely on the grounds of saving taxpayers' money. As so often in the history of American public education, cost-efficiency became the driving force.[17] (Cost-efficiency also served as the excuse for the creation of very big—educationally unsuitable—urban and suburban high schools.)

For a brief period, after World War II, the more progressive approach enjoyed a revival. Once again, educators and child psychologists used the transitional period to respond to the special developmental needs of young adolescents. The percentage of autonomous junior high schools, which had been shrinking during the 1930s, grew rapidly, from 13.6 percent to 31.4 percent of all secondary schools between the years of 1952 and 1971.[18]

CONANT'S WARNING

James Bryant Conant, former president of Harvard, followed in the footsteps of his predecessor, Charles W. Eliot, as a reformer of the schools. In 1959, with a grant from the Carnegie Corporation of New York, he published *The American High School Today*.[19] He offered educators and parents a detailed checklist of the subjects he thought should be studied and the way the schools should be organized.

A year later, in 1960, he turned his attention to the junior high schools. Together with a small staff and with support from the Carnegie Corporation, he spent the 1959–1960 school year visiting 237 junior high schools in ninety districts in twenty-three states. He was aware that "some people have approached the question of education for the twelve to fifteen year olds from a viewpoint that emphasizes recent studies in physiology and adolescent psychology. Others have approached the same questions from a different viewpoint that strongly emphasizes academic subject matter."[20] Given those different viewpoints, he said, he tried to rely mainly on what he had personally observed during his visits.

In assessing the role and the actual performance of the junior high schools, Conant wrote in *Education in the Junior High School Years* that "first, parents and teachers are well aware that early adolescence is a very special period physically, emotionally, and socially. It is a crucial age in the transition from childhood to adulthood and often presents many problems."[21]

Some of what he saw alarmed him. In an address to the American Association of School Administrators in Atlantic City, he charged that instead of enjoying their independence, these schools tended increasingly to imitate the high schools, particularly their weakest features. He accused them of an "almost vicious" overemphasis on competitive athletics and extreme academic pressures for the sake of getting into college. Colleges, he said, "are by and large the worst sinners in this regard" but that "the disease" of athletic rivalry had spread from the colleges all the way down to the junior high schools appeared to him as "a new and shocking revelation."[22]

Specifically, he warned against the danger "that the three-year junior high school may become a replica of the senior high school." He wrote: "Interscholastic athletics and marching bands are to be condemned in junior high schools: there is no sound educational reason for them and too often they serve merely as public entertainment."[23] He also disapproved of graduation ceremonies with diplomas and cap and gown.

Conant predicted "a lot of grief ahead" as parental pressures pushed high school subjects down to pre-high school pupils. He urged that the seventh grade serve as a transition from the elementary school's self-contained classroom with one teacher to the departmentalization of high school.

Conant was surprised that there was little agreement among professional educators about what the junior high school ought to be like. He did find some general agreement about the nature of the youngsters with whom the schools would have to deal: that at their level of maturity, they needed more help in making the transition from elementary school.

Still, Conant, somewhat critical of the child-centered theories of the 1920s and the early advocates of the junior high school, did stress the importance of academic subjects in junior high school—English, social studies, algebra, science, art, music, physical education, and (in the unreconstructed gender-oriented ways of his time) industrial arts for boys and home economics for girls. Conant also called for a well-stocked central library and a full-time librarian for every junior high school.

It was during the education debates of the early 1960s that one of the endemic flaws of the junior high schools first rose to the surface: the lack of sufficient teachers who understood young adolescents, and who saw the junior high school as an institution with its own ideas and goals. The very name "junior high school" may have been a mistake: Who wanted to be junior or subordinated to the real high school? Those teachers who really liked children would be happier in elementary school; those who had academic aspirations often became frustrated and acted like high school teachers. As is still largely true today, few were being prepared, professionally and psychologically, to be committed to the very special task of dealing with adolescents and shaping a curriculum to their ages and interests.

"Because of the transitional nature of these grades," Conant wrote, "teachers with an unusual combination of qualifications are needed. Satisfactory instruction in grades seven and eight requires mature teachers who have both an understanding of children, a major characteristic of elementary school teachers, and considerable knowledge in at least one subject-matter field, a major characteristic of high school teachers." Because such specially qualified teachers are difficult to find, Conant urged teacher-training institutions to take this into account and warned against looking at the junior high schools "as a training ground for senior high school teachers."[24] He called on school boards to do everything in their power to enhance the status and prestige of junior high school teachers. His appeal fell largely on deaf ears: Few of those boards' lay members had any deeper understanding of the junior high schools' mission.

Little came of Conant's comments on the junior high schools, probably because he had invested so much of his time and energies in his efforts to reform the high schools that his critique of the junior highs tended to be overshadowed.

A TEACHER'S VIEW

Nancie Atwell, who taught English in eighth grade (she now runs a K–3 experimental school), wrote in her book *In the Middle*:

> When I listen hard to my junior high students, their message to me is, "We're willing to learn. We like to find out about things we didn't know before. But make it make sense. Let us learn together. And be involved and excited so that we can be involved and excited." When I listen to educators talk about junior high, I hear a different message. I'm told that my role is to keep the lid on . . . and prepare my students for high school.[25]

Atwell understands the underlying problem that the middle grades must face if they are to succeed. She writes:

> Surviving adolescence is no small matter; neither is surviving adolescents. It's a hard age to be and teach. The worst things that ever happened to anybody happen every day. But some of the best things can happen, too, and they are more likely to happen when junior high teachers understand the nature of junior high kids and teach in ways that help students grow.[26]

Some of the brighter, observant students also sense the inferior level the system has reserved for the junior high school. At the end of the year, one of Atwell's students, after saying that he would miss her, added: "Maybe some day you'll be smart enough to teach in the high school."

Conant's critical review may have been the first hard look at the junior high school; it was not the last.

It was a growing dissatisfaction with the junior high school that led in the 1960s to a renaming of that institution as the middle grades or middle school or, in some instances, as in New York City, the intermediate school. The new nomenclature suggests that young adolescents require a school that responds to their important developmental years instead of an advance copy of the high school.

In the 1980s the Lilly Endowment, in Indianapolis, studied the middle grades—increasingly the preferred terminology—because it had found that, particularly among poor and minority youngsters in inner cities, "the number of students who fail in school seems to grow almost uncontrollably from fourth through eighth or ninth grades. As a result, these students fall further and further behind in almost every essential activity, until they either drop out or struggle in remedial programs throughout their high school years." The endowment therefore concluded that something must be done to avoid the drift into a dead end during "these critical formative years." It called for a clear sense of purpose in the middle grades and "a mandate to create powerful experiences for young adolescents."[27]

Middle-grades schools, the endowment warned, too often are viewed merely as "feeder schools" for the high schools instead of being a testing and proving ground "for combining what we know about learning and what we know about early adolescent development."[28]

The Edna McConnell Clark Foundation also directed its attention to the middle-grade schools' potential for dealing constructively with disadvantaged young adolescents, stating: "Even if disadvantaged children have demonstrated academic achievement in elementary school, their achievement gains tend to diminish during the middle grades. For some students, this decline is dramatic. In their remaining school years, they never live up to their academic promise in elementary school."[29]

These problems, the foundation stressed, are compounded by changes in development and behavior youngsters undergo in early adolescence: Peer approval becomes more important and may lead to a downgrading of studying; risk-taking influences much of their behavior; school failure resulting from these changes in attitudes may, in turn, lead to a decline in self-confidence.

At the very time when disadvantaged young adolescents need support, the foundation found, they are placed in institutions that are ill-equipped to respond to their needs. Middle schools are larger and more impersonal; teachers are less accessible; the middle grades are not only academically harder but also often less stimulating than the elementary schools. Just as society, including many parents, often considers adolescence as a phase young people must live through, so the middle years in school are too often treated as something students must simply "get through." As a result, the foundation concluded, "the middle grades become the breeding ground for behaviors and attitudes that cause many students to drop out of school in the ninth or tenth grade."[30]

Yet it is during these very years that damage can be prevented. Next to the first three years of infancy, when the new human being learns to walk, to listen and understand, and to speak, the years of early adolescence are a time of the most dramatic development. The middle grades, therefore, ought to be viewed as a time of special opportunity for positive intervention—shaping adolescents' values, helping them to set goals for themselves, assisting their healthy development. The junior high school, or the middle grades, ought to respond to adolescents' special needs and pay attention to the development of their bodies and minds.

While the original junior high schools depended heavily on the efficiency experts for their organization—determining the best use of space and facilities in a community—the middle school took its marching orders from developmental psychology and the child-oriented philosophy of Dewey and other progressives. The homeroom assumed new importance, with a teacher getting to know a limited number of youngsters and acting as counselor. Pupils were encouraged to probe and discover. Even the idea of team teaching—several teachers with different subject-matter expertise teaching a class together—began to be advocated by reformers. (Team teaching never became a major force in the schools, in part because teachers traditionally are trained to preside over their classroom rather than to engage in collaboration.)

Once again, however, efforts at reforming the way young adolescents learn and are taught became subordinated to outside pressures. The panic set off by the launching of the Soviet Sputnik imposed on many ninth grades a less flexible and more high school–oriented curriculum, especially in mathematics and science. Once again, overcrowding often dictated the way schools were organized.

By the 1980s, more than eighty years after the founding of the first junior high school in Berkeley, the purpose of education in the middle grades continued ill-defined. Many of the schools remained merely an adaptation of either the elementary or the high school. In part, educators' uncertainty about what the middle grades should be and do is the consequence of their, and most adults', uncertainty about how to deal with young adolescents—what and how to teach them, how to affect their behavior, what to prepare them for.

The daunting reality is that the middle grades receive a motley crew of young people: no longer children who essentially accept the teacher's role, and may trust and occasionally even love the teacher. The young adolescents who enter the middle grades school are far less docile: They want to be shown why they should respect the teacher, why they are in school in the first place, what the school can offer them beyond the company of their peers.

With her experience as a junior high school teacher and her sensitivity for the special needs of adolescents, Atwell wrote in 1987: "The American secondary school status quo presents a bleak picture, revealing little evidence of the collaboration, involvement, and excitement in acquiring knowledge that our students crave—that all humans crave." She expressed concern "with the nature of instruction adolescents typically receive in U.S. junior high schools; how our classroom ambience, instructional approaches, and ability groupings do not meet adolescents' needs; and how this is no accident. Our junior high schools are structured to deny, or at least delay, the satisfaction of our junior high school students' needs, physical, intellectual, and social."[31]

By the mid-1980s, experts on both education and adolescence agreed that something was seriously wrong with the way the schools had been dealing with young adolescents. Other factors virtually forced educators and the public to focus their attention and concern on that age group. Serious physical and mental health problems, including depression and suicide, sounded the alarm. So did increasingly younger pregnancies and teenage involvement in violence. The old view that adolescence was merely a phase that would pass seemed no longer acceptable, and the schools had to reexamine the way they were treating the junior high school population.

While the junior high school and subsequently the middle or intermediate school were supposed to ease the transition from elementary to secondary school, there was a lack of understanding of what makes that transition difficult. Instead of arranging a compromise between the one-teacher elementary school class and the departmentalized middle grades, the basic structure turned out to be one of a daily succession of subject-matter lessons, each taught by a different teacher. The pupils moved from class to class; each teacher dealt with a daily average of five to six classes, each with a new cadre of students. Typically, teachers recognized students by the seating chart, not as individuals. Some effort was often made to substitute counselors for the absence of personal contact and guidance, but financial constraints tended to give each counselor so many "clients" that personal meetings had to be limited to acute crises rather than continuous advising.

Moreover, the heritage of the allegedly cost-effective factory model—the big school—compounded the problem of anonymity within the school. Under any circumstances and at any age, anonymity aggravates potential behavior problems: When people are submerged in the impersonal condition of large institutions, they tend to behave at their worst. For teenagers, with their normal insecurities and their natural tendency to explore and test the rules of society, being swallowed up by a large impersonal institution is particularly damaging. Such an organization clashes head-on with Dewey's concept of the school as a community.

At the heart of the problems that an effective school for the middle grades should address is the nature of early adolescence: the risks to which young teenagers are exposed; the temptations they face; the fateful choices they must make in shaping their values and their behavior. The potential dangers include alcohol and other substance abuse, and nicotine; premature, irresponsible, and unprotected sexual activity; poor nutrition; and, increasingly, involvement in violent behavior. Many of their uncertainties lead to depression and other mental disorders and, in the most serious cases, suicide. All teenagers are in need of effective health care.

At the same time, these early years can also be the gateway to lasting success. Helped to make the right choices and to channel energies into productive activities, these youngsters are at the threshold of what can be a lifetime of personal strength and success.

TURNING POINTS

In the late 1980s, the Carnegie Council on Adolescent Development established a task force on the education of young adolescents. In its final report, *Turning Points: Preparing American Youth for the 21st Century*, published in June 1989 by Carnegie Corporation of New York, the task force said:

> Middle grade schools—junior high, intermediate, and middle schools—are potentially society's most powerful force to recapture millions of youth adrift, and help every young person thrive during early adolescence. Yet all too often these schools exacerbate the problems of young adolescents.
>
> A volatile mismatch exists between the organization and curriculum of middle grade schools and the intellectual and emotional needs of young adolescents.[32]

Perhaps the basic corrective of past failure is to reduce the damage done by large, factory-style middle-grade schools. Since big buildings cannot be replaced by smaller ones, the remedy suggested by *Turning Points* and other recent reports is to reorganize the large buildings into smaller units—schools within schools or houses, each with no more than about 120 youngsters.

At the same time, the teaching staff would be reorganized into teams composed of experts in a variety of subjects and would coordinate instruction through cooperative planning. (This is different from the earlier, largely unsuccessful concept of team teaching in which several teachers acted as a team in the classroom.) Under such an arrangement, every teenager would be known well by one adult who would serve as an advisor and confidant on both academic and personal problems. In the words of *Turning Points*, the aim is to "create small communities for learning where stable, close, mutually respectful relationships with adults and peers are considered fundamental for intellectual development and personal growth."[33]

To strengthen those important ties, *Turning Points* recommended that each team of teachers remain with the same group of youngsters for at least two, and possibly three, years. Lack of continuity is one of the basic flaws in American education; lack of continuity in personal relationships is particularly damaging to the development of young adolescents.

Equally important is the creation of a link between school and home. Some effective middle-grade schools have realized its importance and tried to institutionalize it. James P. Comer, Maurice Falk professor of child psychiatry, Yale University School of Medicine, has created a successful model that emphasizes communication with parents and continuing parental involvement in defining the schools' programs for young adolescents. Deborah Meier, the director of Central Park East Secondary School in East Harlem, provides parents with a regular newsletter about school and community-related activities. In stressing the importance of involving parents, particularly of poor adolescents, the Edna McConnell Clark Foundation pointed out that "parents do not have to be well educated to help in their children's education."[34] *Turning Points* underscores this by urging: "Reengage families in the education of young adolescents by giving families meaningful roles in school governance, communicating with families about the school program and student's progress, and offering families opportunities to support the learning process at home and at the school."[35]

Schools must make special efforts to forge links with the community. This may include the involvement of students in community service and the creation of internships in local businesses, hospitals, parks, and other enterprises. While essential for all young people, this is crucial in the case of poor youngsters, who desperately need a link between their often debilitating environment and the world of work.

SCHOOL AND HEALTH

Neglect of today's adolescents' health and fitness is at a crisis state. By age fifteen, about a quarter of all young adolescents are engaged in behaviors that are harmful to themselves and others. Poverty adds to the crisis. In 1988, about 27 percent of American adolescents between the ages of ten and eighteen lived in poor or near-poor families. For nonwhite minorities, the figure exceeded 50 percent. Half of all black and 30 percent of Hispanic adolescents live in one-parent families. As many as 5 million teenagers have no health insurance and therefore are denied access to proper health care, especially of the preventive kind. Poor health and debilitating living conditions make it difficult for these adolescents to succeed in school. Their problems therefore must be addressed by middle-grades educators as well as by the community at large.

The problems of today's teenagers enrolled in middle-grades schools differ dramatically from those of the past. By age sixteen, 17 percent of girls and 29 percent of boys have had sexual intercourse. Between 1960 and 1988, gonorrhea increased four times among ten- to fourteen-year-olds. Suicide rates almost tripled among ten- to fourteen-year-olds between 1968 and 1988. Middle-grades schools cannot ignore these facts.

One of the key recommendations of *Fateful Choices: Healthy Youth for the 21st Century*, a book sponsored by the Carnegie Corporation and based in large part on research underwritten by the Carnegie Council on Adolescent Development, is the creation of school-related health centers.[36] Such centers would provide adolescents with comprehensive health services, from dental care to treatment of injuries and chronic diseases. They would also deal with reproductive issues, including counseling on sexual matters ranging from advocacy of postponed sexual activity to family planning and prevention of sexually transmitted diseases.

Existing school-related health centers serve mainly high schools, too late for many of the critical health issues faced by adolescents. Moreover, the clinics now serve fewer than 1 percent of the age group. Yet the experience of the existing centers shows that they can substantially improve young people's health and prevent health-threatening activities.

In the long run, however, youngsters must be given the information and the skills to safeguard their own health. This is why *Fateful Choices* urges that middle-grades schools, and possibly even the upper elementary grades, include in their curriculum instruction in human biology and the life sciences to provide young adolescents with an understanding of the potential damage to their bodies and minds from alcohol abuse and the use of drugs and nicotine. Such courses also aim at preventing premature sexual activity and lessening the high risk of sexually transmitted diseases, including AIDS.

In an atmosphere of increasing violence, with escalating injuries and deaths among young people, the schools are also urged to make a contribution by teaching the benefits of nonviolent conflict resolution.

CONCLUSION

Why focus on early adolescence? Only because it may well be the most misunderstood and, therefore, the most neglected stage of human development. Parents hope that this too shall pass. Physicians do not want to spend the time and effort necessary to understand, and be understood by, teenagers. Teachers see the assignment to the middle grades as an unwelcome trial at best. Educators have been slow to discover reasons why even youngsters who do relatively well in elementary school so often fail in junior high school.

Yet, even if the institutions that deal with the early teen years constitute weak links in the chain of human development, they are only one segment of what ought to be recognized and treated as a continuum. The human story begins before birth and continues through infancy to the preschool and elementary school years, then on to early and late adolescence, and ultimately to adulthood.

The trouble comes with our tendency to break what ought to be a continuum into nearly self-contained fragments: child care, Head Start, preschool education, elementary school, the middle grades, senior high school. Each segment is dependent on the one that precedes it, yet communication between them—up and down—is defective. Blame for failure tends to be directed downward. In that flawed process, adolescence gets short shrift. Beyond the segregation by age group, there is the larger division between the poor and the affluent.

David A. Hamburg, Carnegie Corporation's president, in "The Urban Poverty Crisis: An Action Agenda for Children and Youth," writes:

> There is much that can be achieved if we think of our entire population as a very large extended family—tied by history to a shared destiny and therefore requiring a strong ethic of mutual aid.
>
> I suggest that the central question is: Can we do better than we are doing now? After all, the casualties in early life are now so heavy that they are beginning to drag down the entire nation. The social and economic costs of severely damaging conditions that distort growth and development are terrible—not only in the intrinsic tragedies of these shattered lives but also in effects that hit the entire society, rich and poor alike—the costs of disease and disability, ignorance and incompetence, crime and violence, alienation and hatred. In a more than microbial sense, these are infections that know no boundaries, that cannot be effectively contained the way we are going now. Surely present knowledge, evidence and experience make clear that we can do better than we are now doing.[37]

In their eighty-year history, the junior high schools (and their successors) have fluctuated between sincere efforts to respond to a growing understanding among experts of the special needs of teenagers and a variety of social and economic issues, from competing more effectively with adversaries in international trade to preparing adolescents for admission to college. Some forward-looking initiatives have been taken, as in the Lilly Endowment's support of schools that integrate the regular school day, from 8:00 A.M. to 3:00 P.M., and after-school activity, from 3:00 P.M. to 6:00 P.M., with schools and youth-serving agencies.

More recently, the Carnegie Corporation has been underwriting follow-up initiatives to implement the recommendations of *Turning Points.* After decades of relative planlessness, there is finally some hope that the middle grades will find a firmer footing within the total scheme of American education—not as a holding pen; not as a device for dropout prevention; not as a utilitarian vocational or prep school in the service of either business or college; but as an academic and developmental home base for young people in the process of moving from childhood to maturity.

I am greatly indebted to Daniel Perlstein and William Tobin of Stanford University for their research reported in "The History of the Junior High School: A Study of Conflicting Aims and Institutional Patterns," commissioned in 1988 by the Task Force on Education of Young Adolescents, in the process of producing Turning Points.

Notes

1 Nancie Atwell, *In the Middle: Writing, Reading, and Learning with Adolescents* (New York: Boynton/Cook, 1987), p. 25.

2 John H. Best, ed., *Benjamin Franklin on Education* (New York: Teachers College Press, 1962).

3 John Dewey, "The School and Society," in *John Dewey: The Middle Works*, ed. Jo Ann Boydston (Carbondale: Southern Illinois University Press, 1980), pp. 19–20.

4 Fred M. Hechinger and Grace Hechinger, *Growing Up in America* (New York: McGraw-Hill, 1975), p. 119 and annotated bibliography p. 427.

5 Ibid., p. 107; and National Education Association Committee of Ten on Secondary School Studies, *Report of the Committee of Ten* (Washington, D.C.: U.S. Bureau of Education, Government Printing Office, 1893), p. 45.

6 Edward L. Thorndike, "Elimination of Pupils from School," in *U.S. Bureau of Educational Annual Report, 1908* (Washington, D.C.: Government Printing Office, 1909), p. 9.

7 Massachusetts Commission on Industrial and Technical Education, "Report of the Sub-Committee on the Relation of Children to the Industries" (Quincy, Mass.: Author, 1909, act of 1906), pp. 47–54, 57–69.

8 H. N. McClellan, "The Origins of the Junior High School" *California Journal of Secondary Education*, February 1935, pp. 168–69.

9 U.S. Bureau of Education, "Special Reports: 'Principles Involved'," Bulletin No. 38. Report of the Committee of the National Council of Education and Secondary of Time in Education (Washington, D.C.: Government Printing Office, 1913), p. 25.

10 National Education Association, "Cardinal Principles of Secondary Education," Report of the Commission on the Reorganization of Secondary Education (Washington, D.C.: U.S. Bureau of Education, Government Printing Office, 1918), p. 18.

11 Ibid.

12 Quoted in Hechinger and Hechinger, *Growing Up in America*, p. 99.

13 Ibid., p. 100.

14 Elwood P. Cubberley, *Changing Conceptions of Education* (Boston: Houghton Mifflin, 1909), pp. 50–51.

15 Leonard Koos, *The Junior High School* (Boston: Ginn and Co., 1927), p. 62.

16 Hechinger and Hechinger, *Growing Up in America*, pp. 66, 67.

17 Samuel Popper, *The American Middle School* (Boston: Houghton Mifflin, 1962), p. 212.

18 Daniel Perlstein and William Tobin, "The History of the Junior High School: A Study of Conflicting Aims and Institutional Patterns" (A paper commissioned by the Carnegie Corporation of New York, 1988).

19 James Bryant Conant, *The American High School Today* (New York: McGraw-Hill, 1959).

20 Ibid., p. 9.

21 James Bryant Conant, *Education in the Junior High Schools Years* (Princeton, N.J.: Education Testing Service, 1960), pp. 16ff.

22 *The New York Times*, February 21, March 2, March 4, 1960.

23 Ibid.

24 Conant, *The American High School Today*, pp. 12–13.

25 Atwell, "In the Middle," p. 36.

26 Ibid., p. 25.

27 Lilly Endowment, Inc., *Middle Grades Improvement Program: A Prospectus for Indiana Major Urban School Corporations* (Indianapolis: Lilly Endowment, 1986), p. 48.

28 Ibid.

29 The Edna McConnell Clark Foundation, "Program for Disadvantaged Youth: Program Statement," working paper (The Edna McConnell Clark Foundation, New York, June 1988).

30 Ibid.

31 Atwell, "In the Middle," p. 36.

32 Task Force on Education of Young Adolescents, *Turning Points: Preparing American Youth for the 21st Century* (Washington, D.C.: Carnegie Council on Adolescent Development, 1989).

33 Ibid., p. 9.

34 The Edna McConnell Clark Foundation, *Program for Disadvantaged Youth*, p. 11.

35 Task Force on Education of Young Adolescents, *Turning Points*, p. 9.

36 Fred M. Hechinger, *Fateful Choices: Healthy Youth for the 21st Century* (New York: Hill and Wang, 1992).

37 Adapted from David A. Hamburg, "The Urban Poverty Crisis: An Action Agenda for Children and Youth," adapted from *Today's Children: Creating a Future for a Generation in Crisis* (New York: Times Books/Random House, 1992).

Schools as Places for Health, Mental Health, and Social Services

JOY G. DRYFOOS
Hastings-on-Hudson, New York

The caring professions, community leaders, parents, and young people themselves are being overwhelmed by the threat of the "big four" adolescent problems: sex, drugs, violence, and depression. In every behavioral and attitudinal survey, these items are at the top of the list of what troubles teenagers and stands in the way of their achieving healthy and safe maturity. In the past, professional attention to these problems has been conducted within entirely separate domains, with categorical programs for prevention of substance abuse, teen pregnancy, and delinquency and promotion of mental health. Each domain has its own experts, interventions, and sources of funds. These programs are isolated from one other and, with few exceptions, are operated separately from the educational system. Only recently has there been an acknowledgement that behaviors such as abusing drugs or engaging in early sexual intercourse are interrelated with and influenced by educational outcomes such as grades, attendance, retention, and graduation. In a reciprocal mode, young people who do well in effective schools are less vulnerable to the "new morbidities" while young people who are protected from problem behaviors achieve academically.[1]

Recognition of the linkages between adolescent health status and educational achievement is leading to the proliferation of new forms of institutional arrangements. Health, mental health, social services, recreation, and arts programs are being brought into schools to augment the services that school systems have put together to deal with the difficult problems arising in today's social environment. The goal of these new efforts is to create "one-stop" service centers in a convenient place where young people can attend to their many needs. The place is the school. The theory is that school is where to find most adolescents, at least before they drop out, and if middle and junior high schools are included in these interventions, almost all young people could be reached through school-based facilities.

This is neither a new nor a radical idea. About a century ago, in response to the massive impact of immigration, urbanization, and industrialization, large numbers of doctors, dentists, and nurses were brought into overcrowded city schools to screen for communicable diseases, treat caries, get rid of pediculosis, and even perform minor surgery such as tonsillectomies and tooth extractions.[2] By the 1920s, the medical profession backed away from these interventions, fearing socialized medicine. Schools hired their own nurses to check for immunization and attendance status, relied on health-education curricula to influence youth to change health behaviors, and assumed that the private sector would take care of adolescent health needs. In the early 1970s, a new generation of pediatricians initiated demonstration projects in a few cities that brought medical and dental units back into schools, but these innovative programs lasted only as long as the grants.[3]

This article describes the resurgence of a school-based services movement, bringing an array of community-health, mental-health, and social services back into schools during another period of social upheaval. The description of these centers and programs is followed by an analysis of the advantages and the limitations of these developments. Finally, a discussion of the future for one-stop adolescent health centers is presented. The focus of this article is on improving the health status of adolescents through school-based initiatives. However, this subject comprehends only one side of an equation; the other side is the restructuring of schools to make them into places in which all young people have an equal opportunity to learn. Schools cannot assume the sole responsibility for producing competent adults if they are to fulfill their primary mission—to educate. Other chapters in this book focus on that mission (see H. Craig Heller, Gordon M. Ambach, Deborah Meier, and James P. Comer, "At the Crossroads," in this book).

SUPPORT FOR THE CONCEPT OF SCHOOL-BASED PROGRAMS

Some twenty-five major reports were published between 1989 and 1991 that addressed the interconnectedness of young people's health status and their educational experience, called for a more comprehensive approach to health, and supported the placement of health-promotion and health-service programs in schools.[4] For example, two organizations representing disparate major interest groups, the American Medical Association and the National Association of State Boards of Education, issued *Code Blue: Uniting for Healthier Youth.*[5] Code Blue is the parlance used in medicine to signify a life-threatening emergency, which is how the organizations' joint commission characterized contemporary health problems of youth. Their recommendations stem from their agreement that *education and health are inextricably intertwined*, that efforts to improve school performance that ignore students' health are ill-conceived, as are health-improvement efforts that ignore the role of education. Thus the commission strongly supported the establishment of health centers in schools, attention to the school climate and issues related to achievement, and the restructuring of public and private health insurance to ensure access to services: "Families, schools, neighborhoods, the health community, and the public and private sectors will need to forge new partnerships to address the interconnected health and education problems our young people are experiencing."[6]

The Office of Technology Assessment (OTA), charged by Congress with reviewing the health status of American adolescents, recognized school-linked clinics as one of the most promising recent innovations to improve adolescent's access to health services. The report proposed as its major strategy that "Congress could support the development of centers that provide comprehensive and accessible health and related services specifically for adolescents in schools and/or communities."[7] The OTA documented that many adolescents are not covered by private health insurance, and that many adolescents in low-income families are not enrolled in the Medicaid system. The report pointed out that all adolescents face age-related barriers to access to confidential medical care because of parental-consent requirements, lack of information about services, a scarcity of providers trained to deal with adolescent issues, and, in rural areas, long distances to travel and inadequate public transportation. The OTA recommended that the federal government provide "seed money" for the development of comprehensive health centers in or near schools and funding for continuation of established programs. They added a strong caveat, noting the limited systematic evidence that school centers improve adolescent health outcomes.

The movement toward creating service centers in schools is being driven by educators as well as health professionals. Studies of school-restructuring issues have highlighted the relationship of good health to educational achievement, and the importance of bringing health services into schools. *Turning Points*, the Carnegie Council on Adolescent Development's challenge to middle-school reform, called for the placement of a health coordinator in every school to organize the necessary resources to ensure that young adolescents would be healthy in order to learn.[8] The task force recognized, however, that the needs of some students might exceed the available resources, and therefore schools should consider options such as school-based and school-linked health centers. They envision a comprehensive services network with the school as the center, and community agencies acting as the lead coordinating organizations.

TRADITIONAL HEALTH AND SOCIAL SERVICES IN SCHOOLS

Every school system has its own board policies, and every state has different legislation covering school health. In general, our nation's 83,000 public elementary and secondary schools rely heavily on school nurses and guidance counselors.[9] School nurses typically provide vision and hearing screening, check for immunization compliance and head lice, arrange for emergency care, give students excuses to go home if they are ill or injured, and help with attendance records. Some schools still test for scoliosis (curvature of the spine), although this is no longer considered cost-effective because of low reliability of case finding and low incidence of serious problems. In most states, school nurses are not allowed to give students medication, even aspirin. Currently, there are about 45,000 school nurses, roughly one for every two schools.[10] The ratio of school nurses to students is approximately one per 1,000, but the geographic distribution is uneven and some schools have no nurses (for example, in New York City) while others exceed the desirable ratio of 1:750. According to Philip Nader, a pioneer in school-based services:

> Economic pressures on schools, a return to the basics and a lack of documentation of the value of school health services has resulted in a trend toward replacement of the professional school nurse by less qualified nurse aides or licensed practical nursing personnel, further diminishing the quality and quantity of school health services available to children.[11]

There are about 70,000 guidance counselors in public schools, about 1 per 600 students. The high school guidance counselor's primary role is to assist students in making decisions about curricular choices and applying to colleges. Because of the large number of students for whom they are responsible, they are not able to provide psychological counseling or deal with behavioral problems. The 1988 *National Education Longitudinal Study* of eighth-graders found that only 11 percent of students had talked to a school counselor or a teacher about personal problems within the previous year.[12] Some school systems employ social workers and psychologists who may work as part of the pupil personnel services team, specifically to attend to more complex problems of students and their families.

School administrators, particularly (but not only) in disadvantaged communities, are increasingly acknowledging that they cannot continue to be the "surrogate parents" for young people with overwhelming health, social, and psychological problems, needs that cannot be met by school personnel. In certain circumstances, parents are not available to help their children; they have too many problems of their own. Existing pupil personnel staff is being stretched to the limit. School systems are confronted with massive budget cuts in which school nurses and other support personnel are among the first to be eliminated. Faced with these daily crises, school administrators are much more open than in the past to allowing local health and social agencies to relocate their services in school building sites.

SCHOOL-BASED HEALTH CLINICS (SBCs)

A school-based health clinic (SBC) is a facility located in a school building or adjacent to a school building where an array of services is provided by medical and social service personnel. In general, the comprehensive package of services includes health screening, physical examinations, treatment of minor injuries and illnesses, and counseling and referral. Attention to reproductive health care and mental-health services varies according to the program. The Jackson-Hinds (Mississippi) Comprehensive Health Center's School-Based Clinics program is typical of the earliest "models," which focused more on reproductive health care than did later ones (see Appendix 1).

In 1984, only ten SBCs could be identified around the country. The first SBC at the high school level was organized in Dallas in 1970 by the Department of Pediatrics, University of Texas Health Science Center.[13] The program included family planning and a decline in the birth rate appeared during the early years of the project. The most publicized model, in St. Paul, Minnesota, was started in 1973 by the Maternity and Infant Care Program of the local medical center. When the program was first initiated in one high school clinic with a focus solely on family planning, it failed to enroll students. After the program was expanded to include comprehensive health services and placed in four sites, enrollment grew. In 1980, it was reported that birth rates had dropped significantly after the initiation of health services including family planning in four high school sites.[14] However, this research did not include a control group or account for abortions.

Between 1985 and 1991, SBCs were organized in high schools and middle schools in almost every state, primarily in urban areas. There is no exact count, but the most recent survey (1991) conducted by the Center for Population Options (CPO) started with a listing of 328 sites.[15] While a major goal of many of the earlier programs was prevention of pregnancy, more recent entries are focused on a wide range of goals, including dropout and substance-abuse prevention, mental health, and health promotion. Because of the early focus on pregnancy prevention, SBCs were dubbed "sex clinics" by the media and detractors, and until recently, this theme has dominated whatever attention school-based health service programs have received. Yet SBCs have not proven to be effective at pregnancy prevention, although they show enormous promise as centers for integrating services such as counseling and general health screening that may indirectly impact on sexual behaviors.[16]

The growth of SBCs has resulted from a variety of forces: demand arising at the community level to help schools deal with the "new morbidities"; popularity of an innovative model for working with high-risk youth; responses to requests for proposals from foundations; and stimulation by state government initiatives. A number of the new program models have been designed by adolescent-medicine physicians and public-health practitioners who want to develop a delivery system of services for adolescents.

In 1986, the Robert Wood Johnson Foundation (RWJ) initiated a grants program to establish SBCs to make health care more accessible to poor children and reduce the rates of teen pregnancy.[17] Some twenty-three health clinics were organized in schools by teaching and community hospitals, county health departments, not-for-profit agencies, and, in some cases, the school systems. However, school systems that received grants had to subcontract with community health providers rather than directly hiring health professionals. According to Lear et al.:

> The primary reason for this approach was the belief that the way to strengthen health services provided in schools is to make those services an integral part of the community's health care delivery system . . . [these] health care institutions are best able to arrange medical referrals, address infection control, arrange laboratory pick-ups, protect medical confidentiality, provide medical back-up when the health centers are closed and respond to the myriad of issues that arise in the daily management of a health center.[18]

Many states provide funds to stimulate the organization of SBCs at the local level, typically through competitive health department grants. Arkansas, California, Connecticut, Delaware, Florida, Georgia, Iowa, Kentucky, Maryland, Massachusetts, Michigan, New Jersey, New York, and Oregon currently support some form of school-centered health and social services for children, youth, and families (see Appendix 2). The California State Education Department has been designated the lead agency for the new $20 million Healthy Start initiative for development of school-based health, mental-health, and social and academic support services, and a consortium of foundations has set up a new nonprofit agency to provide monitoring, evaluation, and technical assistance to California communities and schools. Most state legislation has placed restrictions on the use of state funds for the distribution of contraceptives and referral for abortion on school premises.

No single SBC model has emerged during this developmental stage. A wide array of agencies administer SBCs. According to the Center for Population Options, in 1991 three-fourths of SBCs were sponsored by public-health departments, community-health clinics, and hospitals or medical schools; 6 percent by community-based organizations and private nonprofit agencies;

and 7 percent by the school district itself.[19] Because of the great variety of models and sizes, annual costs range from about $50,000 to $300,000. Most of these funds come from state health departments, Medicaid, city governments, and foundations, not from school district budgets.

The average clinic enrollment is around 700 (with a wide range) and there are about 2,000 visits per year.[20] In most schools, about 70 percent of the students register for the clinic. All schools require parental permission to enroll, with some exceptions covered by state and federal laws for emergency care, reproductive-health care, and drug and mental-health counseling. SBCs are typically staffed by nurse practitioners, social workers, clinic aides, and other specialized personnel (nutritionists, health educators, psychologists). Physicians come in part-time for scheduled examinations and treatment, and are available on call for consultations and emergencies. The clinic coordinator is frequently the nurse practitioner. If the school still has a school nurse, her services are integrated with those of the clinic operations as much as possible. Most clinics provide general and sports physicals, diagnosis and treatment of minor injuries, pregnancy tests, immunizations, laboratory tests, chronic-illness management, health education, extensive counseling, and referral. Over 90 percent prescribe medications.

A 1990 CPO report reveals that 97 percent of high school and 73 percent of middle-school clinics provide counseling on birth-control methods.[21] About three-fourths of the high schools and half of the middle schools conduct gynecological examinations, follow up contraceptive users, and provide referrals to other agencies for methods and examinations. However, only half write prescriptions for contraceptives and only 21 percent actually dispense them. Although the clinics say they are offering these "family-planning" services, only 10–20 percent of the students report using the clinics for family planning. Not surprisingly, the clinics that offer the most comprehensive family-planning services appear to be the most heavily utilized by the students for family planning. One study of six clinics found that at only two sites were more students using contraceptives than in comparison sites without clinics, but there were no differences in pregnancy or birth rates across sites. Kirby et al. concluded that the clinic could not have an effect on pill and condom use unless much higher priority were given to pregnancy or AIDS prevention throughout the program and the school.[22] This implies much greater attention to follow-up of sexually active students to ensure compliance with contraceptive methods.

Program data show that clinic users are more likely to be female, African-American or Hispanic, and disadvantaged (eligible for free-lunch programs).[23] However, a large number of males do use the clinics, especially for physical examinations and treatment for accidents and injuries. Reports from clinic practitioners invariably mention personal counseling as the most sought after service, reflecting the stressful lives of contemporary adolescents. In some clinics, 30–40 percent of the primary diagnoses are mental-health related.[24] The presence of a nonthreatening, confidential advisor apparently opens up communication about such issues as sexual abuse, parental drug use, and fears of violence.

In summary, a movement toward the development of school-based centers has emerged during the past decade reflecting a response to the overwhelming needs of today's students for health services. It is estimated that in aggregate some 400 school-based clinics may now be serving about 300,000 students per year, a minuscule proportion of the total number of enrollees in junior and senior high schools. Nevertheless, these "pioneer" programs prove that such efforts are both possible and feasible, and, in a sense, this cohort may be the "cutting edge" for the implementation of a wide range of service programs, each individualized to the particular needs of the students, the school, and the community.

MENTAL-HEALTH CENTERS IN SCHOOLS

A key finding in surveys of students is the high incidence of depression and suicidal ideation. The OTA estimated that one out of five adolescents age ten to eighteen suffers from a diagnosable mental disorder, including depression, and that one out of four adolescents reports symptoms of emotional distress.[25] Yet few depressed students have access to mental-health care in the community, and the already overextended school psychologists and school social workers cannot possibly meet this critical need. As a result, there is a growing interest in bringing outside services into school sites.

Several different approaches are being used to bring mental-health services into schools: on-site counseling and treatment for mental-health problems by mental-health professionals; building mental-health teams to work with school personnel to develop more effective responses to high-risk children; and development and implementation of competency-building curricula in classrooms.[26] These three kinds of interventions have in common that they are designed, implemented, and funded by community agencies, outside of the school system, and brought into schools in the same way as SBCs, primarily through foundation grants and/or statewide funding.

While all of these models are interesting and important, I will concentrate here primarily on the emergence of centers within schools that provide actual screening, diagnosis, and treatment for psychosocial disorders. These direct-service programs are similar in organization to school-based health clinics but they start out with the specific goal of remediation of psychosocial problems. The School-Based Youth Services Program in New Brunswick (N.J.) is an example of a mental health program operated in a school by a local community mental health center (see Appendix 3).

The work of carving out this subset of activities is being refined by the School Mental Health Project at the University of California–Los Angeles, a national clearinghouse that offers training, research, and technical assistance.[27] This project works in conjunction with the Los Angeles Unified Schools District's School Mental Health Center and based on that experience is in the process of developing a guidebook for practitioners who want to follow a mental-health model. Howard Adelman and Linda Taylor, who direct the project, believe that the major challenge for school-based mental health centers is to identify and collaborate with what is already going on in the school district. Many schools have programs focused on substance abuse and teen pregnancy prevention, crisis intervention (suicide), violence reduction, and "self-esteem" enhancement, and other kinds of support groups. However, these efforts lack cohesiveness in theory and implementation, often stigmatize students by targeting them, and suffer from the common bureaucratic problem of poor coordination between programs. One of the most demanding roles for the mental-health center is to establish working relationships with key school staff members.

In response to the often overwhelming demand for services, mental-health practitioners (primarily social workers or clinical psychologists) have initiated a number of innovative group-counseling approaches. For example, staff at the San Fernando Heights School (Los Angeles) school-based center developed "Biculturation Groups" for helping students from other countries make the transition into a new school and community.[28] Three kinds of problems are dealt with: acculturating to a new environment; coping with common problems of adolescence; and dealing with pre-immigration problems such as war-related trauma or family separation.

A school-based clinic program in four junior high schools in the Washington Heights area of New York City operated by the Columbia University School of Public Health has added mental-health components to the original health model in response to the serious psychosocial problems of the students.[29] Social workers provide individual and group counseling, offer group intervention, and maintain contact with parents, teachers, and other school personnel as needed to meet the needs of the students. The social workers do comprehensive psychosocial assessments on children identified by surveys, medical staff, and school personnel for given problems and follow up with group, individual, or family counseling; home visiting; mentoring; parent workshops; or school consultation with guidance counselors or teachers. As this program has evolved, the social work staff (rather than the nurse practitioners) have assumed most of the responsibility for dealing with sexuality issues. They run groups focusing on decision-making skills, reproductive knowledge, and refusal skills. As part of this activity, they escort sexually active students to the family-planning clinics at the back-up hospital. They are also responsible for following up contraceptive patients to ensure their compliance. Direct and immediate social work intervention is required in all cases of reported or suspected child abuse and psychiatric emergencies.

In addition to the development of direct mental-health services in schools, other initiatives have received considerable attention, particularly the "Comer Process." Developed in 1968 by James Comer at Yale University and currently being widely replicated, this program attempts to transfer mental-health skills to schools, where "change agents" must be created by strengthening and redefining the relationships between principals, teachers, parents, and students.[30] An essential element is the creation of a mental-health team including the school psychologist and other support personnel, who provide direct services to children and advise school staff and parents. A member of the mental-health team plays an active role on the management-oriented School Improvement Team, along with representatives of teachers, teacher aides, and parent groups.

In summary, a variety of mental-health programs are being offered in schools by community mental-health centers, university psychology and social work departments, and mental-health practitioners. A few might be classified as school-based mental health centers but most of the efforts to cope with the rising number of psychosocial problems appear to be attached to existing health clinics or other approaches. It is not possible to enumerate the number and location of schools with discrete mental-health programs (as distinguished from school psychologists and social workers who may counsel students as part of school function).

COMPREHENSIVE MULTIFACETED PROGRAMS

School-based health centers increasingly use the language of "comprehensiveness." As centers open in schools, the demand for many different services arises. As we have seen, programs that started out as pregnancy-prevention rapidly shifted to general health services, and those that provided general health services had to incorporate psychosocial counseling. As the demand for personal counseling grew, the clinics began to assume more of the aura of mental-health services.

Yet when these centers are opened in school sites, they often meet a bewildering array of categorical prevention and treatment programs. One principal of an inner-city junior high school in New York displayed a list of 200 different programs coming into his school from outside community agencies. He stated that he had no idea what they did, and would be happy to replace them with one central facility that coordinated and monitored services provided to his students.

The call for coordinated services is being heard across the land, not only in relationship to adolescent health issues, but in regard to maternal and child health, early childhood services, welfare reform, and practically every other social endeavor.[31] Most of the new plans call for the development of one-stop centers and typically these centers are in or near schools. "Teen Moms" is an example of a comprehensive model that has been in existence for some time. Those interested in alleviating the many problems connected with early teenage parenthood have long been packaging services for teenage parents that include on-site infant care along with educational remediation, parenting skills, health services, and personal counseling.[32] More recent models embrace the concepts of case management with the use of "community women" who are supposed to act as mentors and advocates. A few of these teen-parent programs are located within schools (as in Jackson, Mississippi) but most are operated by school systems as alternative schools.

New York State supports fourteen community schools charged with developing school/community collaborations that use the schools as sites for access to social, cultural, health, recreation, and other services for children, their families, and other community adults.[33] In Rochester, New York, the Chester Dewey School uses a full-time coordinator to encourage community agencies to bring in afterschool care and mentoring, and evening programs and activities for adults. The Community School Project has worked with the Department of Social Services to address the serious housing needs of the parents through workshops on tenants' rights, assisting parents to find better housing and to reduce evictions.

The national Cities in Schools (CIS) initiative has promoted the collaborative model, bringing social services into schools by placing social workers from community agencies as case managers on school sites.[34] Each participating community works out its own version of this approach and there are a number of "spin-offs" that were started by the CIS process but later became independent. One large-scale undertaking in Pinal County, Arizona, the Prevention Partnership, places site directors in twelve schools along with VISTA volunteers who act as service brokers to 120 service providers in the county. This program employs a school-based management system, and referrals are made for counseling, mentoring, parenting skills, employment and welfare assistance, prenatal and preventive health services, and emergency services. The four New Futures experiments being conducted by the Annie Casey Foundation in Pittsburgh, Savannah, Dayton, and Little Rock are attempting to build "oversight collaboratives" that will bring together community leaders, schools, and community agencies to create new institutional arrangements that will alter the way services (including education) are delivered to children.[35] Preliminary reports suggest that these New Future initiatives are "slow going," with little effect on restructuring schools or changing the ways that agencies conduct their business.[36] However, researchers found enhanced dialogue between leaders in schools and community agencies with the potential for improvement in the future. Aside from educational interventions, these programs have successfully implemented supplemental new initiatives such as case management and school-based clinics.

SINGLE-PURPOSE SCHOOL-BASED PROGRAMS

Perceptions about what can be brought into schools by outside community agencies are becoming more and more inclusive. As has been pointed out, many task forces and commissions have recommended comprehensive collaborative community-wide programs. Yet some of these large-scale comprehensive programs are proving difficult to implement (e.g., New Futures) and slow to evaluate (e.g., Cities in Schools). In fact, most of the documented successful prevention programs are categorical and are operated by individuals and/or teams from single community agencies that come into schools and provide specialized counseling, treatment, and referral to outside agencies.[37]

An example in the substance-abuse prevention and treatment field is called Student Assistance. In this effort, social workers from an outside agency are assigned to schools, where they work with the principal, teachers, and other support personnel to identify high-risk students, provide individual and group counseling, facilitate referrals and follow-up, and help create a healthy and safe school climate.[38]

A similar model has proven successful in the teen-pregnancy prevention field. Counselors, usually social workers, from outside agencies are placed in schools, where they conduct individual and group counseling and referral for family planning. Each counselor has a private office in the school and confidentiality is carefully safeguarded.[39] Another school-based pregnancy prevention program, Team Outreach, incorporates a life-planning curriculum, mentoring, and counseling along with volunteer job placements in the community.[40]

The successful categorical programs feature a number of common components such as early intervention, intensive one-on-one individual attention, training in social skills and competency building, exposure to the world of work, and involvement of peers and parents.[41] Many programs that work to prevent social-behavioral problems focus on the acquisition of basic academic skills and schools are essential partners in much of the prevention activity. However, no one component is believed to work miracles. The comprehensive efforts that are currently emerging typically package most of these elements into an integrated intervention.

ADVANTAGES OF PLACING SERVICES IN SCHOOLS

Schools are rapidly becoming the locus of a wide range of collaborative efforts related to health, mental health, and social services. Although these programs are diverse in size, function, organization, and outcome, there are important common features of school-based programs for adolescents. Placing services in schools gives certain students access to care they would not otherwise be able to obtain. Most of the clinic sites are in low-income communities that do not have a large supply of private physicians, and many of the families have no medical insurance. While some qualify for Medicaid, the children in the family may not have confidential access to the Medicaid card. Almost all school-based services are free. A few charge a token fee but collections are minimal.

Adolescent-medicine physicians and public-health practitioners support the concept of school-based services because such services give them access to high-risk populations that do not ordinarily use private-sector medicine or even community-based clinics. Some SBC advocates believe that by utilizing these clinics, adolescents gain a "medical home" while in high school and learn communication skills that will help them access the medical care system in the future. It is probable that the utilization of school clinics lowers the demand on emergency rooms, where adolescents frequently go for crisis care and even general health services. Preliminary data suggest that school-based clinics may be more cost-effective than purchasing comparable care from private physicians (assuming that physicians were available).[42]

Almost all of these programs have been implemented with funds from state, foundation, local, or private sources. Very few school systems are able to finance these kinds of programs, estimated to cost about $100,000–$200,000 per year. However, school systems have contributed matching funds by making space available and providing maintenance and security. In some systems, school personnel such as school nurses and psychologists become integrated with the staff of the clinic or center.

Almost all of the programs are organized and managed by outside agencies that bring in their own funds and protocols. Experience has shown that planning a school-based clinic or center takes at least a year. The selection of the service mix results from planning by a representative committee including school staff, community agencies, parents, and students. In the most effective efforts, one staff member is designated coordinator to give full attention to developing the program, supervising staff, and negotiating between the school and provider agencies.

Evaluation of the effectiveness of school-based centers is still at an early stage. An excellent management-information system, designed by David Kaplan for the Denver school-based clinic program, is now being utilized by more than 100 programs around the country.[43] A number of unpublished papers have been presented at professional meetings, and it should be expected that these findings will soon appear in journals. While the earlier study results were quite optimistic about school-based clinic programs' potential for preventing pregnancy, they were also crude. More recent work has failed to find a consistent effect on pregnancy rates, although it seems clear that in those schools where clinics make contraception available, contraceptive use is higher. As part of their study of SBCs, Kirby and Wascek compiled data on a high school in Jackson, Mississippi (see Appendix 1).[44] Students were asked to check off school-clinic services ever used: About one-third had used the clinic for sports and health examinations, 26 percent for counseling in general, 28 percent for contraceptive counseling, 22 percent for contraceptive supplies, and 15 percent for immunizations. The researchers found few significant differences in pregnancy-prevention practices between clinic users and nonusers; however, they did find that 77 percent of the students who had ever used the school clinic to obtain contraceptives had used an effective method at last intercourse, compared with 48 percent of the students who had not used the clinic for this purpose. Between 1979 and 1990, more than 7,200 adolescents were served by the Jackson school-based program. Among the 180 student mothers followed up, only 10 experienced a repeat pregnancy and the pregnancy-related dropout rate decreased from about 50 percent to zero.

Scattered results from preliminary studies around the country show small positive impacts. One question that is often raised is whether the mere presence of a clinic in a school influences the sexual activity rate. Research on the effect of clinics on the incidence of sexual activity among the students has yielded no evidence that the rates increase after the clinic opens.[45] A two-year follow-up survey in Kansas City revealed almost no change in reported sexual behavior.[46] Following a three-year school-clinic demonstration project in Baltimore, Zabin et al. found a postponement of first intercourse that averaged seven months among program participants.[47]

A survey conducted by the Houston school-based clinic program showed that clinic users were more than twice as likely to use contraception every time they had sex as those who had not been to the clinic and they were less than half as likely never to use contraception.[48] Among students who were already sexually active, clinic patients in Kansas City showed higher rates of contraceptive use than nonpatients, and a striking increase in use of condoms among males. In Baltimore, younger female students and males in the experimental schools were much more likely to use birth control than those in the control schools, and in St. Paul, female contraceptive users had an extremely high rate of continuation: 91 percent were still using the method (mostly the pill) after a year and 78 percent after two years of use.[49] (Free-standing family planning clinics report a twelve-month program dropout rate of close to 50 percent.[50])

The Kansas City program reported a substantial drop in substance use during a two-year period.[51] This program places high priority on teaching healthy life-styles and reducing risk-taking behaviors through group and individual counseling. The Kansas City SBC also reported changes in mental-health outcomes: reductions in hopelessness, suicidal ideation, and low self-esteem. The Pinelands, New Jersey, program reported reductions in suspensions, dropouts, and births among students two years after the program started and the Hackensack, New Jersey, program showed a reduction in fights, which they attributed to conflict-resolution interventions.[52] Almost three-fourths of New York City students who used SBCs thought that the clinic had improved their health and more than a third stated that the clinic had improved their school attendance. Most (91 percent) stated that the clinic had improved their ability to get health care when they needed it and 88 percent stated that the clinic had improved their knowledge of and ability to take care of their bodies.[53]

At this point in time, the primary evidence that school-based programs are having an impact lies in utilization figures, with large proportions of student bodies enrolled and using services. One study found that the highest risk students (with multiple problem behaviors) were the heaviest users of the clinic.[54] Screening and assessments have resulted in extensive case findings —particularly heart murmurs, asthma and other respiratory diseases, need for immunization, sexual abuse, parasites, sexually transmitted diseases, and other problems that beset disadvantaged youth.

The school-based mental-health programs can document extensive hours of counseling and treatment. In New Brunswick, more than one-fourth of the student body has received intensive psychological care. These same students and their families did not use the local community mental health center for services because of costs and perceived inaccessibility. A clinic in Quincy, Florida, reported that about one student a week comes in saying that he or she is either contemplating or has attempted suicide.[55] Most of the cases found in school clinics require counseling and crisis intervention for depression, stress, and severe family problems, rather than long-term treatment for psychoses and conduct disorders.

No data are available about the outcomes of the provision of direct mental-health services to adolescents in schools, nor have new research findings been reported from current replications of the Comer process. We would expect that achievement and attendance rates would improve in communities that recognize the importance of mental-health interventions.

Categorical programs have been identified that can document improvement in categorical outcomes such as pregnancy prevention and lower substance use.[56] Comprehensive programs targeted to a specific population can produce some successes, such as teen parents programs that reduce repeat pregnancies and improve school completion.

Finally, parents, students, teachers, school administrators, and program staffs have extremely positive attitudes toward the concept of one-stop services located in schools. A Harris poll found that 80 percent of parents and 81 percent of teachers believe that developing school programs to provide counseling and support services to children with emotional, mental, social, or family problems would "help a lot" to improve educational outcomes.[57] The public does not fear that attention to reproductive-health issues will increase the level of sexual activity among students. In fact, a survey of public attitudes toward provision of birth control information and contraceptives in schools showed an approval rating of 73 percent.[58] Approval was highest among African-American respondents (88 percent) and unmarried people (86 percent). Fully 80 percent approved of school clinic referrals to family-planning clinics.

The AIDS scare has begun to have an impact on policies regarding the distribution of condoms in schools. In recent months, New York City, Philadelphia, Los Angeles, San Francisco, and Baltimore authorities have revised policies to make condoms available to students. In New York City condoms are being distributed by teachers and other staff who volunteer to be trained for this mission. In Baltimore, the nine school-based clinics initiated a policy to distribute contraceptives after a parent survey showed wide approval.

In summary, school-based programs are developing at a rapid rate because they are providing services to a very needy population, junior and senior high school students who have little access to other sources of care. They bring into disadvantaged school systems committed and caring staff workers who can give all of their atttention to the physical and psychosocial needs of the students. The development of these diverse programs is taking place all around the country despite trying conditions that include competition for scarce resources, acute shortages of nurse-practitioners, and a constant struggle to maintain services.

LIMITATIONS OF SCHOOL-BASED PROGRAMS

Two issues frequently arise in discussions about the merits of placing services in schools: the problem of negotiating governance between school systems and community agencies, and the lack of long-term funding.

GOVERNANCE

Given the complex processes involved when one or more community agencies moves into a school system, it is surprising that these models are being replicated as rapidly as they are. Each party has its own board of directors, policies, funding, accounting procedures, personnel practices, and insurance. There are different union contracts and salary structures in schools and outside health and social service agencies. Working out the details for collaboration requires endless planning and negotiation.

From the point of view of the community agencies, school boards are often inflexible. Many initiatives have been delayed because of difficult policy decisions, for example, the use of school facilities, reproductive-health care, and personnel practices. Often, the host school is already overcrowded and finding adequate space for a clinic requires extensive remodeling. Clinic hours differ from those of the school, necessitating arrangements with the custodial staff. The school nurse may feel threatened by the new facility and raise objections to procedures that conflict with her turf.

One might think that policies regarding birth control create the most conflict. This has not generally been the case. Only one or two clinics have failed to open because of community dissension. So much has been made of this issue that it is typically dealt with early in the planning process. Few school systems allow distribution of contraceptives on site and almost all programs allow for parental consent. These policies have assuaged critics but they have also limited the effectiveness of school-based clinics in their work with sexually active teenagers in regard to compliance with contraceptive methods. As pointed out above, these policies are currently under review in light of the AIDS epidemic.

Operating a school-based clinic requires constant nurturing of the relationship between the clinic program and the school. The key player in these ongoing negotiations is the school principal. As the primary gatekeeper, the principal facilitates access to students, promotes good working relationships between the school staff and the program staff, and makes sure the building is safe and clean. If the principal does not cooperate, the program will not work.

School clinics open the door to many turf issues. One question that frequently arises when a program is placed in a school with existing support personnel such as a psychologist, a social worker, or even a guidance counselor, is who is in charge of mental health "cases." This becomes particularly sensitive in dealing with special education students. Ensuring confidentiality can be very difficult in situations in which school and clinic staff are both involved.

Similar questions have been raised about the "ownership" of health-promotion curricula. If the school-based clinic is providing extensive individual and group counseling, is it necessary to use school time for health-promotion curricula? If clinic personnel are willing to go into classrooms and take on the responsibility for sex-education, substance-abuse and suicide-prevention, and violence workshops, what is the role of school health educator? If the clinic assumes the health-promotion role, is it necessary to train teachers to do sex education and substance-abuse prevention?

Teachers in schools with clinics are sometimes reluctant to allow students to leave classes to make clinic visits. They may also be threatened by the confidential relationship between clinic counselors and students. In some cases, stress-related behavior derives from negative school experiences, and specific teachers have been implicated in lowering student's expectations and accused of failing to teach. Clinic practitioners may have negative views of school discipline policies that rely heavily on suspension and expulsion and practices such as tracking and grade retention that have been shown to undermine achievement.

Many school systems are driven by the desire to raise test scores and lower dropout rates. Teachers are frustrated because they believe that the students' behavioral problems and the social environments of the communities in which the schools are located stand in the way of achievement. School-restructuring efforts try to create a learning community equalizing outcomes for all students. In some instances, the school-based clinic programs have become involved with school restructuring because they see that they cannot successfully treat the students' psychosocial problems without massive changes in the way the students are treated in school.

FUNDING

School-based health and social service programs derive funds from diverse sources. More than half of the funding derives from Maternal and Child Health and other state health department grants.[59] Few programs are adequately funded and almost all of them rely on a mix of resources that require complicated and time-consuming accounting procedures. Each source of funds has its own regulations and eligibility. Foundation support is time-limited. The twenty-three Robert Wood Johnson grants have now reached their limit and those programs have to find other sources of funding, what the foundation calls "institutionalization."

One approach to long-term funding being appraised by RWJ-supported researchers and others is to increase the use of Medicaid funds for eligible students, particularly in light of new provisions to stimulate the use of Early Periodic Screening Treatment and Diagnosis programs. It has been estimated that about one-third of the students served in school-based clinics are eligible for Medicaid but only about 3 percent of the services are financed by such reimbursements. A recent survey found that the major barriers to the use of Medicaid or private insurance by school-based clinics were (1) students did not know whether their families were Medicaid or private insurance recipients; (2) time and costs of paperwork involved in billing were prohibitive; (3) state Medicaid or private insurance companies refused to pay for services; (4) Medicaid did not recognize schools as qualified medical providers; and (5) confidentiality issues.[60] Clinics administered by private community health agencies and hospitals or medical schools were the most likely to be using Medicaid. The tighter the link to a medical base, the more likely a program is to have access to third-party funds. Increasingly, clinics are placing Medicaid eligibility workers on school sites to help students with eligibility determinations. In some communities and states, the concept of declaring an entire school Medicaid-eligible is being explored. This would cut down on the bureaucratic hassle and ensure continuity of funding and confidentiality.

Another important source of support of school-based centers is a line item in the state budget, as in the New Jersey Department of Human Resources and the Kentucky Department of Education. The limitations of this approach are that only enough money may be included for demonstration projects, as in New Jersey, or that the grants may be very small, as in Kentucky. At one point, the state of Michigan developed a plan to fund 100 school-based clinics, but the appropriation so far covers only 20 such programs. The continuity of state funds depends on continuing legislative approval, not easily guaranteed during this period of fiscal constraints, and a change of governor can bring changes in priorities (although the school-based program has weathered changes in administration in most states). A further limitation is that state funds usually have restrictions, particularly prohibiting distribution of contraception and/or counseling regarding abortion.

In summary, many issues remain to be resolved in regard to the creation of one-stop centers in schools, issues that are similar despite the significant differences in the health, mental-health, and social services models. All programs suffer from shortages of funding and most operate in a crisis mode. The demand for services in schools is often overwhelming. Although most of the current school-based programs follow a medical model, starting with assessments, screening, and physical examinations, the most frequently cited unmet need is for mental-health counseling. The acute shortage of emergency psychiatric and day-treatment facilities for adolescents and the shortage of bilingual mental-health clinicians are widespread. As new staff and services are brought into centers, the utilization rates increase.

An observation of one inner-city project showed that

> as soon as the doors of a new clinic site open, mobs of students pour in seeking minor items like bandaids, ice packs and sanitary napkins, producing a steady stream of work for the staff. At the same time, a small number of students are identified who have been battered, are severely depressed, have burdensome family problems, are taking drugs or require a complex mix of many different kinds of services. The new clinics are overwhelmed by the two extreme ends of the spectrum of needs and find little time to reach the vast majority of students in between. Reorganization of the work load, targeting high risk individuals and the development of specialized protocols have alleviated this problem somewhat, but the clinic staff perceive it as one which school based clinics can never overcome. As they say, "it goes with the territory."[61]

The absence of evaluation and the minimal published literature on the subject produce an impression of haphazard diffusion of an idea, implemented at widely disparate levels of effectiveness. With the exception of some of the state-supported programs, each program is packaged in a different way and there is no central system for monitoring quality. A common problem is the complexity of governance in a model that brings the services, staff, and funding from an outside community agency into a school.

OUTLOOK FOR ONE-STOP CENTERS IN SCHOOLS

In disadvantaged communities, schools cannot address the challenge of raising the quality of education and at the same time attend to the problems of young people and their families without a substantial mobilization of health and social services resources. Poverty rates among youth are growing, housing is deteriorating, and violence threatens everyone. These worsening conditions are accelerating the drive among concerned people to find new solutions that incorporate the linkage between educational achievement and adolescent health. While school-based services will not solve the underlying problems of poverty and discrimination, they are perceived by both health and educational practitioners as one potentially cost-effective approach to alleviating the symptoms. Young people can receive support to stay in school, manage their psychosocial problems, prepare for the work force, and experience positive relationships with caring adults. Thus, the idea of packaging services together and putting them in a central place like a school is very attractive.

Thus far, the school-based clinic model has been conceived as an intervention for "high-risk" communities. Many but not all of the clinics are located in metropolitan areas with the highest incidence of the "new morbidities"—teen pregnancy, sexually transmitted diseases, AIDS, drug abuse, violence, and depression—and the highest school failure and dropout rates. Although advocates of this model acknowledge that there are high-risk adolescents in affluent communities as well, there is no consensus on whether every school should have such a center or only those schools that serve disadvantaged populations. Suburban youth, who make up the majority of high school students, increasingly lack parental support and also need the attention of caring adults to help them get through their teen years. They also must learn to deal with a fragmented health, mental-health, and social service system. Suburban schools, because they have larger budgets than city schools, are more likely to employ support personnel including psychologists, speech therapists, school nurses, and guidance counselors. In order to ensure that all adolescents have access to the full range of services they need, suburban schools might take an intermediate step by assigning a staff member in every school to foster coordination with community agencies (as recommended in *Turning Points*[62]). This would entail schoolwide planning for individual counseling, crisis intervention, family involvement, and systematic referrals for services along with follow-up.

My own vision of the ideal community school is a center in a school that brings together those services most needed in that community. At the high school level, these might include health, mental-health, and career-training and job-placement services; after-school recreation and cultural events; parent education; and public-assistance and community police force programs. Most importantly, the center would facilitate arrangements for individual and family counseling. The employment of youth advocates who assist students with family and school problems would ensure that those most in need receive the services they require as soon as possible. Health-promotion activities such as pregnancy and substance-use prevention would become the responsibility of the center staff. The schoolhouse doors would be open most of the time, including evenings, weekends, and summers.

Community schools set up to serve elementary school populations would include preschool and after-school care, parent training, home visiting, educational programs for parents, and other health and social services. Experience to date suggests that once a school community enters the process of thinking about centralizing services in schools, almost any public or private community agency can be transported from its community base into the school facility. Edward Zigler of Yale University has long articulated the need for "Schools of the 21st Century" incorporating these services. His model is being replicated in more than 200 schools throughout the nation (particularly in Kentucky and Connecticut).[63]

The bottom line here, of course, is how to make this vision a reality. If the current crop of school-based clinics are having a hard time maintaining their bases of support, how can community schools be institutionalized on a large enough scale to have any impact? Schools, community agencies, foundations, states, and the federal government have various roles in meeting this challenge. The primary role for school systems is to encourage the development of these collaborative relationships, to make it known that they are willing to use their facilities to host an array of services. The role of the community agencies is to gear up to provide their services in new locations, much as hospitals and health departments organize satellite clinics. Community agencies have to be prepared to deal with the ambiguities and frustrations that arise in negotiations with school systems. Schools and community agencies together have to hammer out the governance arrangements that will assure efficient functioning of the center.

Articulate grass-roots support is an essential component in gaining the ear and pocketbook of both the citizenry and the decision-makers. Parents, students, and community leaders can make their voices heard at budget hearings and planning sessions.

Foundations have already played an important role in funding demonstration projects, but they must be prepared to do more. It is unlikely that evaluation will be conducted on a large enough scale without extensive foundation support. One of the advantages of foundations is that they can assist grantees to monitor programs and document processes.

Many states are already heavily involved in the extension of the school-based clinic model. These state programs, usually placed in state health or human resources departments, need to develop collaborative relationships with state education agencies. In some states, collaboration is legislatively mandated, while in others governors have created child- and youth-services "mini-cabinets" to foster integration of services. Together, state agencies need to be able to provide technical assistance to communities, monitor the quantity and quality of the services, and organize training and conferences. States can promote the development of school-based centers not only through funding, but also by waiving various regulations in regard to Medicaid and other state-controlled resources.

The federal government has played virtually no role in the advancement of these new kinds of service models. Yet the potential for moving from demonstration programs to institutionalization lies within the power of Congress, which in 1990 passed but did not fund the Young Americans Act. This legislation would create a central commission and council for generating a coordinated federal response to the multiple needs of children. Funds would be provided to states for planning and coordination. Congress could also create a new cabinet-level agency and integrate the hundreds of categorical youth-serving programs into a more rational delivery system.

The federal government could be instrumental in changing policies now to allow categorical funds to be used to design and implement community-school collaboratives. Possible sources of funds in addition to Medicaid include Drug Free Schools, Office of Substance Abuse Prevention, Juvenile Justice, Division of Adolescent and School Health of the Centers for Disease Control, and other AIDS prevention monies. It is possible that the mission of Chapter 1 to aid economically disadvantaged children could be expanded to encompass their health and psychosocial needs as well as educational remediation. There are definitely signs in Washington that integration of youth and family services is the direction of the future, but almost all of the proposed school-based efforts are directed toward preschool or elementary school children, prior to the age of puberty.

All health and social indicators confirm that our society will have to move rapidly to enable disadvantaged adolescents to mature into responsible, literate, productive adults. The combined forces of the educational, health, and welfare systems working together are necessary to counteract the effects of the decaying social environment on this generation of youth. The traditional approaches to health and psychosocial problems are not working. New school-based centers of health and mental-health care are emerging but they will remain in the demonstration phase or disappear completely without significant support and attention.

APPENDIX 1
JACKSON-HINDS COMPREHENSIVE HEALTH CENTER'S SCHOOL-BASED CLINICS

The federally funded Comprehensive Health Center in Jackson, Mississippi, currently operates school-based health services in four high schools, three middle schools, and one elementary school. In 1979, when the program was first initiated at Lanier High School, the staff found many conditions that demonstrated the extensive unmet needs of the students, including urinary tract infections, anemia, heart murmurs, and psychosocial problems. In a student body of 960, they found more than 90 girls who were either pregnant or already had a child. Some 25 percent of the pregnancies had occurred while the youngsters were in junior high, leading the program to extend resources to an inner-city junior high school and a second high school the following year. The other clinics were added in the late 1980s.

Clinics are located in whatever rooms schools can make available. At Lanier High School, two small rooms near the principal's office are equipped as clinics. Group counseling and health-education classes are provided in a large classroom with private offices for individual counseling. The infant-care center is located in a mobile unit attached to the school. The staff at Lanier includes a physician, a nurse practitioner, a licensed practical nurse, two nurse assistants, and an educator/counselor, all part-time workers.

The school-based clinic protocol includes a medical history and routine lab tests of hematocrit, hemoglobin, and urinalysis. Each enrolled student completes a psychosocial assessment that reveals risk levels for substance abuse, violence, suicide, pregnancy, sexually transmitted diseases (STDs), accidents, and family conflict. Depending on indications from the health history and assessment tool, the student is scheduled for a visit with the physician and/or counselor. However, the clinic is always open, from 8:00 A.M. to 5:00 P.M., for walk-in visits for emergency care and crisis intervention.

Clinic staff conduct individual and group counseling sessions. If sexually active, students are given birth-control methods including condoms and followed up bi-monthly. Staff also dispense formal health instruction about specific issues such as compliance with medication protocols or treatment of acne, and informal "rap sessions" on parenting, the reproductive health system, birth-control methods, sexual values, STDs, and substance abuse. The counseling and clinic services are closely coordinated. Enrollees in the school clinic are referred to the primary community health center for routine dental screening, cleaning, and fluoride application. This facility is always open to students after school hours and on weekends and holidays.

Arrangements for early prenatal care are made through the obstetrical department of the health center. Teen mothers are carefully monitored throughout their pregnancies with special attention paid to keeping the young women in school as long as possible and getting them back within a month after delivery. Day care is provided at the school. Young mothers are counseled and instructed about child development and parenting skills. The Day Care Center is also used for teaching child psychology to high school students.*

* This description is based on "A Community Based Education and Intervention System," Jackson-Hinds School Based Adolescent Health Program (undated); and Douglas Kirby and Cynthia Waszak, *An Assessment of Six School-Based Clinics: Services, Impact and Potential* (Washington, D.C.: Center for Population Clinics, 1989). Additional information was provided by Dr. Aaron Shirley, director of the Jackson-Hinds Community Health Center on the occasion of a visit to Lanier High School and thereafter.

APPENDIX 2
NEW JERSEY SCHOOL-BASED YOUTH SERVICES PROGRAM

The School-Based Youth Services Program (SBYSP) has served as a model for other states. Following a competitive process, grants were made by the New Jersey Department of Human Services in 1987 to 29 communities for collaborative projects to be operated jointly by the school system and one or more local nonprofit or public health, mental health, or youth-serving agencies and to be located in or near the school. Based on the theme of "one-stop services," each project had to provide core services including mental health and family counseling, drug and alcohol counseling, educational remediation, recreation, and employment services at one site. Health services had to be available on site or by referral. In addition, child care, teen parenting, family planning examinations and referral for contraception, transportation, and hotlines could be provided with the grant (but not contraceptives or referral for abortion services). All centers had to be open after school, weekends, and during vacations.*

* Janet Levy and William Shepardson, "A Look at Current School-linked Service Efforts," in *The Future of Children: School-Linked Services* (Los Altos, Calif.: Center for the Future of Children, David and Lucile Packard Foundation, 1992), pp. 141–42.

APPENDIX 3
SCHOOL-BASED YOUTH SERVICES PROGRAM, NEW BRUNSWICK (N.J.) PUBLIC SCHOOLS

This mental health program was initiated in New Brunswick High School in 1988, funded by the New Jersey School Based Centers program. It is operated by the Community Mental Health Center, which is part of the University of Medicine and Dentistry of New Jersey. The program was stimulated by New Brunswick Tomorrow, a local business-sponsored effort that is trying to revitalize New Brunswick. In 1991, New Brunswick School-Based Youth Services Program (SBYSP) was awarded new state funds to expand services into five local elementary schools.

The SBYSP is a centralized service delivery system that integrates existing school programs, creates new services within schools, and links a network of youth-service providers. Although its primary thrust is mental-health promotion and treatment, it "looks like" a comprehensive youth center in a school setting. Currently, the program has ten full-time core staff members, including eight clinicians (psychologists and social workers), one of whom serves as the director. The staff conduct individual, group, and family therapy and serve as consultants to school personnel and other agencies involved with adolescents. An activities/outreach worker plans and supervises recreational activities and outreach contacts at the high school. Specialized part-time staff include a pregnancy/parenting counselor, a substance abuse counselor, and consultants in suicide prevention, "social problems," and medical care. A number of student interns from Rutgers University Graduate Schools have field placements in this program and there are also some volunteers.

The facility at New Brunswick High School is located in the old band room, fixed up very attractively to resemble a game room in a settlement house, with television, pingpong, and other active games, comfortable furniture, and books and tapes for the students to borrow. Private offices where students can go for individual psychological counseling ring the main room. The center offers tutoring, mentoring, group activities, recreational outings, and educational trips. A number of "therapeutic" groups have been organized: social problem solving, substance abuse, Children of Alcoholics, and coping skills for gifted and talented. Students are referred to the local neighborhood health center for health services and treatment. Children of teen parents are offered transportation to child-care centers.

Of the 650 students in the New Brunswick High School, 91 percent are enrolled in the program and have parental consent statements on file. During the past two years, one in four of the enrolled students has been involved in active mental-health counseling with one of the clinicians. Many of the students, especially the girls, appear to be clinically depressed. According to Gail Reynolds, the director, the demand for services is overwhelming. Many of the problems require immediate and time-consuming interventions with the family, school, and social agencies. After a student has made three visits, parents must come in for counseling sessions. Staff make home visits in order to involve parents.

In the process of setting up the program within the school, the superintendent was a key player and supportive from the start. The first summer was spent overcoming the resistance of the people in the school, preparing the school staff, and working out referral procedures with the school's four guidance counselors and the teachers. Reynolds meets with the counselors once a month and with the principal and vice-principal weekly. Relationships with school staff are complex and vitally important to the functioning of the center. One problem that had to be overcome was convincing the maintenance staff to allow the premises to stay open after 3:00 P.M. The center is open all day and into the evening, and all summer.*

* Based on "School Based Youth Services Program," New Brunswick Public Schools (undated); and visits to program and discussions with Gail Reynolds, director.

Notes

1 Joy G. Dryfoos, *Adolescents-at-Risk: Prevalence and Prevention* (New York: Oxford University Press, 1990).

2 David Tyack, "Health and Social Services in Public Schools: Historical Perspectives," in *The Future of Children: School Linked Services* (Los Altos, Calif. Center for the Future of Children, David and Lucile Packard Foundation, 1992), vol. 2, pp. 19–31.

3 Godfrey Cronin and William Young, *400 Navels: The Future of School Health in America* (Bloomington, Ill: Phi Delta Kappa, 1979).

4 See Alison T. Lavin, Gail R. Shapiro, and Kenneth S. Weill, *Creating an Agenda for School-Based Health Promotion: A Review of Selected Reports* (Cambridge: Harvard School of Public Health, 1992).

5 The National Commission on the Role of the School and the Community in Improving Adolescent Health, *Code Blue: Uniting for Healthier Youth* (Washington, D.C.: American Medical Association and National Association of State Boards of Education, 1990).

6 Ibid., p. 41.

7 U.S. Congress, Office of Technology Assessment, *Adolescent Health-Volume I: Summary and Policy Options*, OTA–H–468 (Washington, D.C.: Government Printing Office, April 1991).

8 Task Force on Education of Young Adolescents, *Turning Points: Preparing American Youth for the 21st Century* (Washington, D.C.: Carnegie Council on Adolescent Development, 1989).

9 This discussion focuses on actual health services. However, schools are involved in other health-related activities such as providing health education, paying attention to nutrition, and maintaining a healthy and safe school environment. An unknown number of school systems employ health educators, school psychologists, and other special-education experts.

10 Julia Lear et al., "Reorganizing Health Care for Adolescents: The Experience of the School-Based Adolescent Health Care Program," *Journal of Adolescent Health* 12 (1991): 450–580.

11 Philip Nader, "School Health Services," in *Maternal and Child Health Practices; Third Edition*, ed. Helen Wallace, George Ryan, and Allan Oglesby (Oakland, Calif.: Third Party Publishing, 1988), p. 464.

12 National Center for Education Statistics, *National Education Longitudinal Study of 1988: User's Manual,* NCES-464 (Washington, D.C.: U.S. Department of Education, 1990).

13 An earlier school-based clinic started in 1965 provided comprehensive health services primarily to young children in Cambridge, Massachusetts. See Philip Porter, "School Health is a Place, not a Discipline," *Journal of School Health* 57 (1987): 417–18.

14 L. Edwards et al., "Adolescent Pregnancy Prevention Services in High School Clinics," *Family Planning Perspectives* 12 (1980): 6–14.

15 The Center for Population Options organized the Support Center for School Based Clinics in 1984, and has surveyed the field annually. Only preliminary data are available from the 1991 survey. See the Factsheet "School-Based and School-Linked Clinics (Washington, D.C.: Center for Population Options, 1991).

16 Joy G. Dryfoos, "School and Community-Based Prevention Programs," in *Adolescent Sexuality: Preventing Unhealthy Consequences*, ed. Susan Coupey and Lorraine Klerman (Philadelphia: Hanley and Belfus, 1991).

17 The Robert Wood Johnson Foundation, *Making Connections* (A Summary of The Robert Wood Johnson Foundation programs, Princeton, New Jersey, n.d.)

18 Lear et al., "Reorganizing Health Care for Adolescents," p. 450.

19 Center for Population Options, "Factsheet," p. 2.

20 Cynthia Waszak and Shara Neidell, *School-Based and School-Linked Clinics: Update 1991* (Washington, D.C.: Center for Population Options, 1992).

21 Center for Population Options, *School-Based Clinics Update 1990* (Washington, D.C.: Center for Population Options, 1991).

22 Douglas Kirby, Cynthia Waszak, and Julie Ziegler, *An Assessment of Six School-Based Clinics: Services, Impact, and Potential* (Washington, D.C.: Center for Population Options, 1989).

23 Claire Brindis et al., "Utilization Patterns among California's School Based Health Centers: A Comparison of the School Year 1989-90 with the Baseline Year of 1988-1989" (Unpublished paper from Center for Reproductive Health Policy Research, University of California, San Francisco, February 1991).

24 For example, see *San Jose School Health Centers 1990–91 Annual Report* (San Jose, Calif.: San Jose Medical Center, 1991).

25 Office of Technology Assessment, *Adolescent Health*, p. 97.

26 Howard Adelman and Linda Taylor, "Mental Health Facets of the School-Based Center Movement: Need and Opportunity for Research and Development," *Journal of Mental Health Administration* (in press). See also *Mental Health Network News*, published by the School Mental Health Project of the Department of Psychology, University of California, Los Angeles.

27 Adelman and Taylor, "Mental Health Facts."

28 Described in *Mental Health Network News* 2 (1991): 1–2.

29 Joy G. Dryfoos, "Bringing Health and Social Services into Inner City Junior High Schools" (Report to Center for Population and Family Health, Columbia University School of Public Health, 1991).

30 James P. Comer, "Improving American Educational Roles for Parents," *Hearing before the Select Committee on Children, Youth and Families June 7, 1984* (Washington, D.C.: Government Printing Office, n.d.), pp. 55–60.

31 See Lavin et al., *Creating an Agenda*; Atelia Melavill and Martin Blank, *What It Takes: Structuring Interagency Partnerships to Connect Children and Families with Comprehensive Services* (Washington, D.C.: Education and Human Services Consortium, 1991); and Heather Weiss, *Family Support and Education, Programs and the Public Schools* (Cambridge: Harvard Family Research Project, 1988).

32 P. Nickel and H. Delany, *Working with Teen Parents: A Survey of Promising Approaches* (Chicago: Family Resource Coalition, 1985).

33 Melaville and Blank, *What It Takes*, p. 42.

34 Dryfoos, *Adolescents-at-Risk*, pp. 214–15.

35 Center for the Study of Social Policy, *New Futures in Pittsburgh: A Mid-Point Assessment* (Washington, D.C.: Center for the Study of Social Policy, February 1991).

36 Gary Wehlage, Gregory Smith, and Pauline Lipman, "Restructuring Urban Schools: The New Futures Experience," *American Educational Research Journal* 29 (1992): 51–93.

37 Dryfoos, *Adolescents-at-Risk.*

38 National Institute of Alcohol Abuse and Alcoholism, *Prevention Plus: Involving Schools, Parents and the Community in Alcohol and Drug Education* (Washington, D.C.: Department of Health and Human Services, 1984), pp. 194–99.

39 Inwood House, "Community Outreach Program: Teen Choice. A Model Program Addressing the Problem of Teenage Pregnancy" (Summary Report, 1987).

40 Joseph Allen et al., "School-Based Prevention of Teenage Pregnancy and School Dropout: Process Evaluation of the National Replication of the Teen Outreach Program," *American Journal of Community Psychology* 18 (1990): 505–24.

41 Dryfoos, *Adolescents-at-Risk.*

42 Lucy Siegel and T. Kriebel, "Evaluation of School-Based High School Health Services," *Journal of School Health* 57 (1987): 323–27.

43 David Kaplan, "School Health Care-Online!!!, School-based Clinic Management Information System" (Denver: The Children's Hospital, 1992).

44 Kirby et al., *An Assessment of Six School-Based Clinics.*

45 Ibid., pp. 9–10.

46 Gerald Kitzi, Presentation at Third Annual Conference of the Support Center for School-Based Clinics, Denver, 1986.

47 Laurie Zabin et al., "Evaluation of a Pregnancy Prevention Program for Urban Teenagers," *Family Planning Perspectives* 18 (May/June 1986): 123.

48 Christine Galavotti and Sharon Lovick, "The Effect of School-Based Clinic Use on Adolescent Contraceptive Effectiveness" (Paper presented at National Conference on School-Based Clinics, Kansas City, Mo., November 1987).

49 Linda Edwards and Kathleen Arnold-Sheeran, Unpublished data from St. Paul presented at American Public Health Association meeting, November 1985.

50 James Shea, Roberta Herceg-Baron, and Frank Furstenberg, "Clinic Continuation Rates according to Age, Method of Contraception and Agency" (Paper presented at the annual meeting of the National Family Planning and Reproductive Health Association, March 1982).

51 Kitzi, Presentation.

52 Thomas Kean, Speech, Carnegie Council on Adolescent Development (Washington, D.C., April 14, 1992).

53 Welfare Research Inc., *Health Services for High School Students, Short-term Assessment of New York City High School-based Clinics* (Report to New York City Board of Education, June 3, 1987).

54 James Stout, "School-Based Health Clinics: Are They Addressing the Needs of the Students" (Master's thesis, University of Washington, 1991), p. 22.

55 *Clinic News* (Center for Population Options) 2 (April 1986): 3.

56 Dryfoos, *Adolescents-at-Risk.*

57 Metropolitan Life, Louis Harris and Associates, Inc., *The American Teacher, 1988* (New York: Metropolitan Life, 1989).

58 Planned Parenthood Federation of America, Inc., and Louis Harris and Associates, *Public Attitudes toward Teenage Pregnancy, Sex Education and Birth Control* (New York: Planned Parenthood Federation of America, 1988).

59 Center for Population Options, Factsheet, p. 2.

60 Sarah Palfrey et al., "Financing Health Services in School-Based Clinics," *Journal of Adolescent Health Care* 3 (1991): 233–39.

61 Dryfoos, "Bringing Health and Social Services," p. 33.

62 Task Force on Education of Young Adolescents, *Turning Points.*

63 Information supplied by Yale Bush Center in Child Development and Social Policy, 1992.

Parent-School Involvement during the Early Adolescent Years

JACQUELYNNE S. ECCLES
University of Michigan, Ann Arbor, and
University of Colorado, Boulder

RENA D. HAROLD
Michigan State University, Ann Arbor

Adolescence is one of the most fascinating periods of development. Other than infancy, there is no other time in life when the individual experiences such rapid and dramatic change. This rapid change opens the door for both positive and negative consequences. On the one hand, there is growing concern about the fate of our adolescents. A myriad of reports have emerged in the last few years pointing to the problems associated with this developmental period—increasing incidence of school failure, growing dropout rates, especially in the large urban school districts, increasing involvement of youth in delinquent and very dangerous activities, increasing violence among youth, and increasing incidence of other indicators of poor adjustment. The recent report *Turning Points*, for example, concluded that at least one-quarter of American adolescents are already in serious danger while another quarter are at risk for major problems.[1] On the other hand, adolescence is also the time when many youth begin a successful and exciting transition from childhood into adulthood. It is a time when children blossom into interesting and healthy young adults if they are provided with supportive and developmentally appropriate social contexts in which to explore themselves and the world around them.

Many reports have suggested that schools could play a critical role in helping to keep (or to put) adolescents on a healthy, rather than risky, developmental trajectory. Adolescents spend more waking time in school than anywhere else, including with their families. They also need close relationships with nonfamilial adults to help them sort through independence and identity issues, especially since achieving increasing independence from one's parents is a primary task of this developmental period. In our society, teachers are likely to be the primary nonfamilial adults in many adolescents' lives. Not surprisingly, then, evidence from a variety of disciplines indicates that teachers can have a major positive impact and may even play a protective role in the lives of adolescents. This is particularly true if they work in concert with the adolescents' parents and other community organizations. This article focuses on the ways teachers could work more effectively with parents to facilitate healthy adolescent development. First, it discusses the general importance of greater parental involvement with children's education. Then it discusses barriers to parent involvement and summarizes specific ways teachers could try to involve parents during their children's adolescent years.

IMPORTANCE OF PARENT INVOLVEMENT

Researchers have known for some time that parents play a critical role in their children's academic achievement as well as in their socioemotional development.[2] It is only recently, however, that researchers have begun to look at the role schools might play in facilitating parents' positive role in children's academic achievement. Critical to this role is the relationship that develops between parents and schools, and between communities and schools. Although this is a relatively new research area, there is increasing evidence that the quality of the links between parents and schools does influence children's and adolescents' school success.[3] In fact, evidence suggests that active parental involvement in the schools is a critical factor in a child's educational success at all grade levels.[4] Good parent-school links also have positive effects on parents and teachers.[5] Thus, it appears that parental involvement is important for students, teachers, and parents alike.

Yet mounting evidence suggests that parents are not as involved as either they or the schools would like. Findings from several studies make it clear that parents want to be more involved with their children's education and would like more information and help from the schools in order to meet this goal.[6] Teachers also report being dissatisfied with current levels of parent involvement.[7] Furthermore, the situation gets worse as children move from elementary school into secondary school. Even though parent involvement is minimal in elementary school, it declines substantially as children move into secondary school.[8]

The message, then, seems clear: Both teachers and parents think that family involvement in the school is important and can have positive effects. So why is it that parents are not more involved with the schools? Lack of family involvement can stem from various parent characteristics and experiences, such as lack of time, energy, and/or economic resources; lack of knowledge; feelings of incompetence; failure to understand the role parents can play; or a long history of negative interactions with the schools that have left parents suspicious of, and disaffected from, the schools. *Even more important*, lack of family involvement can stem from various school and teacher practices and characteristics, such as poor reporting practices, hostility toward the parents, lack of understanding of how to effectively involve parents, and lack of interest in involving parents. In fact, specific school and teacher practices have been shown to be the major factor influencing parent involvement:

> Status variables are not the most important measures for understanding parent involvement. At all grade levels, the evidence suggests that school policies and teacher practices and family practices are more important than race, parent education, family size, marital status, and even grade level in determining whether parents continue to be part of their children's education.[9]

It is also clear that parent involvement can be substantially increased by the efforts of teachers and schools to facilitate the parents' role.[10] The power of schools and teachers to influence parent involvement and to improve parent-school links has been demonstrated even with "hard-to-reach" parents, as well as with white, middle-class, two-parent families.[11]

This very brief summary of the literature suggests that parent involvement is both important and achievable even in the secondary school years. In fact, several of the recent school reform programs incorporate greater family involvement as a key element. Foremost among these is one designed by James P. Comer. This program uses a school-based management approach to try to create a school climate that fosters high motivation, high school attachment, and high achievement. According to Comer, the success of the program depends in large part on changing the school-parent relationship. For example, in his book *School Power*, Comer described the critical role parents played in changing the school culture and redirecting the developmental pathways of the children in the original New Haven Project. His vivid descriptions suggest that changes in the parent-school partnership are critical mediators of the impact of his intervention program. Thus, building a more equal school-parent partnership is one of the key principles underlying the Comer approach.[12]

INFLUENCES ON PARENT INVOLVEMENT AND BARRIERS TO GREATER PARENT INVOLVEMENT

To understand the many barriers to parent involvement in their children's schooling, we need a model of parent involvement. One such model is presented in Figure 1. This model was designed to provide a framework for thinking about the dynamic processes that underlie parents' involvement in their children's education. It treats parent involvement as both an outcome of parent, teacher, and child influences, and as a predictor of child outcomes. It also suggests a framework for thinking more generally about the ways in which both schools and parents influence children's school performance. Although the model was not specifically framed with adolescent children in mind, the constructs included can be thought about from this point of view, as they are in this chapter.

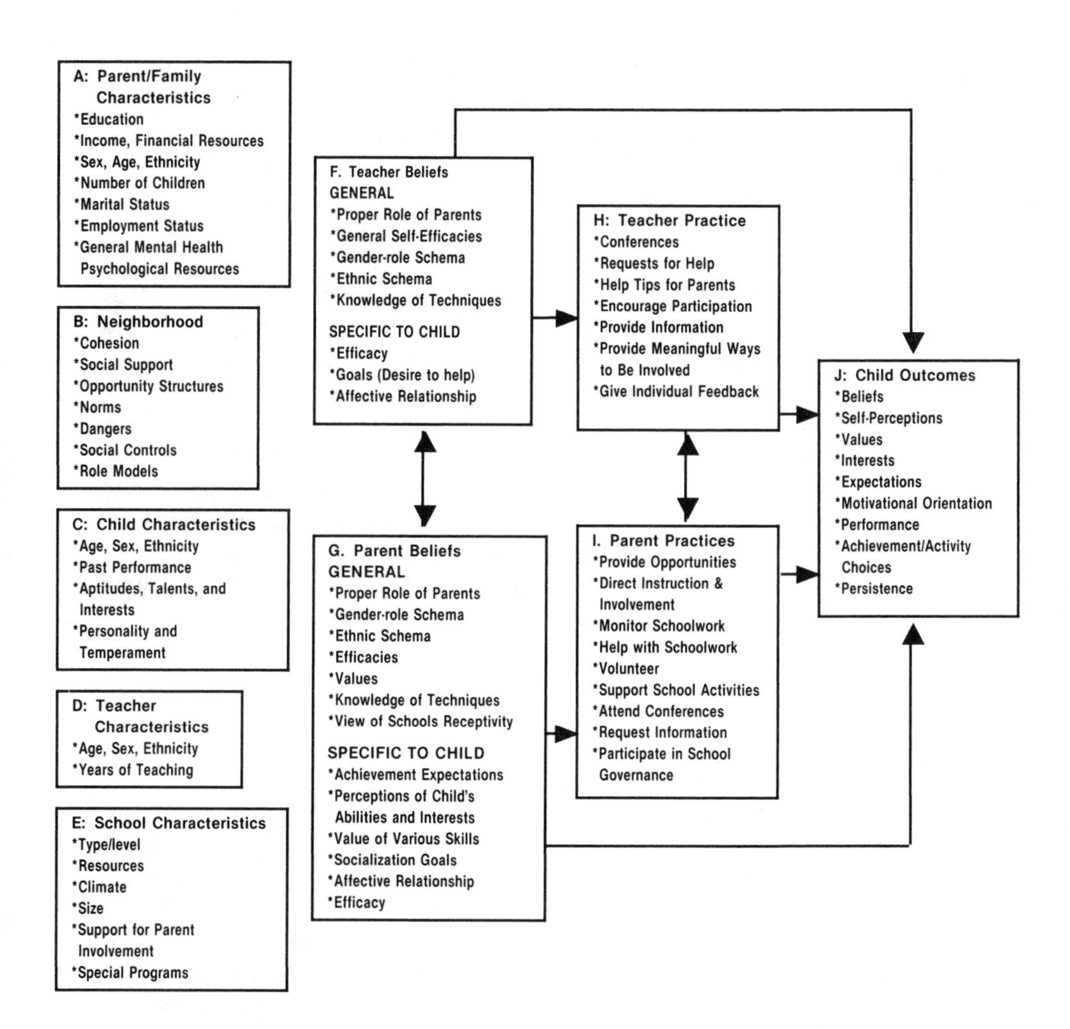

Figure 1. Model of Influences on Parent Involvement and Child Outcomes.

This model hypothesizes that there are a variety of influences on parent involvement. The first set of these influences is commonly referred to as exogenous variables—variables that have global and pervasive effects on parent involvement. These variables are summarized in the left-hand column of Figure 1. They include various characteristics of families and parents, neighborhoods and communities, and teachers and schools, as well of the children themselves. Note that there are no arrows connecting these five boxes with the other boxes in the model. It is assumed that the variables listed in these five boxes influence the variables listed in all of the other boxes in the model. The second column (boxes F and G) includes more specific beliefs and attitudes of teachers and parents. The model assumes that these beliefs and attitudes affect each other as well as the two boxes in the third column, namely, specific teacher practices (Box H) and specific parent practices (Box I). Finally, it is assumed that the variables listed in boxes F, G, H, and I all affect the child outcomes listed in the last column in Box J. The model summarizes a wide range of possible relationships among the many listed influences. For example, the impact of the exogenous variables listed in boxes A, B, C, D, and E on teachers' practices related to involving parents (Box H) are proposed to be mediated by various teachers' beliefs systems (Box F) such as their stereotypes about different parents' abilities and willingness to help their children in the various academic subjects. Some of the child-outcome variables listed in Box I are identical (or very similar) to the child characteristics in Box C. This overlap is intentional and captures the cyclical nature of the relationships outlined in the model. Today's child outcomes become tomorrow's child characteristics and so the cycle continues over time. A more detailed discussion of some of the most important of these many influences follows.

PARENT/FAMILY CHARACTERISTICS

Numerous studies have documented the relation between parent involvement in their children's education and such family characteristics as family income, parents' education level, ethnic background, marital status, parents' age and sex, number of children, and parent's working status. For example, parents who are better educated are more involved in school and at home than parents who are less well educated; parents with fewer children are also more involved at home but family size does not seem to affect amount of involvement at the school; and parents who work outside the home are less likely to be involved at school, but parents' working status does not seem to affect the level of involvement at home.[13]

The following parent/family characteristics are likely to be important:

1. *Social and psychological resources available to the parent*—that is, social networks, social demands on parents' time, parents' general mental and physical health, neighborhood resources and dangers, and parents' general coping strategies.
2. *Parents' efficacy beliefs*—that is, the parents' confidence that they can help their child with schoolwork, parents' view of how their competence to help their children with schoolwork changes as the children enter higher school grades and encounter more specialized subject areas, and parents' confidence that they can have an impact on the school by participating in school governance.

3. *Parents' perceptions of their child*—that is, parents' confidence in their child's academic abilities, parents' perceptions of the child's receptivity to help, parents' educational and occupation expectations and aspirations for the child, and parents' view of the options actually available for their child in the present and the future.
4. *Parents' assumptions about both their role in their children's education and the role of educational achievement for their child*—that is, what role the parents would like to play in thir children's education, how they think this role should change as their children get older, how important they believe participation in school governance is, and what they believe are the benefits to their children of doing well in school and having parents who are highly involved at their school.
5. *Parents' attitude toward the school*—that is, what role they believe the school wants them to play, how receptive they think the school is to their involvement both at home and at school, the extent to which they think the school is sympathetic to their child and to their situation, their previous history of negative and positive experiences at school, their belief that teachers call them in only to give them bad news about their child or to blame them for problems their children are having at school versus a belief that the teachers and other school personnel want to work with them to help their children.
6. *Parents' ethnic identity*—that is, the extent to which ethnicity is a critical aspect of the parents' identity and socialization goals, the relationship between the parents' conceptualization of their ethnic identity and their attitudes toward parent involvement and school achievement, their beliefs about the likelihood that they and their children will be treated unfairly because of their ethnicity, and the extent to which they think the school supports them in helping their children learn about their ethnic heritage.
7. *Parents' general socialization practices*—that is, how the parents usually handle discipline and issues of control versus autonomy, and how the parents usually "manage" the experiences of their children.
8. *Parents' history of involvement in their children's education*—that is, the impact of parents' experiences with their children's elementary schools and teachers on the parents' interest in being involved with their children's middle grade teachers. Virtually no one has studied this long-term impact of parents' early experiences with their children's school.

COMMUNITY CHARACTERISTICS

Evidence also suggests that neighborhood characteristics such as cohesion, social disorganization, social networking, resources and opportunities, and the presence of undesirable and dangerous opportunities affect family involvement.[14] Factors such as these are likely to be associated with both different parent beliefs and practices and different opportunity structures in the child's environment. For example, Eccles et al. have been studying the relation of family management strategies to neighborhood characteristics as part of their involvement with the MacArthur Network on Successful Adolescence in High Risk Environments. These investigators are especially interested in how families try to provide both good experiences and protection for their children when the families live in high-risk neighborhoods—neighborhoods with few resources and many potential risks and hazards. To study this issue, they are conducting two survey interview studies (one of approximately 500 families living in high- to moderate-risk neighborhoods in inner-city Philadelphia and the other of approximately 1,400 families living in a wide range of neighborhoods in Prince George's County, Maryland). Initial results suggest that families actively involved with their children's development and in their children's schooling use different strategies depending on the resources available in their neighborhoods: As one would expect, families living in high-risk, low-resource neighborhoods rely more on in-home management strategies both to help their child develop talents and skills and to protect their child from the dangers in the neighborhood; families in these neighborhoods also focus more attention on protecting their children from danger than on helping their children develop specific talents. In contrast, families in less risky neighborhoods focus more on helping their children develop specific talents and are more likely to use neighborhood resources, such as organized youth programs, to accomplish this goal, in part because such resources are more readily available and accessible in their neighborhoods. Equally interesting, there are families in all types of neighborhoods that are highly involved in their children's education and schooling. There are also very disengaged families in all types of neighborhoods—in fact, just as many of the disengaged families lived in low-risk, relatively affluent neighborhoods as in the high-risk.[15]

Such neighborhood characteristics have also been shown to influence the extent to which parents can successfully translate their general beliefs, goals, and values into effective specific practices and perceptions. Evidence from several studies suggests that it is harder to do a good job of parenting if one lives in a high-risk neighborhood or if one is financially stressed.[16] Not only do parents in such circumstances have limited resources available to implement whatever strategies they think might be effective, they also have to cope with more external stressors than do white middle-class families living in stable, resource-rich neighborhoods. Being confronted with these stressors may lead parents to adopt a less effective parenting style because they do not have the energy or the time to use a more demanding but more effective strategy. For example, several investigators have found that economic stress in the family (e.g., loss of one's job or major financial change) has a negative effect on the quality of parenting.[17] To the extent that schools could help relieve some of this stress, they could facilitate greater parent involvement.

Far less work has investigated the dynamic processes by which these global social factors actually affect parent involvement and children's school outcomes, but it is clear that there is substantial variation in parental involvement within any of these social categories, and that teachers can successfully involve even the hardest-to-reach parents.[18] To do this, however, schools and teachers need to take the difficulties these families face into account in designing appropriate strategies for increasing parent involvement. More research is badly needed to identify the characteristics of parents and schools associated with effective parent involvement in underrepresented ethnic groups and high-risk neighborhoods, and especially for adolescent children.

CHILD CHARACTERISTICS

Numerous studies indicate that parents' involvement in their children's school achievement is affected by the characteristics of their children. We know, for example, that the child's sex and age influence the extent of parent involvement.[19] Age is especially relevant for this discussion. As noted earlier, parent involvement drops off rather dramatically as children move into junior high school or middle school. Why? It is likely that some of this decrease reflects the stereotypic belief that parents should begin to disengage from their adolescents as they move into secondary school. Parents may feel that young adolescents both desire and need independence, and thus feel that their involvement in their children's education is not as important as it was earlier. They may also feel that the children do not want them to come to school, as evidenced by a common adolescent plea not to have their parents chaperone school activities. Although there may be an element of truth in this belief, it is too extreme. Adolescents may indeed want greater autonomy, but they still need to know that their parents support their educational endeavors. They need a safe haven in which to explore their independence, a safe haven in which both parents and schools are actively involved. It is important that schools do what they can to strengthen the role available to parents during these years.

The decrease in parent involvement as children move into secondary school may also result from a decrease in parents' feelings of efficacy as their children grow older. It may be that parents feel less able to help their children with schoolwork as the schoolwork becomes more advanced and technical, in part because they are, in fact, less knowledgeable in some of the subject areas. No longer are children working on basic reading and spelling skills, or drilling on math facts. Parents may not know the material being taught in more advanced and specialized courses. Parents may also feel that the methods used in teaching various subjects (e.g., math) are very different from the methods used when they were in school; as a consequence, they may worry that will mislead or confuse their children if they try to help. Finally, research has shown that parents believe they have more influence over their children in general, as well as in terms of specific behaviors, when the children are in the elementary grades than they will when their children reach adolescence.[20] There are things schools could do to help parents be more effective tutors and mentors for their adolescent children. Examples of promising approaches to this problem are presented later.

At a more general level, it seems likely that the child's previous academic experiences and the child's personality also affect parent involvement. For example, parents may be more likely to try to help a child who is having trouble than a child who is doing very well, especially if that child has done well in the past; alternatively, parents of high-achieving children may be more likely to participate in school governance and school activities than parents of lower-achieving children; parents should also be more likely to continue trying to help a child with whom they get along than a child with whom they have many conflicts. Finally, it seems likely that the parents' experiences with helping the other children in the family will also have an impact on the parents' involvement in the education of subsequent children as they pass through the school system.

SCHOOL AND TEACHER CHARACTERISTICS AND PRACTICES

From an intervention perspective, it is important to think about the school and teacher characteristics that influence parent involvement. As noted earlier, work by Epstein and her colleagues suggests that school factors are *the* primary influence on parent involvement. In fact, the strongest predictors of parent involvement in several studies are the specific school programs and teacher practices being used (or not used) to encourage parent involvement: When parents feel that schools are doing things to involve them, they themselves are more involved in their children's education.[21]

Two school characteristics are especially important to the point of view offered in this article: the physical and organizational structure of secondary schools, and the beliefs and attitudes of school personnel. Level of schooling is a key variable affecting parent involvement.[22] Change in the physical and organizational structure is one of the primary differences parents and students confront as children move from elementary school into secondary school. Junior high schools and middle schools are much bigger; they serve a wider range of communities and social/ethnic groups; they are typically much more bureaucratic in their governance and management systems; and they are typically departmentalized—resulting in less personal contact between specific teachers and both students and families. Changes such as these could result in the increase we find in parents' feelings of alienation from the school. These changes are most certainly associated with greater feelings of alienation on the part of the adolescents themselves. Parents who are involved in their neighborhood elementary schools may see this involvement as part of their connection with their community and friends. The "home" elementary school may seem like an extension of the family, particularly in neighborhoods where the population is relatively stable. Parents and teachers get to know each other over the years their children are in the school. As children leave their home schools and several elementary schools merge into one middle school, there is likely to be a decrease in the extent to which the families feel connected to the school. Junior high schools and middle schools expand the physical community, without expanding the emotional sense of community. The sense of belonging and investment may decrease, and as a result, parents may feel less able and less inclined either to be involved or to try to affect change in the educational experiences of their children. Additionally, children typically spend six or seven years in an elementary school and only two or three in a middle school. The attachment that has formed over the elementary years when parent help seems more essential has less time to form and may seem less necessary in the early secondary school grades.

Alternatively, school personnel may inhibit parent involvement by their own beliefs and attitudes about parent involvement. Like parents, teachers and school personnel at this level may think it is better for the adolescent to have less parental involvement. They may also think it is too much trouble to involve parents at this level because parents are busy or disinterested or "ignorant." As a result of these beliefs, school personnel at this level have been found to actively discourage parent involvement in the classroom and the school.[23] This appears to be especially true in low-income and minority neighborhoods where parents may be seen as part of the problem in educating their children, rather than as a resource.[24] The negative interactions that these parents are likely to have with the schools, combined with potentially negative recollections of their own educational experiences, serve as a major barrier to parent involvement in ethnic communities and high-risk inner-city school districts. The following teacher and school characteristics are likely to be important predictors of the school's response to parent involvement: (a) beliefs about the appropriate amount and type of parent involvement, (b) beliefs about influences on parents' levels of participation, particularly their beliefs as to why parents are not more involved, (c) sense of efficacy about their ability to affect the parents' level of participation, (d) knowledge of specific strategies for getting parents more involved, (e) plans for implementing these strategies, and (f) support for implementing specific plans.

INCREASING PARENT INVOLVEMENT AND PROVIDING MEANINGFUL AGE-APPROPRIATE OPPORTUNITIES FOR PARENT INVOLVEMENT IN THE EARLY ADOLESCENT YEARS

This section outlines general and specific ways to involve parents of early adolescents in their children's education. There are several general approaches schools can use to increase parent involvement. First, schools can offer parents more meaningful roles in school governance. Comer suggests that parents need to understand and agree with school goals in order to reinforce them at home.[25] If parents are meaningfully involved in the basic planning and governance of the school, they are more likely to be invested in school goals, and will therefore be more likely to maintain a strong positive connection with the school. This is such an important part of school climate that Comer has made increasing parent involvement a key dimension of his intervention program. To meet this goal, this program calls for parents to be included on the School Based Management Team. This feature of the Comer program ensures that parents are directly involved in the development of the Comprehensive School Plan. The program also calls for the creation of the Parent Program Team, charged with the responsibility of developing a comprehensive parent-participation program designed to increase the involvement of the parents as volunteers in the classroom and the school building, as well as in after-school "social" activities. Comer assumes that these kinds of activities will eventually lead to greater involvement of parents in their children's education both at home and at school, which, in turn, should lead to better outcomes for the children.

Keeping parents informed is a second method to enhance family connections to the school in the middle years. Communication should begin prior to the child's making the secondary school transition in order to preempt the forces that lead to a decline in parents' involvement at this point in their children's schooling. Furthermore, it is essential that schools go beyond the more traditional approaches to communication, such as conferences and open houses, to an approach that sets up a personal relationship between particular teachers and each parent. For example, the school could assign an advisor to each student/family; this advisor could then serve as the contact person for both the student and his or her parents, and could make sure parents are given ample information about the school in general and about their adolescent in particular. This relationship could also provide the entree for parents into the school, and thus establish an environment that feels both safe and encouraging for parent involvement.

Finally, and perhaps most importantly, there must be opportunities for parents to support the educational process at school and in the home in ways that work and are helpful for the developmental stage of their early adolescent children. As stated above, research has demonstrated that parents are most involved when schools actively try to encourage their involvement.[26] It follows, then, that planning programs that demonstrate important and appropriate ways to be involved with their early adolescents' educational experiences should help ensure continued parent involvement as the children progress from the elementary to the middle grades.

Below are more specific suggestions structured around the following typology of parent involvement, suggested by Epstein and her colleagues: (1) basic obligations of families to provide for the safety and health of their children; (2) basic obligations of schools to communicate with families about school programs and the individual progress of their children; (3) parental involvement at school; (4) parental involvement in learning activities at home; (5) parental involvement in decision making at school, and (6) collaboration and exchange with community organizations. Most school-based programs focused on parent-school involvement include at least one of these types of involvement.[27] A discussion of this typology and the potential application in school settings for early adolescent children follows.

1. *Basic obligations of families to provide for the safety and health of their children*: We know that both healthy social development and school achievement depend on the home environment. Schools can play a role in helping parents provide a good environment at home. School-family programs that teach parenting skills and effective monitoring strategies like providing the child with a specific space to do homework and working out a homework schedule at home are an example of efforts to facilitate this type of involvement. Unfortunately, the nature of many existing programs makes it much more likely that they will be found in the elementary grades, but this does not need to be the case. There are important developmental changes taking place in children as they move into and through the secondary school years, and families need information on how to cope effectively with these changes.

Many of the things parents worry about in their adolescents' behavior are quite normal and can be handled fairly easily with age-appropriate interventions. Parents need to know about these changes and about effective means of handling the changes they are seeing in their children's behavior. In addition, several health issues (such as AIDS; sexually transmitted diseases; eating disorders; increased levels of depression; ingestion of health-compromising chemicals like nicotine, alcohol, drugs, and steroids; and increased exposure to violence) become more relevant during the early adolescent period. Many parents are quite anxious about their ability to handle these issues. Schools could offer educational programs to provide parents with guidance in dealing with these issues, including how to identify potential danger signs and find appropriate help in their communities—programs on topics such as teaching children about the importance of safe sex and good nutrition, and about the dangers associated with the use of substances such as cigarettes, alcohol, drugs, and steroids; as well as programs that help parents organize their own time to help their children with study and time-management skills. These "programs" could be in the form of organized presentations, discussion groups held at school or in the community, or lending libraries that make videotapes (e.g., Claude Olney's "Where There's a Will, There's an A") and books (e.g., The Home and School Institute's *Survival Guide for Busy Parents*) easily accessible to parents with demanding work and family schedules.

Schools could also help parents find safe places for their adolescents to spend time away from home. Schools are community buildings that could be used as program sites by youth organizations and social service agencies. Streets in many communities are very dangerous places and parents are finding it increasingly difficult to fulfill their obligation to protect their adolescents from dangerous situations without locking them up in the house—a strategy that is neither very practical for adolescent children, nor congruent with adolescents' need for autonomy and developing their identity outside of their family. Schools could help families and communities deal with this problem and at the same time build better connections between the school and the community/family. The use of the school building for extracurricular activities might also result in the student's having more positive feelings about the school.

2. *Basic obligations of schools to communicate with families about school programs and the individual progress of their children:* Parent-teacher conferences, curriculum nights, open houses, phone contacts, report cards, and standardized test results are typical examples of this type of parent-school connection. This communication begins in the earliest grades and usually continues through high school, although the nature and frequency of the contacts may change as the child goes through the school system. As students move to the middle grades and have more than one core teacher, "capsule" nights are often used to provide parents with information about each class and an opportunity to meet each teacher. Such programs involve attending a miniaturized version of the child's daily schedule, for example, fifteen minutes in each classroom, and are generally held in the evening to accommodate working parents. Unfortunately, such programs do not provide much opportunity for parents and teachers to get to know each other and to talk about specific children. Different types of programs are needed to facilitate more direct and personalized parent-teacher communication.

It is also important at this time to increase the amount of information given to parents about curricular choices that may be related to eventual career/occupation choices. As children move into junior high school or middle school, they begin to make course choices that have both short- and long-term implications for their future options. Often neither the full range of choices nor the implications of various choices are made clear to parents. For example, in one of the school districts we have studied, we were told that the parents make the decision regarding which math class their child is placed into in the seventh grade. When the parents in this school district were interviewed, the majority did not know they had a choice because the sixth-grade teacher typically sent home a form that was already filled in with the teacher's recommendation regarding the child's math placement; the parents also did not know the long-term consequences of being placed in the various seventh-grade math courses. Apparently, the school had not communicated their policy clearly enough for the parents to really make this important decision. Nonetheless, early course choices in subjects like math and science can play a major role in shaping the curricular track students find themselves on in high school. If parents do not fully understand this connection, they cannot effectively play the role of advocate for their children.

Further, it is incumbent on the schools to increase personalized communication with the families, especially when there is an increase in the number of teachers with whom the early adolescent student interacts. Some school districts have attempted to do this by "teaming" teachers, thereby encouraging discussion among the student's core teachers. Typically, such districts also assign one of the team members to be an "advisory" teacher (i.e., the one who communicates most directly with the student and his or her family) for each student in order to increase the likelihood of good communication between school and family.

There is a need for coordination across teachers at this grade level to ensure effective monitoring of the child and to alert the parents to any danger signs or special talents that may be identified. There is also a need for teachers to help parents help their children make wise and informed choices about future educational and occupational goals. Because teachers both see many adolescents and interact with each student regularly, teachers are well positioned to identify an individual student's talents and intellectual strengths. In turn, teachers are uniquely situated to help both students and parents think about each adolescent's unique talents and aptitudes in terms of future educational and occupational choices. Parents often do not know very much about the relation between particular academic skills and future job options, particularly if they themselves do not excel in the same subject areas as their adolescents, or if they hold stereotypic beliefs about what their children might be good at or might like. For example, females are less likely than males to consider going into applied mathematics (e.g., engineering) and physical science; consequently, girls are less likely to take advanced math and physical science courses in secondary school. Females appear to be selecting themselves out of these intellectual domains, and they do so at great cost to themselves. Avoiding these courses in high school makes it difficult to take many college majors and courses, including some they might be interested in pursuing—for example, nursing, economics, or ecological sciences.

It also significantly decreases the opportunity to major in engineering or the physical sciences. Parents often do not understand these implications, and parents may not notice that a daughter is exceptionally good in math and science.[28] Bright females typically do quite well in all of their courses and may not give their parents any reason to believe that they are unusually good in math and science. In addition, parents may not understand that there are many good jobs in these fields and that females are more likely to be paid an equitable salary in these fields than in many other occupational fields. Teachers can provide parents with this type of specific information relevant to a child's future. They can also let parents know about special programs for which their child is eligible. Providing this type of information to parents increases the number of female and minority students who enroll math and science in high school and consider occupations requiring these courses and requiring a college education.[29] Information such as this is especially important for families in high-risk neighborhoods and for families who have recently immigrated to this country or to the state or city in which they are currently living.

3. *Parental involvement at school:* Parents and other family members may assist teachers in the classroom in a variety of capacities, including tutoring, teaching special skills, and providing clerical or supervisory help. Unfortunately, this type of involvement is most likely to decrease as the child enters the middle grades. It is still very important, especially in the inner city. As noted above, parents are desperate to find safe places for their adolescents to gather. There is also a pressing need for tutorial programs, for tutors, and for places to house tutorial programs for adolescents. Finally, as noted above, adolescents in particular need exposure to many different types of adult models as they try to form their own identities—models of different occupational choices, models of effective problem solving, models of different ethnic traditions, models of community involvement and good citizenship, models of overcoming adversity and resisting the lure of illegal activities, and models of healthy life-styles. Parents can provide all of these. For example, they can bring their own talents and family histories into the school by speaking at assemblies on life histories or careers, by offering a mini-course or workshop in an area of their expertise, or by assisting in specialized areas such as teaching computer skills, coaching a team, or planning and coordinating field trips and other outings. Such programs are increasingly relevant as adolescents begin to make plans for their lives.

Parents can also help to bring in other community resources and to coordinate finding placements in the community for adolescents to spend time engaged in meaningful adult activities. The Carnegie report *Turning Points* stresses the importance of increasing the school-community connection particularly for early adolescents.[30] This report recommends greater opportunities for community placement in volunteer service organization and in job settings. Schools, understandably, resist this suggestion because creating and monitoring such opportunities is a time-consuming task—but it is exactly this kind of task that parents are especially well situated to take on. It is also possible to involve parents in the school in other roles. For example, schools could provide parents with the opportunity to watch their child's performance in activities such as sports, music, and drama and to participate in more traditional activities like fund-raising.

4. *Parental involvement in learning activities at home:* Family members are often requested to work with their own children on learning tasks that will facilitate and promote the child's class work. This may be done at the state level, for example by producing guides for parents such as the "Calendar of Reading, Writing, and Mathematics Skills" developed by the Michigan State Board of Education, or at the district level by individual schools and teachers. Schools often provide information at the beginning of the semester, or on a more regular basis, on learning goals and ways in which parents can be helpful to their children in achieving these goals. This practice generally begins in early elementary school and continues through secondary school, although the kind of information provided and the tasks that are targeted for help usually change across grade levels. As children get older, teachers often send home "contracts" at the beginning of a term (e.g., letters that detail their expectations, their grading system, and/or assignments) that both students and parents are asked to sign. But teachers seem less likely to ask for parent help with specific skills such as reading or learning math facts as children get older. This may be due to perceptions held by both teachers and parents that students should have mastered basic skills by this point, and that parents are less able to help now than they were before. Neither of these perceptions is necessarily true; consequently, there is still a need for parents to be involved in these types of activities. In addition, however, they can be helped to play an active role with more specialized course material. Given the concerns that many teachers raise about parents' expertise and ability to help their children with homework as the subject matter being taught becomes more technical, it would be helpful for schools to consider ways to provide parents with some supplementary educational training so that parents can both be more helpful and feel more confident in their ability to help. "Family Math" and "Family Computers" (programs developed at the Lawrence Hall of Science) are two exemplar programs with this goal: Both seek to provide supplementary educational experiences for students and parents, both are run at school by teachers in the evenings and on weekends, both have generated great enthusiasm among parent and teacher groups, and both are relatively inexpensive to introduce and sustain in a school system.

Teachers could also increase parent involvement in learning activities at home by developing assignments that provide a meaningful role for parents to play. During adolescence children are increasingly interested in things like their cultural heritage, their parents' experience while growing up, and their community's history. They are also interested in how people make important life decisions and how people learn from their mistakes. Teachers could take advantage of these interests by giving assignments that involve interviewing one's parents and other community members, or accompanying one's parents on important activities like work or volunteer activities. Assignments such as these might accentuate the areas in which parents have special expertise and information rather than highlighting the areas in which their knowledge is dated or limited.

5. *Parental involvement in decision making at school*: Parent-Teacher Associations or Organizations (PTA or PTO) are the most common ways for parents to be involved in governance or advisory processes. Again, this type of involvement usually begins in elementary school and sometimes continues into the secondary school years, although it tends to decrease as children move from elementary school into secondary school. In the upper grades, an augmented group that includes students (e.g., PTSA/PTSO) may replace the other governance model in an attempt to get students and their parents (re)invested in the school. In response to districtwide changes or mandates from accrediting bodies, school-improvement teams comprised of school staff and parents have been formed in some areas to address specific programmatic concerns, and to develop and implement changes. Forming advocacy groups for special interests such as the rights of special-education students is another way parents can influence the process of decision making in schools. There is now a lot of interest in increasing this type of parent involvement. Many intervention programs call for active parent participation in school governance and some school districts have mandated the shift of control from school personnel to parent boards (e.g., the Chicago School District). The results of these experiments are not yet known but their existence clearly indicates the need for increased parent involvement in school management at all levels.

6. *Collaboration and exchange with community organizations:* Agencies and businesses may join with the schools to support children's educational experiences. For younger children, this may take the form of child-care services, or activity groups at recreational facilities. Mental and physical health services offered by a school-linked or school-based clinic such as those provided by Healthstart (an agency in St. Paul, Minnesota) may be an example of this kind of community collaboration in the later grades. Insights into careers offered through experiences provided by community and business personnel would be increasingly important and interesting as the student progresses through school. Some schools have formed partnerships with local businesses, which then provide some financial backing for special projects as well as offer students a look at different aspects of the work world. This notion

of the school-community link is therefore especially relevant to the middle grades. Parents can play a central role in helping to create and maintain these links.

CONCLUSION

This chapter has attempted to accomplish three goals: First, to document the importance of parent involvement in their children's schooling, particularly during the early adolescent years; second, to discuss the various influences on parental involvement and the many barriers to parent involvement during the adolescent years; and third, to provide some concrete recommendations for ways to increase parent involvement, particularly during the adolescent years. It began by noting the critical role parents and teachers can play if they work together to support healthy adolescent development. Unfortunately, the collaborative relationship between parents and schools seems to decrease rather than increase as children move into their adolescent years, and into secondary schools. This downward trend can be reversed. There are effective ways to involve parents in a collaborative relationship with the schools even during the secondary school years. Furthermore, there is every reason to believe that parent involvement is just as important, if not more important, during these years. This is particularly true in high-risk communities. Adolescents are at particular risk in these communities, and we are losing many of them to the dangers of the street culture. Increased family/community/school cooperation is essential if we are to reverse this trend. Early adolescence may well be our last best chance to promote healthy development—a chance that can be realized only through parent-school collaboration.

Preparation of this article was supported by a research grant from the National Institute of Child Health and Human Development and by the MacArthur Network on Successful Adolescence in High Risk Environments. Reprints can be obtained from the authors at 5201 Institute for Research, University of Michigan, Ann Arbor, Michigan 48106-1248.

Notes

1 Task Force on Education of Young Adolescents, *Turning Points: Preparing American Youth for the 21st century* (Washington, D.C.: Carnegie Council on Adolescent Development, 1989), pp. 1–10.

2 Jacquelynne S. Eccles et al., "School and Family Effects on the Ontogeny of Children's Interests, Self-perceptions, and Activity Choice," in *Nebraska Symposium on Motivation, 1992*, ed. Janis Jacobs (Lincoln, Neb.: University of Nebraska Press, in press), pp. 1–10.

3 Cf. James P. Comer, *School Power* (New York: The Free Press, 1980); Joyce L. Epstein, "Student Reactions to Teacher Practices of Parent Involvement" (Unpublished report, Baltimore: The Johns Hopkins University Center for Research on Elementary and Middle Schools, 1982); and Edward Zigler, "Project Head Start: Success or Failure?" in *Project Head Start: A Leg-*

acy of the War on Poverty, ed. Edward Zigler and J. Valentine (New York: The Free Press, 1979), pp. 495–507.

4 Joyce L. Epstein, "What Principals Should Know about Parent Involvement," *Principal* 66 (1987): 6–9; Eccles et al., "School and Family Effects," pp. 4–10; and Janis H. Jacobs, "Parent Involvement: Remarks" (Eric Document Reproduction Service No. ED 241 175, 1983) pp. 1-4.

5 Cf. Reginald Clark, *Family Life and School Achievement* (Chicago: University of Chicago Press, 1983); Comer, *School Power*; Epstein, "What Principals Should Know about Parent Involvement"; and Joyce L. Epstein, "Parents' Reactions to Teacher Practices of Parent Involvement," *The Elementary School Journal* 86 (1986): 277–94.

6 James P. Comer, "Educating Poor Minority Children," *Scientific American* 259 (1988): 42–46; and Sanford M. Dornbusch and P. L. Ritter, "Parents of High School Students: A Neglected Resource," *Educational Horizons* 66 (1988): 75–77.

7 Cf. *The Condition of Teaching: A State by State Analysis* (Princeton, N.J.: The Carnegie Foundation, 1988).

8 Epstein, "Parents' Reactions to Teacher Practices," pp. 277-80. See also, for general discussion, Task Force on Education of Young Adolescents, *Turning Points*.

9 Joyce L. Epstein, "School and Family Connections: Theory, Research, and Implication for Integrating Sociologies of Education and Family," in *Families in Community Settings: Interdisciplinary Perspectives*, ed. D. G. Unger and M. B. Sussman (New York: Haworth Press, 1990), p. 109.

10 Epstein, "Parents' Reactions to Teacher Practices," pp. 277-90.

11 Cf. Comer, *School Power*; and idem, "Educating Poor Minority Children," pp. 42–46.

12 Cf. Comer, *School Power*; idem, "Educating Poor Minority Children," pp. 42–46; and idem and Norris M. Haynes, "Parent Involvement in Schools: An Ecological Approach," *The Elementary School Journal* 91 (1991): 281–77.

13 Eccles et al., "School and Family Effects," pp. 4–15; see also for general discussion Robert D. Hess and Susan D. Holloway, "Family and School as Educational Institutions," in *Review of Child Development and Research, Vol 7: The Family*, ed. Ross D. Parke (Chicago: University of Chicago Press, 1984), pp. 179–222; Kevin Marjoribanks, *Families and Their Learning Environments: An Empirical Analysis* (London: Routledge and Kegan Paul, 1979); and idem, *Ethnic Families and Children's Achievements* (Syndey: Allen & Unwin, 1980).

14 Cf. James Coleman et al., *Equality of Educational Opportunity Report* (Washington, D.C.: Government Printing Office, 1966); Frank Furstenberg, "Adapting to Difficult Environments: Neighborhood Characteristics and Family Strategies" (Symposium paper presented at the Biennial Meeting of the Society for Research on Adolescence, Washington, D.C., March 1992), pp. 1–8.

15 Jacquelynne S. Eccles et al., "How Parents Respond to Risk and Opportunity" (Symposium paper presented at the Biennial Meeting of the Society for Research on Adolescence, Washington, D.C., March 1992), Table 10.

16 Glen H. Elder, Jr., and Avasolm Caspi, "Economic Stress in Lives: Developmental Perspectives," *Journal of Social Issues* 44 (1985): 25–45; Glen H. Elder, Jr. et al., "Families under Economic Pressure," *Journal of Family Issues* 13 (1985): 5–37; and Rena Harold-Goldsmith et al., "Objective and Subjective Reality: The Effects of Job Loss and Financial Stress on Fathering Behaviors," *Family Perspective* 22 (1988): 309–26.

17 Ibid.

18 S. L. Dauber and Joyce L. Epstein, "Parents' Attitudes and Practices of Involvement in Inner-city Elementary and Middle Schools," Unpublished report no. 33 (Baltimore: Johns Hopkins University, Center for Research on Elementary and Middle Schools, 1989), pp. 1–5.

19 Dornbusch and Ritter, "Parents of High School Students," pp. 75–77; and Eccles et al., "School and Family Effects," pp. 15–40.

20 Carol R. Freedman-Doan et al., "Looking Forward to Adolescence: Mother's and Fathers' Expectations for Change" (Symposium paper presented at the Biennial Meeting of the Society for Research on Adolescence Washington, D.C., March 1992), pp. 4-10.

21 Epstein and Dauber, "Parents' Attitudes and Practices of Involvement," pp. 289-305.

22 Ibid.

23 Epstein and Dauber, "Parents' Attitudes and Practices of Involvement," pp. 289-305; and K. V. Hoover-Dempsey et al., "Parent Involvement: Contributions of Teacher Efficacy, School Socioeconomic Status, and Other School Characteristics," *American Educational Research Journal* 24 (1987): 417-435.

24 Cf. Comer, *School Power*.

25 Cf. Ibid; and idem and Haynes, "Parent Involvement in Schools," pp. 271-77.

26 Epstein, "What Principals Should Know about Parent Involvement," pp. 6-9; and Epstein and Dauber, "Parents' Attitudes and Practices of Involvement," pp. 289-305.

27 Eccles et al., "School and Family Effects," pp. 15-40; and Jacquelynne S. Eccles, "Bringing Young Women to Math and Science," in *Gender and Thought: Psychological Perspectives*, ed. Mary Crawford and Margaret Gentry (New York: Springer-Verlag, 1989), pp. 36-57.

28 Ibid.

29 Comer, *School Power*; and idem and Haynes, "Parent Involvement in Schools," pp. 271-77.

30 Task Force on Education of Young Adolescents, *Turning Points*.

Improving the School-to-Work Transition of American Adolescents

ROBERT W. GLOVER AND RAY MARSHALL
The University of Texas at Austin

America has the worst approach to school-to-work transition of any industrialized nation.[1] Put simply, we have no systematic processes to assist high school graduates to move smoothly from school into employment. Our secondary schools and counseling efforts are focused primarily on encouraging youths to continue their education in college and obtain a degree. Yet almost half of each graduating class—roughly 1.4 million young people each year—directly enters the labor market without enrolling in college, and only one-quarter of each graduating class ultimately obtains a baccalaureate degree. Most high school graduates not going to college are left to sink or swim—without advice or career counseling and without any job-placement assistance. A 1981 survey by the Educational Testing Service (ETS) revealed that almost half of all high school students never talked to a counselor about occupations and only 6 percent of high school counselors reported spending more than 30 percent of their time helping students find jobs.[2] Budget cuts during the 1980s eliminated federally funded job counseling services through the public Job Service, which at its peak (in 1964) had served 600,000 youths annually in half of the nation's high schools.[3]

The Commission on Skills of the American Workforce summarized the problems for youths going to work immediately after high school: "There is no curriculum to meet the needs of non-college bound youth, no real employment service for those who go right to work, few guidance services for them, no certification of their accomplishments and . . . no rewards in the workplace for hard work at school."[4]

THE CONTEXT

While school-to-work transition is among the weakest links in the American learning system, it is important for Americans to consider why we must be concerned about improving all of our learning systems. By our definition, the term *learning systems* includes families, community institutions, work places, media, and political processes—in addition to formal schools. Among the key questions we must address are: Why have learning systems become so much more important? How do American systems compare with those of other countries? What are the implications of, and policy actions required by, technological change and a more competitive global economy?

ECONOMIC CHANGE

The need for increased learning and thinking skills is driven by some very fundamental economic developments. The main problem for the United States has been a shift from an economy based mainly on natural resources and economies of scale made possible by mass production for a large, relatively insulated American market to a more competitive global-information economy where economic success depends mainly on the quality of human resources. The United States had enormous advantages in the traditional mass-production economy, and although we retain advantages based on our past successes, we have serious disadvantages in the increasingly competitive global economy. These disadvantages relate to the obsolescence of our traditional learning systems, which were closely related to the skill requirements of a mass-production system.

A basic feature of the traditional American economy was the fact that it afforded very rapid increases in productivity and standards of living. This has been mainly due to an abundant supply of cheap natural resources, economies of scale, and reinforcing processes whereby market forces shifted resources to higher productivity uses (e.g., from agriculture to manufacturing) and caused improvements in one industry to lead to improvements in others (e.g., as when reduced steel costs improved auto and other industries, leading to higher sales and greater scale economies).

This mass-production system had its problems, but it ushered in the longest period of sustained, equitably shared prosperity in the history of the United States—perhaps even in world history.

The main forces eroding the mass-production system's basic institutions were the closely interactive effects of technology and international competition. Technology reduced the importance of physical resources and changed the nature of mass-production processes. Information technology and flexible manufacturing systems make it possible to achieve many of the advantages of economies of scale without large producing units. Technology—best defined as how things are done—is basically ideas, skills, and knowledge embodied in machinery and structures. Technological progress therefore represents the substitution of ideas, skills, and knowledge for physical resources. Schultz demonstrated this process in agriculture, where there have been great increases in output since the 1920s despite the use of less land, physical capital, and labor.[5] Moreover, other economists have demonstrated that almost all of the improvements in productivity since the 1920s have been due to factors associated with human capital and technology—natural resources account for none of the increase and physical capital for only 20 percent or less.

LEARNING SYSTEMS FOR A MASS-PRODUCTION ECONOMY

The skill requirements of the mass-production system resulted mainly from the hierarchical, fragmented nature of the work (or Taylorism) combined with the assembly line. This system required a few educated managerial, technical, or professional employees; most of the work was routine and could be performed by workers who needed only basic literacy and numeracy. Indeed, much work could be done by illiterates. Because the system was so productive, workers with limited education could earn enough money to support their families at levels that were relatively high by historical standards. This was especially true after the New Deal policies of the 1930s provided safety nets for those who were unable to work, collective bargaining to make it possible for workers to improve their share of the system's gains, and monetary and fiscal policies to keep the system running at relatively low levels of unemployment.

Learning systems reflected the mass-production skill requirements. Managerial, professional, and technical families prepared their children for occupations through family information networks and elite learning processes in public or private schools. With some notable exceptions, public schools were organized primarily to provide basic literacy and numeracy skills to lower-income native and immigrant students expected to work in mass-production factories or on farms. Although the system provided more upward occupational mobility than those in most other countries, especially after the reforms of the 1930s and 1940s, both family and school learning systems basically perpetuated the mass-production, resource-oriented occupational structure. This included education and training for the skilled trades through postsecondary school apprenticeship programs. The school-to-work transition processes were informal and largely family related but were perpetuated through formal learning systems.

COMPETING IN THE NEW ECONOMY

Information technology has combined with international competition to alter conditions for economic viability and success. In a more competitive, consumer-driven system, quality—best defined as meeting consumers' needs—becomes much more important; mass-production systems were producer-driven and emphasized quantity, not quality. Moreover, in competitive markets economic success depends heavily on productivity in the use of all resources, not just economies of scale. Competitive systems thus must be more flexible in adjusting to changing market and technological conditions.

In a more competitive environment, companies or individuals can compete in two ways: They can reduce their wages or improve productivity and quality. The easiest approach, the one we have followed in the United States, is the low-wage strategy. Most other industrialized nations have rejected this strategy because it implies lower and more unequal wages, with serious political, social, and economic implications.[6]

Japan and Western European countries take several actions to encourage companies to pursue high-wage strategies. First, they build national consensus for such a strategy. The essential instruments to encourage companies to pursue high-wage strategies include wage regulation, full-employment policies, trade and industrial policies, and adjustment policies to shift resources from low- to high-productivity activities.

Japan and Western European countries promote various forms of worker participation to encourage companies to organize for high performance (i.e., for quality, productivity, and flexibility). It has been well documented that these organizations have lean management systems that decentralize decisions to front-line workers as much as possible. In order to encourage worker participation and decentralized decision making, other countries encourage collective bargaining and require or promote worker participation in management decisions at various levels, including boards of directors, but almost always in work-place decisions.

High-performance organizations likewise develop and use leading-edge technology. The mass-production systems depended on standardized technologies and relatively unskilled labor. As it has become clear that this combination is not competitive in high-wage countries, some American companies have attempted to automate—combining advanced technology with unskilled labor, an approach that rarely succeeded. High-performance organizations require well-educated workers who can adapt and constantly improve leading-edge technology in a process the Japanese call "giving wisdom to the machines."

Because high-performance organizations give workers much discretion, positive incentive systems are basic requirements for success. The incentives for front-line workers in mass-production organizations are often negative (e.g., punishment for failure) or perverse—penalizing workers for superior performance, as when workers lose their jobs when they improve productivity. Positive incentives include group bonuses for superior performance, participation in decisions, internal unity, and employment security.

Above all, high-performance organizations require workers who can analyze data, communicate with precision, deal with ambiguity, learn rapidly, participate in what were considered management decisions in hierarchical management systems, and work well in teams. These have come to be called "higher-order thinking skills," formerly possessed only by the managerial, professional, and technical elites.

Most industrialized countries have developed policies to ensure that a majority of their workers have higher-order thinking skills. These include high performance standards all young people are required to meet before they can leave secondary schools. It is each school's responsibility to see that these standards are met. Standards are important because they provide incentives for students, teachers, and other school personnel; information to employers and to postsecondary institutions; and a means for policymakers and the public to evaluate schools.

Standards are likewise important factors in strengthening school-to-work transition systems, because students who meet high standards are prepared for work, technical training, or other forms of postsecondary education. Since the United States has no national standards for secondary school leavers, our students in nonacademic tracks too often find their options to pursue higher levels of postsecondary education and training severely constrained.

Other countries do several other things that strengthen their learning systems. First, most have family policies to support children. The United States alone among industrialized countries has no child-support, universal preschool, or parental-leave programs. The absence of such policies makes many of our families—especially our low-income families—very poor learning systems. Many of our children therefore start school far behind their more advantaged counterparts, and subsequently receive inadequate learning opportunities at home as well as in school. Families are not only basic learning systems but also provide information and services linking young people to labor markets. Families in most industrialized countries have experienced considerable structural change and stress since the 1960s that have reduced their effectiveness as learning systems. However, most other industrialized countries have done much more than the United States to provide public and community processes to help families compensate for these changes.[7] Second, most other countries also have well-developed labor market institutions and information systems to help match workers and jobs. Third, most other countries provide systematic postsecondary education and training opportunities for school leavers. Finally, they offer incentives for companies to provide on-the-job training for front-line workers. American systems in all of these areas are not very well organized or systematic. Few American companies provide formal education and learning systems for their employees and, as would be expected in Tayloristic work organizations, most of the systems they do have are devoted mainly to training managers—not front-line workers.[8]

IMPLICATIONS OF INADEQUATE SCHOOL-TO-WORK TRANSITION

The lack of a systematic bridge between school and work most adversely affects poor and minority students. They have access to few resources or information networks to obtain mainstream jobs that lead to meaningful careers. In labor markets, word-of-mouth contacts among people who know and trust each other match learners with learning opportunities and jobs with job-seekers. Many middle-class parents have the contacts and resources to be good job developers for their children. However, low-income parents are not so well positioned, especially if they are black or Hispanic. The problems are often compounded by powerful negative stereotypes youths and employers may have about one another. Employers often are influenced by what they see in the media about inner-city youths. Likewise, many minority youths have negative ideas about industry hiring practices. In addition, the location of available jobs may pose significant problems for inner-city and minority youths in isolated rural areas where they lack transportation to the available employment or training opportunities.

U.S. Bureau of Labor Statistics data on the employment status of recent high school graduates confirm these Hispanic and black labor market disadvantages. Unemployment rates for whites, Hispanics, and blacks were 14.9 percent, 29.1 percent, and 50.3 percent respectively. In addition, more black youths were out of the labor force and thus not counted as unemployed. Indeed, only 28.5 percent of blacks but 53.5 percent of white male high school graduates had jobs in October after graduation.[9] These data refer to whether youths have jobs at all without any reference to the quality of those jobs. The realization that relatively few minority youths obtain any job—let alone a good job—even if they study hard and obtain a diploma provides little incentive to excel in school.

Problems in making the transition from school to work are not confined to minorities or the poor. Negotiating the labor market is a difficult task for many American youths who have decided not to pursue a baccalaureate degree. In other countries youths are provided occupational counseling, employment information, and job placement through local schools or labor-market institutions, and employers take an active role in youth development activities. The United States, by contrast, has no system for getting youth from school into work, and the employer community takes little responsibility for youth.

School dropouts and high school graduates are most at risk of unemployment, low incomes, and unsatisfying work. However, even college-bound youths often do not receive adequate career counseling. The result is high proportions of college students who are "undeclared" as to their major. College students are often ignorant of the options available. Many college graduates appear at a loss in making occupational choices; some even enter law or graduate school not so much out of choice but from lack of knowledge of other options.

America is thus not serving many of her youth well and is particularly neglectful of the needs of the three-quarters of her future work force who do not obtain baccalaureate degrees. At the same time, it is becoming clear that the new, high-performance work organizations require that *all* workers be more highly skilled. Stated another way, in the modern global-information economy, few people will obtain a good job that pays well without significant learning beyond high school. The triple demands of efficiency, quality, and flexibility require line workers who have high levels of basic skills and who learn quickly. In short, the quality of America's front-line workers is the bottom line in our nation's economic future. In this light, a closer comparison of American school-to-work transition practices with those of Japan and Germany is especially instructive.

JAPAN

The largest and best Japanese firms, such as Toyota, Mitsubishi, and Sony, actively recruit not only the best university graduates but also the best high school graduates. They aggressively seek out the best high schools and request school staff to recommend students to them.[10] This gives high school students incentives to work hard and perform well in school and it puts power into the hands of teachers, whose recommendations carry significant weight.[11] After hiring them, Japanese firms typically put these eighteen-year-old high school graduates into well-developed learning systems both on the job and off. Japanese foremen and other supervisors are evaluated in part by how well they instruct the workers they supervise; teaching is simply an integral part of their job. In addition, most firms expect their employees to continue learning on their own in self-development programs, conducted through correspondence and other professional development processes. Many employers circulate lists of recommended course opportunities and reimburse half of the tuition to any employee who passes such a course.

GERMANY

The involvement of German firms in the development of the teenage work force is even clearer and more explicit than in Japan. Under the German apprenticeship system, youths beginning at age sixteen spend four days per week in an industry-devised, nationally approved program of occupational instruction with an employer and one day in school. Because apprenticeships involve two learning tracks—on the job and in school—the German system is commonly known as the "dual system." The program of structured training normally lasts for three years. Germany's biggest and best companies participate and actively recruit the best achieving youths. Americans on study tours of the German apprenticeship system are likely to find themselves at factories operated by firms such as Siemens or Daimbler Benz, or even subsidiaries of American firms, including Ford Motor Company or Corning.

The German dual system is supported by an impressive counseling and guidance system operated largely by the public employment service, so that German youths are acquainted with available options and are able to make decisions about careers as adolescents. Youths also have available to them a variety of exploratory activities, ranging from plant tours and job-shadowing experiences to "sniffing apprenticeships," in which youths spend two weeks in a selected apprenticeship on a tryout basis.

The German apprenticeship system is a socialization process as much as it is a training program. Through apprenticeships, the majority of German adolescents at ages sixteen, seventeen, and eighteen spend most of their day in an adult environment—learning such work-readiness behaviors as coming to work on time and valuing quality in their workmanship. As in Japan, German youths are able to participate effectively in these on-the-job learning systems because they are required to meet high academic standards for graduation from secondary schools.

In both Germany and Japan, when young workers complete their formal training, they enter well-developed work-place learning systems. Teaching is an explicit, high-priority component of the training for foremen and other supervisors and work is consciously organized as a learning system.

AMERICAN EMPLOYERS AVOID RESPONSIBILITY FOR YOUTH FORMATION

The contrast with U.S. practices could not be sharper. Whereas Germany and Japan have systematic incentives and high expectations for performance of their adolescents and their expectations are generally fulfilled, Americans expect little of adolescents and our expectations are equally fulfilled.

America's preferred employers—those who offer good wages, attractive benefits, and career potential—ordinarily do not hire high school graduates immediately after graduation, even if they have good academic records. America's biggest and best corporations avoid hiring youths at all. Only a handful of the Fortune 500 firms hire fresh high school graduates for entry jobs offering career opportunities. Even member firms of the Business Roundtable, who so actively advocate school reform and form partnerships with schools, do not hire teenagers. Although almost all of these firms eventually employ high school graduates, they normally wait until the job applicants are "mature and settled down" in their mid-twenties and have accumulated some work experience. Other employers emulate the practices of our largest firms. Thus American apprenticeship sponsors act like any other American employer in a position to be selective about applicants; they choose *against* youth. The average starting apprentice in the United States is in his or her late twenties. This delay in hiring for career-track jobs results in many youths spending five or six years floundering in jobs that offer opportunities neither for learning nor for advancement.[12] More important, these conventional American hiring practices have at least four critical consequences for school-to-work transition:

1. The delay in hiring American youths provides German and Japanese youths a five- to ten-year head start in gaining access to significant occupational skill training.
2. These practices remove some of our best learning systems—our finest corporations—from the processes that develop our youth. By shunning any responsibility for hiring teenagers, the best American employers have effectively disengaged from the process of instructing and socializing their future workers.
3. The delay in hiring high school graduates eliminates a natural communication loop for employers to feed clear information back to schools about what skills are needed in the work place.
4. Most important, effort and achievement in school are disconnected from rewards in the work place, thus undermining student incentives to work hard and achieve in school. Improving the school-to-work transition is thus an essential school reform issue.

Recent research by John Bishop and James Rosenbaum has demonstrated that effort and achievement in high school are not effectively rewarded for students who do not plan to go to college.[13] Few employers ask for high school transcripts, and most of those that do find that they cannot obtain them on a sufficiently timely basis to make hiring decisions. The high school diploma appears to be valued by employers mainly as an indicator of persistence rather than as a measure of achievement. Although a high school diploma makes a big difference in earnings over the long run, it appears to make little difference in the type of employment and wages offered in initial jobs after high school graduation. Because many youths have a short time horizon, near-term employment prospects offer much more powerful incentives than do abstract arguments about lifetime earnings.

American employers currently are not communicating what they need very clearly either to schools or to students. Employers must therefore do a better job of identifying the skills they require of job applicants and reach agreement with schools about how to assess and certify those skills. Equally important, employers must act to hire youths with such skills, once certified. Surveying employers to find out what skills they say they need is not enough;

the effort must be tied to action. A promising vehicle for achieving employer commitment to action is a formal agreement, an idea that started with the Boston Compact in 1982. Legislation introduced in October 1991 by Senators Edward Kennedy (D-Massachusetts) and Mark Hatfield (R-Oregon) and Congressmen Richard Gephardt (D-Missouri) and Ralph Regula (R-Ohio) contains provisions establishing community youth employment compacts in Title III B. Entitled the "High Skills, Competitive Workforce Act of 1991," this legislation was drafted to implement the recommendations of the Commission on Skills of the American Workforce.

IMPORTANT DESIGN FEATURES OF A COMMUNITYWIDE SCHOOL-TO-WORK INITIATIVE

It is clear that we cannot simply transport the German or Japanese approach to American shores, nor should we want to. Each is embedded in its culture and has its own flaws and deficiencies. Rather, we should learn from the approaches used in other countries and adapt the best aspects into our own homegrown solutions.

The design for the systematic yet flexible model envisioned here is based on several principles. *The first of these is to connect achievement in school with rewards in the labor market.* Incentives are important for everyone. Students must know that achievement in school pays off unmistakably in terms of economic opportunity.

Second, no single program or training approach can meet the needs of all youths or of all employers. Thus it is important to make available a variety of training and learning services and opportunities, including work-based learning options.

Third, a system is needed that is available to all youths, rather than a series of short-term demonstrations for special populations. The initiative must be institutionalized with regular financing and thus not dependent on ad hoc grants for continued support. It requires a sustained commitment from the business community, which must see that it is in its own interest. To avoid stigmatizing the participating youths, the initiative must not be reserved exclusively for disadvantaged populations. Of course, helping minority youths and the disadvantaged is a key concern, but there are better ways to help assure their participation than by making poverty an eligibility criterion. Targeting can be achieved by selecting school districts with heavy poor and minority enrollments and by building in strong recruiting and outreach components to assure that poor and disadvantaged youths are well served by the system. Also, *an integral part of any school-to-work system is to serve those who have dropped out of school and who have enrolled in second-chance learning programs, connecting achievement and performance in these programs with rewards in the labor market.*

Fourth, in several respects, information is a key element of the proposed system. To manage the system properly, accurate feedback is needed about youths after they leave school. In order to provide the community with information about its young adults, an information system should be developed to follow young people who have left high school, graduated, and entered the labor market or postsecondary education or training programs. Such data are not commonly available now, and they are essential for accountability and for monitoring progress against goals. Information also is needed on the performance of various public and private training providers, including proprietary schools, community colleges, and other postsecondary training options. In order to make informed decisions about which path to take, youths need to know about the efficacy of various training options after high school. Such data should be collected regularly and made accessible to students and their parents, as well as policymakers and the general public. Finally, graduating youths need a better way to document their competence than conventional school transcripts. Skill certification procedures that are both user-friendly and meaningful to employers need to be developed.

Fifth, if adolescents are expected to be in a position to make decisions about careers, providing better and earlier occupational information and guidance is essential. To be successful in the job market, moreover, students need better information on how to get and keep a job. Students must be able to present themselves on paper and in person; they must have opportunities to practice their interviewing skills.

Sixth, vocational options need to have a strong academic content. Critics of vocational-technical education often draw a false distinction between "vocational" and "academic" education. Properly taught, technical education always has required considerable academic content—and technical education will contain even more academic content in the future, as higher theoretical and conceptual skills are required. Most abstract and academic subjects can be taught more effectively through hands-on experience than through classroom lectures. In fact, learning probably is always more effective with the unity of thought and action. The importance of learning by doing has been rediscovered by much recent research.[14] Academic content is necessary also in providing a foundation for adaptability and learning how to learn. Narrow job training or task learning soon becomes obsolete in the changing world of work. It is essential that youths learn how to learn in order to constantly upgrade and improve their skills to match the needs of the work place.

Finally, the system should not foreclose the option for higher education. Although students may identify themselves as "non-college-bound" in high school, many subsequently may decide to pursue further schooling. Attending college is not a one-time-only decision. In view of the need to promote continued learning as a valued skill essential in almost all jobs that pay well, it is best not to close the options unnecessarily for any youngster. Participation in the program should not preclude college attendance. On the contrary, a major objective of the initiative should be to foster lifelong learning of all types.

THE COMPACT: A FOUNDATION FOR AN AMERICAN SCHOOL-TO-WORK SYSTEM

The problem of bridging the transition between school and work requires a systematic regional and community response. One promising approach is to organize job collaboratives or compacts between businesses, schools, and community leaders along the lines of the Boston Compact.[15] Compacts have been established in several cities, but many are simply unfocused collections of business-education partnership activities. What we have in mind here is a version far more specific—geared to results in integrating school and employment and in creating incentives for learning.

The essential mission of the job collaborative is to stimulate academic achievement and career readiness among students. All of the parties in the compact agree to commit themselves to a set of measurable goals or outcomes and to a system for evaluating each through time. A primary aim is to provide students with incentives to stay in school and perform well in order to be eligible for jobs and financial assistance for higher education. Participating students agree to maintain certain standards of performance. For example, in Boston they must obtain certification that they are working hard from two teachers, must stay out of trouble with the law, and must maintain at least an 85 percent school attendance level. In return, businesses agree to preferential hiring of students who meet the specified standards. For their part, school authorities agree to make specific improvements in the participating schools.

To build a bridge between school and the business community, Boston copied the model of the British Careers Service, an arm of the local educational agency with responsibility for counseling and job placement, now a part of the Youth Training Scheme. Young counselors were placed in schools to help train youths in presenting themselves effectively to employers and to help connect participating students with jobs.

Begun in 1982 and renegotiated in 1988, the Boston Compact brought together the resources of the public schools, businesses, universities, labor unions, and the mayor's office to improve student academic achievement and work preparation in exchange for increased opportunities for both employment and higher education. This compact has been most successful in gaining jobs for high school graduates. In 1989, through the compact 1,107 graduates (in a class of just under 3,000) found full-time jobs averaging $6.75 per hour in over 900 businesses.[16] Over 85 percent of the youths placed are reported to have been satisfactory employees. Perhaps most impressive of all, among high school graduates employment of blacks reached parity with that of whites at a level substantially above the national average. Youth unemployment rates in Boston were significantly lower than in other places, and the difference between the proportions of black and white unemployed youths was almost negligible—an achievement virtually unparalleled in any other major city.[17]

Even though Boston's booming economy during the 1980s was a helpful factor, the compact's accomplishment in raising employment for black high school graduates to the level of employment of whites was due as much to the efficacy of the concept as to economic conditions. The Boston project focused on a fundamental difference between middle-class white youths and those from poor black families: namely, that white middle-class youths have better information and networks to obtain jobs than do poor black youths. Young people from poor homes lack the network of employed fathers and mothers, aunts, and uncles that smooths the transition for the better connected. The recession of the early 1990s has diminished the program's number of placements, but the compact is still performing and evolving, with discussions underway in 1992 to form a vocational-technical school connected directly to a variety of apprenticeship paths into the work place, with related training provided by area community colleges.

The Boston experience has revealed important lessons that should be incorporated into any program to help young people move successfully from school to work. Youth—especially those from disadvantaged families—must have access to information and job networks in order to find employment. Such networks can be established on an institutionalized basis within the high schools through establishing careers services or similar functions. Assistance from an intermediary—including training in effective job-search techniques—is an important component. Job-related standards should not be ignored in student recruitment and selection, and special efforts are needed to articulate relevant standards on a clear, objective basis and to communicate those standards to schools, young people, and their families. Incentives are important for everyone. For students, it must be unmistakably clear that school pays off in terms of economic opportunity and personal satisfaction.

Establishing commitments to performance goals with measurable objectives, regularly measuring performance against those goals, and publishing the results are all critically important. Students need to be contacted after graduation to find out how well the compact is working and to provide feedback to improve future operations.

Of course, no uniform prescription is appropriate for all localities. Each process must be adapted to the needs, resources, and circumstances of both the employers and the youths in the community served. Successful compacts are not just single programs—rather, they become frameworks to organize a wide variety of initiatives or partnerships. Such efforts can refine job-entry requirements, foster the availability of effective mentor arrangements between youths and adults, create meaningful training and career paths for youths, improve occupational counseling, and offer training and education on a joint basis between schools and work sites, thereby putting learning into a practical context more likely to motivate students. In short, the process of bridging the school-employment gap must be systematic, focused, comprehensive, and flexible.

BUILDING EFFECTIVE LEARNING PATHS FROM HIGH SCHOOL TO CAREER-TRACK JOBS

A compact with measurable outcomes and a good information base offers the foundation for a community school-to-work initiative. Under its umbrella, a variety of effective training paths can be developed from high school leading directly to jobs and careers. No single training approach will suit the needs of every youth, every employer, or every occupation. The best arrangement may be to establish a portfolio of promising options including apprenticeships, cooperative education, vocational academies, tech prep programs, and national youth service, along with other learning systems that have not yet been envisioned.

APPRENTICESHIPS

Conceptually, the apprenticeship model offers many advantages in remedying the employment problems of young people. First, unlike most other forms of training, apprenticeship provides a built-in opportunity for youth to earn while they learn. Second, its mode of training—practical learning by doing—has natural appeal to many young people who are weary of conventional classroom instruction. Third, learning occurs in a real job setting, in direct contact with employers and older workers who can help socialize youths to the work place. Apprenticeships thus offer built-in incentives and opportunities for mentor relationships.

The effectiveness of apprenticeship is well documented by research. Studies have demonstrated that craft workers trained through apprenticeship learn new skills faster, are promoted faster and more often, suffer less unemployment, and earn more than their counterparts trained in other ways.[18] Likewise, follow-up surveys of former apprentices have indicated that as many as 15 percent have become business owners themselves.[19]

Since apprenticeship regulations specify a minimum age of only sixteen years, it is technically possible for apprenticeship to serve teenagers in the United States. However, there are some impediments to using the American apprenticeship model for youth younger than eighteen. The child-labor provisions of the Fair Labor Standards Act and insurance regulations, for example, prohibit youth below that age from working in some hazardous apprenticeable job classifications in construction and other industries.

Another impediment is employer reluctance to hire youth as apprentices, especially disadvantaged youths. Sponsors feel that they are making a major investment in apprentices who may leave them before their investments are recouped. Like other investors, apprenticeship sponsors avoid risk. One public policy solution to this problem is to make disadvantaged youths less risky investments for employers, as has been done with a variety of preapprenticeship initiatives such as those provided in the Job Corps, programs registered by the state apprenticeship agencies in North Carolina and Florida, and a wide range of apprenticeship outreach and skill-development programs.[20] However, the approach of expanding preapprenticeship programs is limited by what might be called a "funnel problem." Few apprenticeship positions are available and competition for many of these is intense. A means of expanding the number of apprenticeships, along with getting more youths into them, is therefore needed. One approach—school-to-apprenticeship linkage—has demonstrated that it can accomplish both. The concept of school-to-apprenticeship linkage is simple. High school seniors are employed on a part-time basis as registered apprentices with transition to full-time apprenticeships after graduation, when they become regular apprentices working full time while they complete their related training, ordinarily taken through special classes at local community colleges or vocational schools.

Experience to date reveals some weakness with school-to-apprenticeship programs, especially arranging post–high school related training opportunities for apprentices with small employers who sponsor only one or two apprenticeships, making it difficult to meet the minimum class size requirements in community colleges and vocational schools. An ideal solution to this problem is to get employers to join together in associations to sponsor apprenticeships. However, since many school-to-apprenticeship sponsors are new and inexperienced, this is easier said than done. Considerable work is involved in establishing effective programs of related study at the high school level and beyond.

Thanks in part to the work of a number of individuals and organizations, interest in apprenticeship recently has increased dramatically.[21] In 1991, the states of Arkansas,[22] Wisconsin, and Oregon established a series of state-funded apprenticeship projects. Several bills have been introduced in the U.S. Congress to establish a major national demonstration of youth apprenticeship. Forces driving this movement include a new interest in the German apprenticeship system, the rediscovery by cognitive psychologists of the effectiveness of learning by doing, work by anthropologists in Third World countries confirming the success of informal apprenticeships, and the reaffirmation of the apprenticeship concept by the U.S. Department of Labor's "Apprenticeship 2000" initiative during 1988–1989.[23] In order to distinguish them from traditional apprenticeships, advocates usually call their new programs "youth apprenticeship" or "work-based learning."

COOPERATIVE EDUCATION

Although apprenticeship is not well established in American high schools, another work-study training scheme, cooperative education, has a better foothold. Approximately 600,000 high school students, nearly one-tenth of all students who are enrolled in vocational education programs, participate in cooperative education.

Cooperative education differs from apprenticeship in that cooperative education is more school-based than industry-based, its training typically ends with high school, its work stations are designed to be training stations rather than permanent jobs, and it is best established in a different set of occupations than apprenticeship—primarily in retailing and clerical work. Cooperative education at the postsecondary level has grown significantly over the past two decades, especially among community colleges. Thus, there would appear to be great potential to link the two to offer more advanced training—especially in conjunction with the establishment of tech prep programs (see below). However, at the present time, collaboration between cooperative education at the secondary level and at the postsecondary level is remarkably uncommon.

Existing evaluations of cooperative education programs have yielded mixed results and incomparable findings, but these evaluations have been methodologically flawed.[24] A key problem with cooperative education is the great variation in quality from program to program. One solution is to tie the programs to a certification scheme such as that used in German apprenticeships, in which the skills and knowledge of the program's graduates are tested in performance, written, and oral tests appropriate to the occupation.[25]

VOCATIONAL ACADEMIES

Restructuring high school vocational-technical education is a critical component of any system to improve the linkages between school and work. One promising approach is the career academy, originated in Philadelphia and replicated extensively in California.

Under the basic academy model, at the end of the ninth grade, students at risk of failure are identified and invited to volunteer for a program based on a school-within-a-school format, with a separate team of teachers for a portion of their courses. The resulting cadre of students and teachers remains together for three years. Students spend the tenth grade catching up on academics and integrating computers and field trips into the curriculum. In grade eleven, every student has a mentor from industry who introduces the student to his or her work place and joins the student for recreational activities at least once a month. By the end of the eleventh grade, the student obtains a summer job with one of the business partners. Students who stay with the program are promised a job on graduation from high school.

The academies have worked well because the students have a context for their learning and they have "found a home" in the small academies (about 100 students or less). Evaluations to date indicate that academies have an effect on reducing dropout rates.[26] Plans for a careful evaluation of the longitudinal effects of career academies using a random assignment design are being formulated by the Manpower Demonstration Research Corporation.

Partnership academies were subsequently funded in twelve school districts across California with matching grants of $67,500 from the state. By 1991, several additional California sites were being developed around occupational clusters in hospitality, media, health, or finance, depending on the local economy. Efforts were being made to expand even further.

Industry variations of the academy idea also have emerged. The American Express Corporation, for example, developed the Finance Academy in Phoenix, Arizona, to prepare youth for careers in banking and finance. The program has been replicated in other cities in collaboration with other financial service firms. American Express also began its Academy in Tourism and has established a foundation to promote the academy model generally. However, some of these examples simply involve adding a few vocational courses independent of academic courses without attempting academic-vocational integration or establishing multiyear school-within-a-school arrangements.

The partnership or career academy model offers several advantages over the traditional ways of organizing high school vocational education. First, clustering vocational education by industry rather than by occupation facilitates industry involvement while leaving open a wide array of occupations to which students can aspire. Second, partnership academies are less likely to become stigmatized than are vocational education programs organized along occupational lines. An academy in the health occupations, for example, includes students who aspire to be physicians as well as those who wish to become nurses' aides. Third, partnership academies reach at-risk youths earlier and more effectively than other approaches alone. Identifying and beginning to work with students as early as the ninth grade may prevent some at-risk youths from dropping out. Using the small group school-within-a-school format provides a more personal setting for learning. All of these features make the partnership academy an attractive component of a school-to-work initiative.

TECH PREP PROGRAMS

Promoted by Dale Parnell and by the Center for Occupational Research and Development (CORD), "tech prep" provides an alternative to the "college prep" curriculum. The aim is to prepare youths for technical careers by aligning high school and community college curricula into a coherent, unduplicated set of courses.[27] These were formerly called "2 + 2 programs" because they combine the last two years of high school with two years of community college. Tech prep requires the development of formal agreements between the secondary and postsecondary partners for integrating or articulating high school and postsecondary curricula. Unlike the predecessor 2 + 2 program, which could shorten the length of time required to complete work for a certificate or an associate degree because they were designed as a more efficient learning process, tech prep programs intend to provide students with more advanced skills within the traditional time period than do separate high school and community college programs. Students successfully completing the tech prep sequence obtain a high school diploma and a two-year associate degree or a certificate. Tech prep programs are flexible; they can include components for work-site training and work experience, and can even be combined with two-year apprenticeships.

The Carl D. Perkins Vocational and Applied Technology Education Act of 1990 authorized $125 million annually for planning and demonstration grants to consortia of local education agencies and postsecondary institutions to formulate a three-year plan for the development and implementation of tech prep programs. With such federal encouragement and funding, tech prep will become more pervasive.

While tech prep will certainly foster better school-to-school linkages between secondary and postsecondary institutions, its effectiveness in improving school-to-work transitions is yet to be proven. The effectiveness of tech prep in improving school-to-work connections is likely to rest on the degree to which the programs involve meaningful participation by industry, develop work-based learning that effectively integrates school and employment, and integrate academic and applied learning in new ways that engage students and bring life to the instructional process. It is hoped that the federally supported evaluations now under way will provide evidence of the effectiveness of tech prep approaches.

NATIONAL YOUTH SERVICE

The implementation of an effective program of National Youth Service could help improve the transitions from high school to work and to college or postsecondary training. National Youth Service obviates the need to find employers for all youths in need of work and opens up many more options. Such a program could offer special advantages if through participation in national service, youths could gain financial assistance for college or postsecondary training along the lines of the GI Bill. In addition, National Youth Service volunteers could be used to strengthen schools and second-chance learning systems. Service to others builds unity among youths from diverse backgrounds while offering valuable learning experiences for the volunteers.

CONCLUSION

We need to build on such successful experiences as school-to-apprenticeship linkage, cooperative education, the Boston Compact, the partnership academies, and tech prep. A primary objective should be to establish a scaled-up school-to-work initiative that makes a difference for substantial numbers of youths, including minorities and youths from poor families. In short, we propose a system that encompasses a variety of training/learning options. It would begin by providing earlier and better occupational knowledge and guidance for students (and their teachers)—starting at least in middle-school years. Secondary-level vocational education would be restructured along the partnership academy model. High school students would have the opportunity to participate in a compact in which employers promise preferential access to career jobs in return for meeting achievement standards in school. Students not intending to pursue a baccalaureate degree would have a variety of attractive training opportunities, including academies, youth apprenticeships, tech prep, and cooperative education. Adoption of the Commission on Skills of the American Workforce's recommendations to establish high national standards that all high school students would be expected to meet would help keep the options open for all students and therefore greatly facilitate the transitions to work, technical education, or four-year colleges.

Occupational guidance should be systematically improved, beginning as early as elementary school. By tenth grade, youths would be sufficiently prepared to choose a career academy that would provide a context for learning in their subsequent high school years. Career awareness and goal setting should be followed by career exploration, development of preemployment skills, and mentor relationships. Beginning in the eleventh grade, at least some of the academic training would be conducted in a functional context, using problems and real-life situations encountered on the job. Each participating school would have the equivalent of a careers service staff member on site to help conduct the preemployment training, counseling, and matching of mentors and summer jobs.

At the end of the eleventh grade, the program would branch into a variety of flexible options, including apprenticeships, cooperative education work stations, and tech prep programs. In choosing the tech prep option, students would be required to complete two years of community college. Likewise, apprenticeships would require student participation in related training beyond high school. In most cases such training would be conducted in community colleges.

These options would be presented to students, parents, and employers as high-quality opportunities that do not preclude possibilities of attending college later, especially for students who met world-class academic standards for high school graduation. Students would have to earn admission by achieving certain standards in basic skills and other competencies needed for employment. The training would be competency-based, offering a variety of instructional strategies including an individualized, self-paced mode using instructional materials in a variety of media formats (including print materials, audiovisuals, and computer-assisted instruction). Group work would also be undertaken. The curriculum would need to be substantial and challenging, with a high academic content. For example, knowledge of mathematics (at least through algebra) is required for several apprenticed trades. Competency certification throughout and upon the completion of training would be an integral feature.

Fearing for their own survival in an increasingly competitive world, many American businesses are desperately seeking ways to improve public schools. Numerous partnerships and "adopt-a-school" arrangements have been initiated, and education issues are receiving greater attention from business lobbies. A key political theme from business is to make teachers and administrators accountable for student outcomes, but mandating that educators be "accountable" ignores the fact that learning is a joint enterprise involving both teachers and students. While good teaching can facilitate learning, it is ultimately the responsibility of the student to learn. Learning cannot occur without students' taking action. Motivation is a key to effective learning.

Unfortunately, businesses often overlook a major lever in their own hands for motivating students: They control the most important incentive for work-bound youngsters—access to jobs—yet most do not use it. In addition, businesses have not articulated clearly to schools their needs in terms of learner outcomes or skills required, nor have American businesses organized to develop a consensus on such standards—even for vocational education students. Within limits, many businesses have simply adjusted requirements to the job applicants available. Further complicating this picture is firms' disparate expectations from schools. Business is highly heterogeneous in terms of management practices and other important dimensions. Moreover, skill requirements change through time, and the demands of the global-information economy are raising standards significantly for line workers.[28]

The issue of standards raises difficult questions. Which firms should set the standards? Ideally, should standards be set by the most progressive or leading-edge firms? If so, which firms are leading-edge and how is such an identification made? How often should the standards be updated and what are the processes for doing so? What are the roles of governments, schools, and other "outsiders" in establishing standards? These questions have no simple answers.

Given these complexities, a good place to start is with a compact that promises students who achieve at a specified level preferential consideration for jobs in the summer, after school, and, most importantly, at graduation.

In most communities, employers begin this process by focusing on students' grades and attendance. However, after accumulating experience with the first few graduating classes, recognition generally sets in that grades and attendance are not enough. Simple grade-point averages, for example, do not take into account that some courses are more rigorous than others. Even more fundamental, it is not clear that grades are useful indicators of the skills employers seek. Businesses must specify what skill assessments and certifications of performance they trust. Both the standards and the measures used to assess them must be reasonable, clear, and objective.

A primary requirement for success in any school-to-work initiative is getting employers committed to the effort. Business needs to recognize that inadequacies in the preparation of American youth are not just problems for schools. The development of a quality work force requires active participation of many outside the schools, including parents, public officials, communities, and employers. Ultimately, American employers must shoulder part of the responsibility for the development of youths—their future workers. It is, however, the responsibility of government at every level to provide the incentive context within which employers operate. The federal government should build consensus for a high-skills development strategy, but business and labor representatives should be active participants in that consensus-building process. An effective process to facilitate the transition from school to work for the great majority of our young people who do not pursue baccalaureate degrees must be an integral component of any high-skills development strategy.

We are grateful to the Charles Stewart Mott Foundation and Jobs for the Future for generous financial support for Robert Glover during the preparation of this manuscript. For helpful comments on previous drafts of this paper, we want to thank Paul Barton, Jana Carlisle, Kenneth Edwards, Barbara Green, Samuel Halperin, Suzanne Hershey, Christopher King, Cheryl McVay, Edward Pauly, Ellen Sehgal, John Stevens, Ruby Takanishi, Ken Tolo, Joan Wills, and two anonymous reviewers.

Notes

1 The William T. Grant Foundation Commission on Work, Family and Citizenship Youth and America's Future, *The Forgotten Half: Pathways to Success for America's Youth and Young Families* (Washington, D.C.: The William T. Grant Foundation, November 1988), pp. 26–28; Gordon Berlin and Andrew Sum, *Toward a More Perfect Union: Basic Skills, Poor Families, and Our Economic Future* (New York: The Ford Foundation, 1988), pp. 22–23; U.S. General Accounting Office (GAO), *Training Strategies: Preparing Noncollege Youth for Employment in the U.S. and Foreign Countries* (Washington, D.C.: Government Printing Office, May 1990), pp. 33–41; Commission on Skills of the American Workforce, *America's Choice: High Skills or Low Wages!* (Rochester, N.Y.: National Center on Education and the Economy, 1990), pp. 46–47; Paul Osterman, *Getting Started: The*

Youth Labor Market (Cambridge: MIT Press, 1980); and idem, *Employment Futures: Reorganization, Dislocation, and Public Policy* (New York: Oxford University Press, 1988), pp. 111–14.

2 W. Chapman and M. Katz. *Survey of Career Information Systems in Secondary Schools* (Princeton, N.J.: Educational Testing Service, 1981).

3 Paul E. Barton, "The School-to-Work Transition," *Issues in Science and Technology* 7 (Spring 1991): 50.

4 Commission on Skills of the American Workforce, *America's Choice*, p. 47.

5 Theodore W. Schultz, *Investing in People: The Economics of Population Quality* (Berkeley: The University of California Press, 1981).

6 Commission on Skills of the American Workforce, *America's Choice*; pp. 40–41.

7 Ray Marshall, *Losing Direction: Families, Human Resource Development, and Economic Performance*, The State of Families, 3 (Milwaukee: Family Service America, 1991).

8 Commission on Skills of the American Workforce, *America's Choice*, p. 4.

9 U.S. Bureau of Labor Statistics, "Nearly Three-fifths of High School Graduates of 1988 Enrolled in College" (U.S. Department of Labor News Release 89-308, June 1989).

10 James E. Rosenbaum and Takehiko Kariya, "From High School to Work: Market and Institutional Mechanisms in Japan," *American Journal of Sociology* 94 (May 1989): 1334–65.

11 James E. Rosenbaum, "What If Good Jobs Depended on Good Grades?" *American Educator* 13 (Winter 1990): 12.

12 See Paul Osterman, *Getting Started: The Youth Labor Market* (Cambridge: MIT Press, 1980); and The William T. Grant Foundation Commission, *The Forgotten Half*, pp. 26–28.

13 See John H. Bishop, "Why the Apathy in American High Schools?" *Educational Researcher* 18 (January-February 1989): 6–10, 42; James E. Rosenbaum, "Empowering Schools and Teachers: A New Link to Jobs for the Non-College Bound," in *Investing in People*, Report of the National Commission on Workforce Quality and Labor Market Efficiency, U.S. Department of Labor (Washington, D.C.: Government Printing Office, 1989), pp. 193–97; and idem, "What If Good Jobs Depended on Good Grades?," pp. 10–15, 40, 42, 43.

14 See, for example, Lauren Resnick, "Learning in School and Out," *Educational Researcher* 16 (1987): 13–20; American Association for the Advancement of Science, *Project 2061 Report* (Washington, D.C.: AAAS, 1988) p. 146; and Pat Hutchings and Allen Wutzdorff, eds., *Knowing and Doing: Learning through Experience* (San Francisco: Jossey-Bass, 1988).

15 See William J. Spring, "From 'Solution' to Catalyst: A New Role for Federal Education and Training Dollars" (Working paper prepared for the National Center on Education and the Economy, 1989), pp. 4–17; and idem, "Youth Unemployment and the Transition from Youth to Work," *New England Economic Review*, March/April 1987, pp. 3–16.

16 Commission on Skills of the American Workforce, *America's Choice*, p. 107.

17 National Alliance of Business, *The Compact Project: School-Business Partnerships for Improving Education* (Washington, D.C.: National Alliance of Business, 1989), p. 3.

18 Ray Marshall, William S. Franklin, and Robert W. Glover, *Training and Entry into Union Construction*, Manpower R & D Monograph No. 39, U.S. Department of Labor, Manpower Administration (Washington, D.C.: Government Printing Office, 1975); Stephen N. Hills, "How Craftsmen Learn Their Skills: A Longitudinal Analysis," in *Job Training for Youth*, ed. Robert E. Taylor, Howard Rosen, and Frank C. Pratzner (Columbus: National Center for Research in Vocational Education, The Ohio State University, 1982), pp. 203–40; Duane E. Leigh, "What Kinds of Training 'Work' for Noncollege Bound Youth?" (Report prepared for the U.S. General Accounting Office, October 1989); and Robert F. Cook et al., "Analysis of Apprenticeship Training from the National Longitudinal Study of the High School Class of 1972" (Report prepared for the Bureau of Apprenticeship and Training, U.S. Department of Labor, and the National Training Program of the International Union of Operating Engineers [Rockville, Md.: Westat, Inc., March 1989]).

19 Dorothea Maier and Harold Loeb, *Training and Work Experiences of Former Apprentices in New York State* (New York: Division of Research and Statistics, New York State Department of Labor, 1975).

20 Kenneth Tolo, Robert W. Glover, and John Gronouski, *Preparation for Apprenticeship through CETA* (Austin: Lyndon B. Johnson School of Public Affairs, University of Texas at Austin, 1980).

21 Stephen F. Hamilton, *Apprenticeship for Adulthood: Preparing Youth for the Future* (New York: The Free Press, 1990); idem, "Apprenticeship as a Transition to Adulthood in West Germany," *American Journal of Education* 95 (1987): 314–45; The William T. Grant Foundation Commission on Work, Family and Citizenship Youth and America's Future et al., *States and Communities on the Move: Policy Initiatives to Create a World-Class Workforce* (Washington, D.C.: The William T. Grant Foundation, 1991); Robert I. Lerman and Hillard Pouncy, "The Compelling Case for Youth Apprenticeships," *The Public Interest* 101 (Fall 1990): 62–77; and William E. Nothdurft and Jobs for the Future, *Youth Apprenticeship, American Style: A Strategy for Expanding School and Career Opportunities* (Somerville, Mass.: Jobs for the Future, Inc., 1991).

22 Jobs for the Future, Inc., *A Feasibility Study of Youth Apprenticeship in Arkansas* (Somerville, Mass.: Jobs for the Future, Inc., April 1991).

23 U.S. Department of Labor, *Work-based Learning: Training America's Workers* (Washington, D.C.: Government Printing Office, 1989).

24 David Stern et al., "Work Experience for Students in High School and College," *Youth and Society* 21 (March 1990): 355–89.

25 U.S. General Accounting Office (GAO), *Transition from School to Work: Linking Education and Worksite Training*, GAO/HRD 91-105 (Washington, D.C.: Government Printing Office, August 1991), p. 13.

26 David Stern et al., "Combining Academic and Vocational Courses in an Integrated Program to Reduce High School Dropout Rates: Second-Year Results from Replications of the California Peninsula Academies," *Educational Evaluation and Policy Analysis* 10 (Summer 1988): 161–70; and idem, "Benefits and Costs of Dropout Prevention in a High School Program Combining Academic and Vocational Education: Third-Year Results from Replications of the California Peninsula Academies," *Educational Evaluation and Policy Analysis* 11 (Winter 1989): 405–16.

27 Dale Parnell, *The Neglected Majority* (Washington, D.C.: The Community College Press, 1985); and idem and Daniel Hull, eds., *The Tech Prep Associate Degree: A Win-Win Strategy* (Waco: Center for Occupational Research and Development [CORD], 1991).

28 Commission on Skills of the American Workforce, *America's Choice*, pp. 37–42.

Adolescence and Schooling in Germany and the United States: A Comparison of Peer Socialization to Adulthood

ANNE C. PETERSEN AND NANCY LEFFERT
University of Minnesota, Minneapolis

KLAUS HURRELMANN
Universität Bielefeld

Adolescence is a phase of life in which young people develop from children into adults. Biological development to maturity also proceeds fairly uniformly in all sociocultural contexts except under conditions of severe starvation. But all other aspects of development during adolescence—cognitive, psychological, social—are strongly influenced by the contexts in which they take place. Therefore, the societal arrangements for socializing young people to adult roles can have significant impact on the young adults that emerge.

Schooling is one of the most important socializers in modern technological societies. Societies presumably engage schools to educate and otherwise socialize young people for the roles, especially work roles, they are expected to take as adults. To consider the ways that societies socialize their young to adulthood, we will compare the schooling processes in the United States and in Germany. Through this comparison, we hope to illuminate key features of the schooling process to achieve good outcomes in the preparation of productive adults.

ADOLESCENT DEVELOPMENT

Given the expectations for adults in a technological society, it is not surprising that the period of adolescence, in which children learn to function as adults, is one characterized by great change.[1] One of the major changes is the biological change of puberty. Although the meaning of becoming biologically mature may vary from society to society, the fact of biological maturation is quite uniform cross-nationally.[2] The biological changes of puberty also stimulate the individual to become aware of impending adulthood and especially of becoming a man or a woman. These changes affect identity, sex-role identity, self-esteem, and body image. The research suggests similar processes of adolescent development in the United States and Western Europe.[3]

SOCIAL CONTEXTS

There is also some cross-national similarity in the functioning of social contexts. We will consider each in turn.

FAMILY

The family as a central institution for the adolescent's upbringing has changed considerably because of economic, social, and cultural factors. Today, families are relatively small units of only a few members; increasingly they are households of one or two persons. Families as social systems have become highly susceptible to disturbance, mainly because of an increasing instability in marriage, which is the social heart of the family's relationships. In a recent German youth survey, about 20 percent of the responding adolescents were affected by parental separation or divorce.[4] The German rate for youth experiencing parental divorce prior to adulthood may be similar to that in the United States. For example, one current estimate suggests that about 30 percent of adolescents are likely to have experienced parental divorce.[5] Divorce effects on the adolescent range from minimal to significant.[6]

Family relationships remain the adolescents' emotional and social "home port." At the same time, it is one of the developmental tasks of adolescence to become increasingly involved emotionally, socially, and economically with peers and society beyond the family. Today this process of moving beyond the family is very complex. Because of the longer period of economic dependence on parents, evoked by extended academic and vocational education, and sometimes, at least in the United States, because of the lack of paid work, the transition out of the familial home usually takes place later in life than it did a generation ago. At the same time, adolescents of today very early develop a life-style independent from that of their parents, especially within the area of leisure time and consumption. They tend to move earlier into communities with peers or partners of the other sex. As the process of shifting attachments takes place in different areas at different times, the relations with the family of origin become complicated. The family's significance as an economic support and also as an institution that adolescents relate to when career decisions occur is very high, whereas its role in life-style issues (e.g., music and leisure-time preferences) is small during adolescence.

PEER GROUPS

Comparative historical studies in West Germany show that during adolescence the role of the peer group as a significant social reference group has intensified. Allerbeck and Hoag showed that the relative importance of peer relations has increased over the past twenty years.[7] Whether the same is true in the United States has not been examined but seems likely. Developmental research demonstrates that the strength of adolescent relationships to best friend increases while the strength reported for relationships to either parent decreases over the adolescent decade of life.[8]

In both Germany and the United States, the peer group's influence on consumption and leisure-time activities at adolescence is significant. Peer groups provide standards for consumption and, in doing so, establish standards for adolescent behavior. Peer groups are important in that they offer equal opportunity for participation to their members, which family or school do not provide to the same extent.[9] Peer groups are an important social organization that enable adolescents to experience self-determination.[10]

Average financial resources at the disposal of adolescents are significantly greater today relative to earlier times. The majority of adolescents in both West Germany and the United States live in material comfort. They are able to satisfy many of their consumptive and leisure desires to a degree that their parents would not have considered and could never have achieved. As marketing departments have realized for many years, there is a distinctive accumulation of purchasing power among adolescents.

Adolescents today live fairly independently relative to friends, partners, media, and consumption. In Germany, they do so on the basis of their parents' financial contributions, as relatively few adolescents are themselves gainfully employed. In the United States, part-time employment for adolescents is common and primarily serves needs for "spending money."[11] Nevertheless, the social position of adolescents allows for a wide spectrum of personal development and offers a high degree of autonomy, spontaneity, creativity, and individuality. In West Germany, there are many different reports showing a self-confident way of organizing life different from adults in fashion and clothing, music, leisure-time activities, language usage, and political expression.[12] A similar pattern has been observed in the United States.[13]

However, we have to be aware that adolescents develop their spontaneity and individuality in a social context that is insecure, unstable, and hardly accountable. The adolescent decade involves many risks.[14] The arenas for individual expression in adolescence do not typically lead to adult roles or skills. Therefore, the freedom of adolescents is embedded in their lack of a social role, their marginality.[15]

VARIATIONS IN TIMING TO ADULT ROLES

The modal pattern for the timing of adult roles in Germany is in the mid-twenties or later. In the United States, this would be typical of those who go to college; at least half of the youth cohort do not go on to college but also do not find meaningful work roles, usually until the mid-twenties. Therefore, the timing of the transition is similar in the two groups but the non-college group does not have a role respected by the society for almost a decade. This pattern has clear consequences for youth behavior.

In the United States, but much less so in Germany, there is a sizable group of young women who take on adult parenting roles at relatively early ages (e.g., mid-teens). In these cases, further education and employment are usually put "on hold." From one perspective, this pattern is adaptive as it at least provides a societal role, in comparison with the marginality of young unemployed men. On the other hand, adolescent parenting has been linked to serious negative consequences over the longer term.[16]

As we discuss in more detail below, there are distinct differences in the two countries in the extent to which the society facilitates the transition to adult roles. In the United States, the only clear pattern is that for college-going youth, and increasingly, even a college degree may not lead to appropriate work roles, depending on the area of the degree. Non-college youth have no meaningful role to play and are marginal to the society. In Germany, there is a greater likelihood of attaining a valued role in society during this age period.

SOCIETAL INVESTMENTS IN SOCIALIZATION TO ADULT ROLES

It would seem that societies would invest in the crucial transition of their young people's becoming productive members of the adult society. On this issue, the United States and Germany are quite different, as asserted above. It is noteworthy that societal investment in youth is clearer in the entire European Community (EC) than in the United States. For example, a recent EC commission prepared a report at the request of the ministers of member states with responsibility for youth affairs.[17] It describes youth policy and youth research of member states and makes recommendations for EC action. Notably, "all member states pay policy attention to the transition from education/training into the labour market; to programmes for prevention and protection of young people from social risks; and to youth information and guidance services of various kinds."[18] There is no youth policy, no government organization with coordinating responsibility, and no focus for youth research in the United States. Although the size of the United States might be considered an impediment to a national youth focus, we know of no state that has a focus on youth in a way comparable to member states in the EC.

The dramatic difference in attention to youth issues in Germany, as in the rest of the EC, compared with the United States would surely have implications for transitions to adulthood.

Apart from national traditions, there have been historical changes in investment in children and youth.[19] Coleman has described three phases for societal investment in youth.[20] The first phase entails the use and frequently economic exploitation of children by subsistence-level families. Phase two involves familial investment in children as a resource for the future. Marginalization of children characterizes phase three, when families no longer need children for economic well-being and the role of families is reduced to that of child rearing. In phase three, Coleman argues, schools are important for supplying social capital in order to produce the human capital that society needs, taking the place of the role previously occupied by families. This entire characterization, and especially phase three, is likely to generate considerable debate.

Of interest to us here is that the examples of Germany and the United States have created very different models for schooling to achieve what are presumably similar societal goals. Whereas schools in the United States operate as "command economies," providing the opportunity to gain a general education,[21] school opportunities in the Federal Republic of Germany (FRG) are more explicitly linked to particular students and to occupations. We turn now to the organization of schools in these two countries.

SCHOOLING ARRANGEMENTS

GERMANY

The current policy for youth in West Germany is based on the Federal Youth Plan of 1950. Both schooling and vocational education are integrated into personal and professional development for youth. Schooling in Germany is the responsibility of the several states.[22] Students must attend school full-time for at least nine years in most states, ten in the remainder, and then at least part-time for two to three additional years (in combination with work experience).

In the mid-1980s, 73 percent of the men and 64 percent of the women in the cohort age 26–35 years had received some sort of vocational training.[23] In this same cohort, 13 percent of the men and 11 percent of the women had attended university or college. This difference in vocational versus higher or postsecondary education suggests that vocational training is viewed as more important to the society than is a university education. Vocational training and the placement of apprentices are the responsibility of the Federal Employment Services.

The choice of school type is based primarily on a formal proposal from primary school teachers. If parents object to this proposal, the student may take a two-week examination administered by a neutral board of teachers. Occupational Preparation School (*Hauptschule*) completes compulsory education and prepares students for blue-collar occupations; 30 percent of students are selected into this type of school. Intermediate School (*Realschule*) provides a middle level of education as a basis for higher-level training in nonacademic white-collar occupations; 25 percent are selected for this track, of whom 53 percent are women. Grammar school (*Gymnasium*) is the school track required for admission into the university; this is the choice of 30 percent of the students, half of them women. A newer school type, available only in some areas, is the comprehensive school (*Gesamtschule*); only 10 percent attend this type and students are tracked within this school, with tracking based on teachers' records and recommendations. Of the remaining 5 percent, 1 percent are in private schools and 4 percent attend special schools for the disabled.[24]

About 90 percent of students in the first two school types—occupation preparation school and intermediate school—pursue vocational training. Intermediate-school graduates may go to senior technical schools for more specific training in a field. On graduation from these two types of school, 25 percent are fully credentialed while the remainder continue on to apprenticeships or technical school.

Because of the early age at school tracking, the resulting tracks tend to be based primarily on parental social status.[25] Nevertheless, there has been dramatic historical change in the percentage of students attending grammar school and continuing to higher education, from 6 percent in the early 1950s to 22 percent in the early 1980s and 32 percent in the early 1990s. This trend reflects a dramatic shift away from apprenticeship and toward an academic, college-bound track. There are no fees for a college education.

Although in principle no student in the non-college tracks (some 68 percent of all students) enters work without vocational training, in fact, 10 percent fail to receive such training. This small group includes some who choose no training and some who could not find training places because they lack appropriate school credentials, or lack credentials for available work options. Almost one-third of them are children of foreign workers (workers hired from poorer countries for low-level jobs unwanted by Germans).

The so-called dual system for apprenticeships provides on-the-job learning four days a week, with one day at vocational school. Most jobs in Germany fall into this system, which includes industry and commerce (46 percent), trades (41 percent), professional positions (7 percent), public administration (3 percent), and agriculture (3 percent). Training costs are paid by employers and include training stipends to apprentices, which range from 20–40 percent of the initial wages of a skilled worker and increase over the two to three-and-a-half years of training. Apprentices are drawn 60 percent from occupational preparation schools, 30 percent from intermediate schools, and 5 percent from grammar schools.[26]

UNITED STATES

In the United States, the dominant model for education at the high school level is the comprehensive school. A small and declining percentage of students attend vocational schools. Variations exist in the grade spans in a school, but most adolescents attend high schools that include grades 9–12. Middle-grades education is more variable, with junior high schools (grades 7–8 or 7–9) and middle schools (grades 5–8 or 6–8, typically) about equally common; a small and declining percentage attend grammar schools extending from kindergarten through eighth grade.[27]

Although the United States has no system of tracking into types of schools, schooling is frequently homogeneous relative to social class because of the neighborhood basis of schools and local taxation systems. Despite the attempts to reduce this social stratification of schooling in the 1970s, most adolescents in the United States today receive their education with others of similar class.

A second factor that reinforces social stratification is tracking within schools. Most high schools track students into groups that take different curriculums that function in ways similar to the school tracks in Germany. Indeed, it has been argued that only college-bound students have any incentive to achieve in high school because employers ignore the level of high school achievement and only request evidence of the diploma marking high school completion.[28]

Class rank, high school grades, and test performance all affect the colleges to which one is admitted and may influence whether financial assistance is provided for college fees. Therefore, college-bound students are given incentives for achievement in high school.

Work-bound students have no similar incentives.[29] Aptitude, class rank, course grades, and other school information have little relationship to employment, job attainment, and wages of high school graduates who enter the work force directly.[30] Interestingly, in Japan and in Germany, course grades have large effects on jobs.[31] Although some studies find that vocational schools provide better access to jobs,[32] most studies find no difference.[33]

In recent data, 85 percent of youth in the United States earn the high school diploma and about 50 percent continue on to postsecondary education. (Estimates of college completion rates vary broadly depending on the number of years allowed for completion; one-fourth of each high school graduating class ultimately obtains a baccalaureate degree.[34]) Despite the predominance of the comprehensive high school in the United States and the requirement of at least a high school diploma for most jobs, the mission of the high school is still seen as college preparation.[35] Although the mission has broadened throughout the twentieth century,[36] college-preparatory classes receive more material and human resources.[37] There is also evidence that whereas more than 80 percent of college-track students go on to college, less than 5 percent of those in the non-college tracks do so.[38] Beyond these quantifiable differences, the quality of instruction in the lower tracks is considered to be inferior.[39]

COMPARISONS OF THE TWO SYSTEMS

Cross-national data suggest that average educational attainments are higher in Germany than in the United States.[40] Do the two different systems account for these differences? The U.S. system has been characterized as one of "contest mobility" whereas the West German school system's competition is more a form of "sponsored mobility,"[41] realized through early allocation to one of the different school tracks varying in the future prospects they offer. Such early, career-influencing "branching points" take effect at the beginning of the initial secondary stage by assigning individual students, on the basis of institutional recommendations and parents' wishes, to different forms of secondary school. These forms have been described as a "sponsored mobility system, in that once the branching point has been reached, the rest of the student's career is set, and the student who passes this point is sponsored through successive levels without much attrition."[42] Since the tracks afford different postscholastic career opportunities and since there is little between-track mobility after the first assignment, it is rational for the family to pursue a track that will ensure the child's long-term career prospects. Consequently, this form of institutionalized mobility heavily affects the social-recruitment processes into secondary school tracks and, hence, permanently shapes the school context and the classroom community in terms of family background characteristics. The higher the family status, the greater the probability that the family's children will attend the type of secondary school offering the best postscholastic career prospects, which is the grammar school (*Gymnasium*). The lower and middle classes are concentrated in the school tracks leading to occupations with the lowest future income and status opportunities (*Hauptschule* and *Realschule*).

Though the German system is not completely fixed, the secondary school type to which the student is assigned largely determines the student's ultimate career destination. Attendance at the *Hauptschule* or the *Realschule* limits the range of options significantly in the higher levels of the system.[43] In contrast, the U.S. school system is characterized by a full-scope contest mobility with limited selection of school types except with the private, college-preparatory school option, typically with significant tuition costs. Almost all adolescents in the United States attend schools with college-bound and non-college-bound students. Because public school budgets are largely supported by school district taxes, however, location of a family's residence becomes a factor in the quality of schooling received. A recent national study of schooling opportunities found that there are not equal opportunities across race, class, and locale in the United States for a good education in science and mathematics.[44] Similarly, a recent study of middle-grades schools found that better schooling practices were less frequent in disadvantaged schools.[45] Although there has been a great deal of attention in the United States to providing equality of opportunity, through practices in some communities such as busing and giving parents choice of school selection rather than restricting schools by house location, the children themselves are not yet receiving equal opportunities. Contest mobility describes the intent of the school system in the United States but not the reality, because the contest is not yet held on a level playing field.

An important point of divergence from the U.S. school system is that secondary schools in the Federal Republic of Germany are strictly academic institutions. Classes meet until early afternoon and then pupils go home for lunch and to do their homework. Activities that take place in secondary schools in the United States (e.g., "extracurricular" activities such as athletics, clubs, music, theater) are conspicuously absent. Neighborhood organizations, rather than schools, sponsor such activities. The system of guidance and counseling in cases of behavior disorders has a very limited presence in comparison to the United States.[46] These differences have implications for both family and community life for adolescents. To our knowledge, these dramatic differences in school hours and the services provided by schools have not been examined.

The Federal Republic of Germany is characterized by a continuing commitment to the belief that there is a societal responsibility for the vocational preparation of its youth. This commitment is manifested in both the differentiated secondary school system and the dual system of vocational training in which enrolled adolescents, after completion of secondary school, combine training as apprentices in business, trades, and industry with part-time attendance in vocational schools financed and run by the states (*Lander*). The apprenticeship (*Lehrstelle*) part of vocational training takes place in both privately owned and state-owned and operated enterprises. These apprenticeships provide the primary access to the labor market for those students who do not attend a university.

Since the middle seventies in Germany, because of tight employment, the higher-level school careers are in even more demand. All parts of the population have endeavored to provide their children with the best position for professional careers. This has led to the development of explicit strategies for "optimizing" future careers in which members of all social classes use the material, social, and cultural resources at their disposal to compete for desired outcomes.[47]

In contrast, there is no clear "system" in the United States that maps secondary education onto career paths.[48] Even youth who complete high school do not achieve career-entry positions until their early to mid-twenties. For those adolescents who drop out of high school, the job prospects are even dimmer. Interestingly, the U.S. research literature on the transition to work has, until recently, focused on occupational choice and individual characteristics influencing these choices.[49] The available opportunities received relatively little attention until the more recent emphasis on disadvantaged youth.

Part-time work while attending secondary school is common in the United States, but studies show that these jobs do not track into careers, and the expected benefits for developing job-relevant skills appear not to emerge for most young people.[50] Further, the life-styles available to youth with more disposable income earned at part-time jobs appear to entail significant health risk and decrease the likelihood that further education will be pursued.[51] Therefore, part-time work in the United States does not appear to constitute a substitute for the apprenticeship model prevalent in Germany.

Some states in the United States do have more effective links between school and work. In Minnesota, for example, vocational high schools and postsecondary institutions provide a real alternative to the normative academic courses. In addition, there are active programs of apprenticeship and on-the-job training combined with education. Co-op programs involving work experience combined with pursuit of a college degree are also prevalent.

SCHOOL STRUCTURE AND SOCIAL DISADVANTAGE

Several evaluation studies have tackled the question of whether the comprehensive school in Germany has succeeded in decreasing social disadvantage. The results from all studies are very clear: In comprehensive schools, working-class children reach higher levels more often than in the traditional school system. Social selection, however, has not yet altogether disappeared in comprehensive schools, although it has been considerably reduced. The studies of Fend, where intelligence was controlled for, are particularly interesting. They showed that only 10 percent of working-class children with an IQ of more than 100 were admitted to the *Gymnasium* at ninth grade; in contrast, 36 percent of middle-class children did so.[52] Therefore, social origin more than individual ability decides who can take part in a "higher" level of education in the traditional schools. When intelligence is held constant, the connection between social strata and achievement level almost disappears. Those who gain most from the comprehensive school system, then, are working-class children who can develop their abilities fully in a more open and contest-oriented system.

Thus, the open, contest system of schooling in the United States should stimulate the learning activities of students from working-class and minority families more than does the German system of sponsored mobility. The effects of social stratification on attainment processes should be much more expressed in Germany than in the United States. Studies in the United States, however, would suggest that neighborhood effects and discrimination prevent the United States school system from achieving this potential.[53] As discussed earlier, the tracking system in the United States is similar to the German system in its effects on student attainment.

Because the tracked system of separate schools and the system of comprehensive schools in Germany exist side-by-side, interesting comparisons of the effects of the different systems are possible. Fend and colleagues compared comprehensive schools with schools having the traditional systems. This study encompassed 6,600 students and used a quasi-experimental design matching each comprehensive school with a group of traditional schools (*Hauptschule, Realschule, Gymnasium*). The study shows that homogeneous achievement grouping in comprehensive schools offers the possibility of postponing decisions about future careers until the ninth or even the tenth grade. Thus, the comprehensive school can make use of these organizational advantages. Fend showed that comprehensive schools offers the possibility for students to change their minds about careers, depending on changes over time in their academic achievement. A change of 10 percent of the academic careers of the traditional school system compares with a change of 30 percent in comprehensive schools. This mobility favors most those children for whom low academic attainment was predicted by the end of primary school. Of those students who entered the *Hauptschule* after primary school, only 18 percent attained a certificate at the end of the tenth grade, which is higher than one normally gets in the *Hauptschule*; 46 percent of the students who were categorized as being suitable for the *Hauptschule* attained, in the comprehensive school, a tenth-grade certificate. In other words, every second student in comprehensive school who, at the end of the fourth grade, was predicted for no more than a ninth-grade leaving certificate could do better; within the traditional school system only every fifth student did better.[54]

As far as we know, there are no studies available that compare the achievement levels and the effects of different aspects of schooling in the two countries directly. However, judging from a recent comparison of the German and the British school system,[55] which is mainly a contest system like that of the United States, we can cautiously speculate on the following effects:

> The German schooling system provides a broader curriculum, combined with higher levels of mathematical and mother-language attainment, for a greater portion of the students than does the U.S. system; the differences are particularly marked at the lower half of the ability range, where the achievement level is higher in Germany.

> German schools provide more prevocational instruction than do U.S. schools, with a definite commercial and industrial emphasis; this difference again particularly affects the lower half of the ability range (based on teachers' judgments) and gives them some preparation for the occupation market.
>
> Only about a tenth of all students in Germany leave school without a certificate attesting to the satisfactory completion of their studies covering a broad range of basic subjects. This contrasts with the United States, where the figure for dropouts is about 20 percent.

These achievements are accompanied by comparable resources in Germany and the United States: Pupil-teacher ratios are similar and the proportion of gross domestic product absorbed by education seems to be almost equal. However, curricula are more sharply focused in the tripartite German system. The U.S. school system pays much more attention to the developmental and social needs of adolescents.

IMPLICATIONS FOR THE FUTURE

There is general agreement that future work forces must be more skilled than their predecessors.[56] Few of today's school-leavers will escape the consequences of inadequate preparation.[57] There are several aspects to the rise in skill requirements. The situation is not simply that an increasing proportion of jobs will be at traditionally skilled levels. Skilled jobs themselves are becoming more skilled than in the past. The most rapid current growth in employment is not in traditional crafts but at the technology-dependent technical and professional levels. Moreover, there are important qualitative differences between traditional and new skills. Most important is the need for adaptability. Adaptability is required by the increasing pace of technological change, which means that the size and shape of successful firms, and the requirements of specific jobs within them, will change more rapidly than in the past. It is not new technology itself that imposes these requirements so much as competitive pressures that require firms either to exploit all the capabilities of the latest technologies, or fail.

In terms of the system's ability to cope with the trends and pressures of the 1970s and 1980s, there is no doubt that Germany's dual system proved to be effective. The main challenges in that period were posed by recessions and the growing size of school-leaving cohorts. In the Federal Republic of Germany, virtually all young people could be accommodated through higher retention rates in education and a parallel expansion of the apprentice system. Youth unemployment rates throughout Europe appear to reflect the nature of schooling and attention to the school-work transition.[58] We note, however, that the German system reduced, to some extent, youth unemployment by transferring joblessness to an older age group. It also would be wise to consider future needs in planning youth education, as any system's ability to respond to the crises of the past is no guarantee that it will meet future challenges.

Indeed, the stresses of recession and the population increases in the 1970s and 1980s could have concealed some longer-term problems in Germany. There has been a trend among young West Germans away from the dual system toward remaining full-time students on the academic route to higher education. Approximately 35 percent now follow this route, at least until age eighteen or nineteen. There has also been a steady decrease in the numbers attending *Hauptschulen*, the traditional base for apprenticeship, and a corresponding rise in the number attending *Gymnasia* and *Realschulen*. The attractions of the more academic types of education are clear enough; the academic trajectory leads to the most rewarding jobs in terms of status, pay, and promotion prospects. As the size of the youth cohort decreases, and as increasing skill requirements strengthen employers' appetites for highly qualified recruits, including those with the Abitur (the degree from the *Gymnasium*), the Federal Republic of Germany's dual system could become locked in a downward spiral, deserted by young people and employers alike. The traditional route of *Hauptschule* to an apprenticeship in the dual system would then be seen as inferior, taken only by those at the bottom end of the educational scale.

Of course, the dual system still commands tremendous domestic confidence and international admiration, and up to now these have been among the system's special assets. Germany's employers have been and remain willing to train and to recognize the qualifications that young people earn. Trade unions wish to preserve and strengthen the system. For their part, German school-leavers continue to regard apprentice training as a desirable route into working life. Many still regard it as the best of all possible starts. Parents similarly endorse it as a valued stepping-stone to employment. Many *Gymnasium* graduates opt for apprentice training either prior to or in preference to entering higher education.

Apprenticeship has been and is still considered a necessary stage in the transition to adulthood for younger German school-leavers. Americans have a similar regard to graduating from high school. We suspect that this regard for formal training would survive in Germany even if all regulatory bodies and legal recognition of qualifications were scrapped. Our surveys show that the standard response of West Germans on reaching age sixteen is still to seek an apprenticeship. Some of Hurrelmann's study respondents had returned to education only because they were unable to obtain suitable apprenticeships.[59] The prospect of gaining an apprenticeship made staying on in vocational secondary schools for an extra year seem worthwhile. These attitudes underpin the West German training system. They have given it a solidity and resilience, and blend into a training culture that is among the nation's assets.

However, recent surveys tapped latent dissatisfaction, even frustration.[60] Most of the young Germans who had sought apprenticeships had made multiple applications. Many of the young Germans were eventually settling for training in occupations and with firms that the individuals considered second- or third-best. This was because many had lost out in the competition for high-grade apprenticeships with their more qualified contemporaries. It is true that very few apprentices voiced overall dissatisfaction with their training, but this seemed partly a product of a general willingness to come to terms with reality. Many of the German apprentices felt that their training allowances were unjustly low.

On reaching the end of their compulsory schooling, young Germans cannot be confident about their occupational destinies. They cannot rely even on obtaining the apprenticeship of their choice. In any case, many do not proceed to practice the occupations in which they are initially trained. The entire system depends on young people's confidence that the system will deliver what they want. Up to now they have been prepared to accept what they have been offered, usually the dual system, and have relied on this route to shape and deliver their future prospects.

The fact that *all* the German apprentices in this survey were confident of completing their training successfully raises further queries about standards. Americans ask similar questions of their high schools and colleges. Is Germany's education and training sufficiently demanding to satisfy future skill requirements? Certainly up to age sixteen the majority of German young people perform consistently better than their American counterparts on standard achievement tests. But is this carried through sufficiently into vocational training? Young people have to master prescribed skills and pass examinations in order to qualify. This ensures minimum standards and quality control. Apart from the danger of curricula being outdated by the pace of technological and occupational change, there could be an overemphasis on specific skills at the expense of nurturing the flexible capacities that are increasingly required. These problems have now been addressed in engineering training, but there are many other areas, such as the building trades, where reforms have proved more difficult to achieve. The German emphasis on "recognized" training and "formal" qualifications can make the system vulnerable to the "diploma disease," where qualifications are required and provide access to occupations even when they do not measure their holders' ability to perform competently. Meanwhile, individuals with uncertified talent are held back.

Another question for Germany concerns the absence of "respectable" routes into nonskilled work. The routes where such jobs were the most likely outcome were filled by young people who were there not by choice, but as a result of failing on other trajectories, or their inability to obtain anything else. In the Federal Republic of Germany such young people are a small minority, analogous to high school dropouts in North America. Rising skill requirements could leave this disadvantaged minority lagging further behind. Yet even the most technologically advanced economies will continue to generate unskilled jobs in manufacturing and, in particular, in service industries. During recent decades such jobs have been rejected by native-born adult males in most Western countries. If locally educated young people are to be channeled into these positions, both the routes and the occupations may have to be upgraded.

Finally, the German dual system is based on early choices in an educational career—between *Gymnasium*, *Hauptschule*, and *Realschule*. The routes from these different secondary schools are becoming more blurred as pressures for access to a variety of post-sixteen routes build up and traditional pathways close. It is difficult to see how any major reforms to the Federal Republic of Germany dual system can take place without reviewing, and if necessary overhauling, what precedes it as well.

Germany, like Austria, Switzerland, and other European countries, appears to have made a sound decision in the 1960s to retain the apprenticeship system rather than to expand the university system, as happened in the United States and other countries.[61] Although the dual system has some problems, it has provided a clear pathway to adult work roles for a much larger percentage of the population. Another advantage of the linkage between school and work may be the stronger investment by adults in youth. We may question, however, which is the chicken and which the egg in relationship between societal investment in youth and an apprenticeship system. In any case, there is ample evidence in the United States of an inadequate investment in youth.[62]

It is difficult to compare two national systems because of the many variables involved. For example, does the relative homogeneity of German society make their system work there? What is the effect of cost? In Germany, all education is free, whereas postsecondary education has at least some cost at all institutions in the United States. Does this factor have an effect on choices made by or for adolescents?

Can we recommend one system over the other? That depends. There can be no doubt that the German system is much more effective at providing youth with skills that permit them to enter the work force. The prestige historically attached to apprenticeship attracts young people to the *Hauptschule*/apprenticeship route—the dual system. It is non-college-bound youth who are less well served by the U.S. system. A skilled labor force would seem to require much more than is currently provided to this half of the youth population in the United States.

Although we recognize the merits of the German system for those not pursuing postsecondary education, we also noted its limitations. It does involve more rigid tracking into careers, with the assumption that the choice of a career is made for life. Increasingly, it is clear that career flexibility and mobility are needed, requiring a solid academic background and beginning skills in a specific area but recognizing the need for more continual learning over the life course. Careful attention to an appropriate balance between the labor force needs of the society *and* the developmental needs of individuals is called for.

Notes

1 Anne C. Petersen, "Adolescent Development," in *Annual Review of Psychology*, ed. M. R. Rosenzweig (Palo Alto: Annual Reviews, 1988), pp. 583-607.

2 See W. A. Marshall and J. M. Tanner, "Variations in the Pattern of Pubertal Changes in Girls," *Archives of Diseases in Childhood* 44 (1969): 291-303; and idem, "Variations in the Pattern of Pubertal Changes in Boys," *Archives of Diseases in Childhood* 45 (1970): 13-23.

3 One notable exception to this general similarity differentiates Germany from the United States and some other Western European countries: Whereas early-maturing girls appear to have some difficulties in most countries, presumably because they develop the normal fat distribution of mature women, which contrasts with the lean and long-legged ideal, early-maturing girls in Germany (specifically Berlin) had positive body- and self-images (see R. K. Silbereisen et al., "Maturational Timing and the Development of Problem Behavior: Longitudinal Studies in Adolescence," *Journal of Early Adolescence* 9 [1989]: 247-68). Apart from this exception, that nature of developmental progressions and processes in cognitive, psychological, and social development appear to be similar cross-nationally, at least in early (10-14 years) and middle adolescence (15-17 years).

4 Jurgen Mansel and Klaus Hurrelmann, *Jugendliche im Alltagstreb* (Weinheim: Juvena, 1991).

5 V. R. Fuchs and D. M. Reklis, "America's Children: Economic Perspectives and Policy Options," *Science* 225 (1992): 41-46.

6 Mavis Hetherington, "Presidential Address: Families, Lies, and Videotapes," *Journal of Research on Adolescence* 1 (1991): 323-48; and Pamela A. Sarigiani, "A Longitudinal Study of Relationship Adjustment of Young Adults from Divorced and Nondivorced Families" (Ph.D. diss., The Pennsylvania State University, 1990).

7 K. Allerbeck and W. Hoag, *Jugend ohne Zukunft* (Munchen: Piper, 1985).

8 Anne C. Petersen, Nina White, and Mark Stemmler, "Familial Risk and Protective Factors Influencing Adolescent Mental Health" (Paper presented at a symposium at the biennial meeting of the Society for Research in Child Development, Seattle, Washington, 1991).

9 B. Bradford Brown, "Peer Groups and Peer Culture," in *At the Threshold: The Developing Adolescent*, ed. S. S. Feldman and G. R. Elliott (Cambridge: Harvard University Press, 1990), pp. 171-96.

10 D. Baacke, *Die 13-18 Jahrigen* (Weinheim: Beltz, 1991).

11 Ellen Greenberger and Laurence Steinberg, *When Teenagers Work: The Psychological and Social Costs of Adolescent Employment* (New York: Basic Books, 1986).

12 J. Zinnecker, *Jugendkultur 1940-1985* (Opladen: Leske and Budrick, 1987).

13 Brown, "Peer Groups and Peer Culture."

14 See Lisa Crockett and Anne C. Petersen, "Biological and Psychosocial Development during Adolescence," in *Promoting Adolescent Health*, ed. S. G. Millstein, A. C. Petersen, and E. O. Nightingale (New York: Oxford University Press, in press); and K. Hurrelmann and F. Losel, eds. *Health Hazards in Adolescence* (Berlin: DeGruyter, 1990).

15 Laura E. Hess and Anne C. Petersen, "Narrowing the Margins: Adolescent Unemployment and the Lack of a Social Role" (Paper prepared for the World Scout Bureau, 1991).

16 See, for example, S. L. Hofferth and C. D. Hayes, eds., *Risking the Future: Adolescent Sexuality, Pregnancy, and Childbearing, Volume 1: Working Papers and Statistical Reports* (Washington, D.C.: National Academy Press, 1987); and Crockett and Petersen, "Biological and Psychosocial Development during Adolescence."

17 Lynne Chisholm and Jean-Marie Bergeret, "Young People in the European Community: Towards an Agenda for Research and Policy" (Paper prepared on behalf of the Commission of the European Communities, June 1991).

18 Ibid., p. 4.

19 See, for example, P. Aries, *Centuries of Childhood* (New York: Knopf, 1962).

20 James S. Coleman, "Social Capital, Human Capital, and Investment in Youth," in *Youth, Unemployment, and Society*, ed. A. C. Petersen and J. Mortimer (New York: Cambridge University Press, in press).

21 Ibid.

22 Rosemarie George, *Youth Policies and Programs in Selected Countries* (Washington, D.C.: The William T. Grant Foundation, 1987).

23 Ibid.

24 Klaus Hurrelmann, "The Importance of School in the Life Course: Results from the Bielefeld Study on School-Related Problems in Adolescence," *Journal of Adolescent Research* 2 (1987): 111–25; and H. E. Rolff et al., eds., *Jahrbuch der Schulentwicklung*, Vol. 5 (Weinheim: Jarenta, 1988).

25 George, *Youth Policies and Programs in Selected Countries*.

26 S. F. Hamilton, *Apprenticeship for Adulthood* (New York: The Free Press, 1990).

27 Joyce Epstein and Douglas J. MacIver, *Education in the Middle Grades: National Practices and Trends* (Columbus, Ohio: National Middle School Association, 1990).

28 James E. Rosenbaum, "Are Adolescent Problems Caused by School or Society," *Journal of Research on Adolescence* 1 (1991): 301–22.

29 Ibid.

30 J. L. Griffin, K. L. Alexander, and A. L. Kalleberg, "Determinants of Early Labor Market Entry and Attainment: A Study of Labor Market Augmentation," *Sociology of Education* 54 (1981): 206–21; R. H. Meyer and D. A. Wise, "High School Preparation and Early Labor Force Experience," in *The Youth Labor Market Problem*, ed. R. B. Freeman and D. A. Wise (Chicago: University of Chicago Press, 1982); and J. E. Rosenbaum and T. Kariya, "Do School Achievements Affect the Early Jobs of High School Graduates in the United States and Japan?" *Sociology of Education* 64 (1991): 78–95.

31 Hamilton, *Apprenticeship for Adulthood*; and Rosenbaum and Kariya, "Do School Achievements Affect the Early Jobs?"

32 See, for example, L. Hotchkiss and L. E. Dorsten, "Curriculum Effects on Early Post-High School Outcomes," in *Research in the Sociology of Education and Socialization*, vol. 7, ed. A. Kerckhoff (New York: JAI Press, 1987), pp. 191–219.

33 See, for example, J. Oakes, *Keeping Track: How Schools Structure Inequality* (New Haven: Yale University Press, 1985).

34 Robert W. Glover and Ray Marshall, "Improving the School-to-Work Transition of American Adolescents," *Teachers College Record* 94 (Spring 1993): 588–610.

35 Rosenbaum, "Are Adolescent Problems Caused by School or Society?"

36 M. Trow, "The Second Transformation of American Secondary Education," *International Journal of Comparative Sociology* 2 (1961): 144–65.

37 B. Heyns, "Selection and Stratification within School," *American Journal of Sociology* 79 (1974): 1434–51; and Oakes, *Keeping Track.*

38 James E. Rosenbaum, *Making Inequality* (New York: Wiley, 1976).

39 See, for example, Oakes, *Keeping Track.*

40 See, for example, S. J. Prais and K. Wagner, "Schooling Standards in England and Germany: Some Summary Comparisons Bearing on Economic Performance," *National Institute of Economic Review*, May 1985, pp. 53–76.

41 R. H. Turner, "Sponsored and Contest Mobility and the School System," *American Sociological Review* 25 (1960): 855–67.

42 Randall Collins, "The Credential Society," in *The Forgotten Half: Non-College Youth in America*, The William T. Grant Foundation Commission on Work, Family, and Citizenship, (Washington, D.C.: The William T. Grant Foundation, 1988), p. 91.

43 Max-Planck-Institut fur Bildungsforsehung, *Bildung in der Bundesrepublik* (Reinbek: Rowohlt, 1990).

44 Jeannie Oakes, *Multiplying Inequalities: The Effects of Race, Social Class, and Tracking on Opportunities to Learn Mathematics and Science* (Santa Monica, Calif.: Rand Corporation, 1990).

45 Epstein and MacIver, *Education in the Middle Grades.*

46 Hamilton, *Apprenticeship for Adulthood.*

47 P. Bourdieu, *Distinction: A Social Critique of the Judgment of Taste* (London: Routledge & Kegan Paul, 1984); and Klaus Hurrelmann and Uwe Engel, eds., *The Social World of Adolescents: International Perspectives* (Berlin: DeGruyter, 1989).

48 See, for example, The William T. Grant Foundation Commission on Work, Family, and Citizenship, *The Forgotten Half.*

49 J. T. Mortimer, "Social Class, Work, and Family: Some Implications of the Father's Occupation for Family Relationships and Son's Career Decisions," *Journal of Marriage and the Family* 38 (1976): 241–54; and S. H. Osipow, *Theories of Career Development*, 2nd ed. (Englewood Cliffs, N.J.: Prentice-Hall, 1973).

50 Greenberger and Steinber, *When Teenagers Work.*

51 Hess and Petersen, "Narrowing the Margins."

52 H. Fend, *Gesamtschule im Vergleich. Bilanz der Ergbnisse des Gesamtschulversuchs* (Weinheim: Beltz, 1982).

53 Oakes, *Keeping Track.*

54 Fend, *Gesamtschule im Vergleich. Bilanz der Ergbnisse des Gesamtschulversuchs.*

55 J. Bynner and K. Roberts, eds., *Youth and Work: Transition to Employment in England and Germany* (London: Anglo-German Foundation, 1991).

56 See, for example, Glover and Marshall, "Improving the School-to-Work Transition of American Adolescents."

57 Bynner and Roberts, *Youth and Work.*

58 Michael White and David J. Smith, "The Determinants of Unemployment," in *Youth, Unemployment, and Society*, ed. A. C. Petersen and J. Mortimer (New York: Cambridge University Press, in press).

59 Hurrelmann, "The Importance of School in the Life Course."

60 Bynner and Roberts, *Youth and Work: Transitions to Employment in England and Germany.*

61 H. Bertram, "Youth: Work and Unemployment," in *Youth, Unemployment and Society*, ed. Petersen and Mortimer.

62 See, for example, Fuchs and Reklis, "America's Children."

Adolescents and the Mass Media: From "Leave It to Beaver" to "Beverly Hills 90210"

DONALD F. ROBERTS
Stanford University

"Rising to the Challenge," a video produced by the Parents' Music Resource Center to warn about dangers to adolescents inherent in violent and sexually explicit music videos, opens with excerpts from "Sesame Street."[1] Images of muppets and preschoolers flash by as a narrator proclaims that "Sesame Street" has "proven" that music, words, and images are powerful teachers of children. Attention then switches to scenes from several relatively horrific, heavy-metal music videos that either suggest or explicitly portray sex, rape, violence, drug use, and other objectionable activities. A question that serves as a constant refrain throughout the video frames the juxtaposition of these two kinds of scenes: "At what age does a child cease to learn from music, words, and images?"

Obviously the question functions less as interrogatory than as rhetorical device. Learning from music, words, and images continues throughout life; survival of the species probably depends on it.

But the rhetorical question is instructive in its obvious presumption that exposure to "negative" media images is synonymous with negative audience effects. Similarly instructive is the pairing of the question with shots of children who have clearly fallen prey to such negative images. Leather- and lace-clad, prepubescent Madonna-wannabees grin for the camera; sweaty, glassy-eyed, teenaged, rock-concert audiences strain maniacally to touch, perhaps embrace, equally maniacal heavy-metal musicians. The point, of course, is that children and adolescents are viewed as particularly likely to be influenced by mass media messages.

Both themes—that "objectionable" media messages (be they visual images, sound bites, printed slogans, or rock lyrics) teach objectionable beliefs and behaviors and that young people are particularly vulnerable to such messages—have a long history. Steven Starker's *Evil Influences* presents a fascinating catalogue of critical comment about the dangers to youth (and also to adults) of mediated messages of any kind, comment that predates even the introduction of movable type.[2] Unhappiness with the potential for each new communication technology to wreak havoc on youth begins at least as early as Plato's banishing of storytellers in his *Republic* and progresses through various justifications for bowdlerizing such works as *Grimm's Fairy Tales* and various eighteenth- and nineteenth-century novels to more recent condemnations of film, radio, comic books, and television. Similarly, beginning with studies of motion pictures and youth sponsored by the Payne Fund in the 1930s, and continuing still, concern with negative effects on children, concern that mediated messages will teach them to be violent or prejudiced or materialistic, or to engage in casual sex or drug use, or to develop gender stereotypes, has motivated most scientific research in this area.[3]

But what has that research shown us, particularly about adolescents and the mass media? Given that it goes almost without saying that teenagers learn from mass media—as they did when they were children and as they will when they are adults—what does the empirical evidence have to say about the degree to which mass media operate as a force for good or ill in adolescent lives? Particularly, given today's concerns, what does the research say about the influence of violence and sex in the media on adolescents?

Such questions require confronting two commonly held, albeit questionable, public beliefs. One characterizes adolescence as a period of continuous *storm and stress*, persistent turmoil and conflict, which the average teenager is fortunate to survive. The other holds that mass media engender *massive effects*, immediately, directly, similarly—and usually negatively—influencing an audience's knowledge, attitudes, and behavior. Such beliefs, of course, are the stuff of popular discourse. General-interest magazines, radio talk shows, television specials, parent-teacher discussions, all tend to promulgate views of turbulent teenage years and of manipulative, almost irresistible mass media. But if we turn from newspaper and magazine headlines or televised "special reports" to look at empirical research on either topic, neither characterization seems quite so clear-cut.

ON ADOLESCENCE

A long history of classical theorizing about adolescence, coupled with the news media's taste for conflict and "bad news" (e.g., teen pregnancy, suicide, drug use), contributes to popular treatment of the teen years as a period of persistent turmoil and conflict—years of identity crises, generation gaps, anxiety, and difficult and persistent family strife. While it is true that many individuals do encounter major problems as they navigate the years between ten and twenty, and that almost all teenagers experience some difficulty with some of the tasks of adolescence, little of the research literature supports a *Sturm und Drang* characterization.

At the Threshold: The Developing Adolescent, Shirley Feldman and Glen Elliott's recent collection of research reviews, suggests that although the dominant characteristic of adolescence is change—change in physical, social, emotional, and intellectual functioning—there is scant evidence of unrelenting family conflict and dramatic, debilitating crises.[4] Of course conflicts emerge, but these tend to concern less fundamental issues: dating, tidiness, punctuality, and leisure activities, including use of and apparent responses to the mass media. Generally, however, considerable intergenerational continuity exists between most parents and their adolescent children in fundamental values concerning morality, marriage and sex, race, and religious and political orientations.

Reification of "adolescent" (e.g., "the average adolescent," "the typical teen") adds to the problem by leading to assumptions that all adolescents think, act, develop, and respond to mass media in the same way. Nothing could be further from the truth. Change may be the hallmark of adolescence, but it is change marked by great variety in form and outcome.

Most theories of adolescent development recognize a number of central issues or tasks that each youngster must address—forming an identity, developing a positive body image, acquiring and honing formal problem-solving capabilities and autonomous moral reasoning, more completely defining gender roles and cross-gender relationships, achieving independence from family and from other adults, establishing workable peer relations, preparing for future occupational, family, and civic roles, and so on. Although almost all adolescents deal with each of these issues, they do so in no particular order and at no particular time. Some work on cross-gender relationships before they confront issues of independence from adult authority, while others reverse the sequence; some confront cross-gender relationships as early as the end of primary school, while for others the issue emerges late in the high school or even college years.

It is also evident that whenever an adolescent faces a particular issue, it can almost "consume" him or her in the sense that it simultaneously creates a deep thirst for information about the task of the moment and a filter that influences interpretations of perceived events and messages. Consider, for example, a thirteen-year-old girl who has discovered boys and a sixteen-year-old boy working on establishing independence from parental authority. Each seeks information about his or her task from any available source, including the mass media; each is quite likely to respond differently to the same message depending on his or her concern. Thus, a television portrayal of a youth arguing with parents about dating may be about authority to the boy and about true love to the girl. Finally, adolescents confront these developmental tasks just as they begin to reason independently and just as parental and other adult controls on information seeking in general and media use in particular begin to weaken—increasing the media's importance as an information source.

ON MASS-MEDIA EFFECTS

The second popular notion holds that mass media exert powerful influences on masses of people. However, William McGuire, in an insightful paper entitled "The Myth of Massive Media Impact," concludes that empirical research on media effects fails to support a massive impact model.[5] If we construe "massive" effect to mean that large numbers of people respond to a particular message (advertisement, program, editorial) all in the same way, then no research demonstrates massive impact. For example, relatively few in the electorate change their vote as a result of political pamphleteering, editorial endorsements, or television advertising. Similarly, most attempts to use mass media to engender social change are more noted for their failures than their successes, and although most of our children view a great many portrayals of crime and violence, relatively few become criminals. And in spite of the folklore, very few people fled the Martian invaders Orson Welles brought to earth in 1938.

This is not to say that mass media engender no effects. Clearly they do, and sometimes they are important and dramatic. Mass media do influence some people to change their vote or to give up smoking or to imitate agression—and some obviously did flee the Martians. Typically, however, only a small portion of any audience responds in the same way. Rather, a given message influences relatively small audience subgroups in a variety of different ways. Massive effects in the sense of similar reactions from most of the audience seldom occur.

McGuire posits several reasons that the massive-effects notion survives in spite of contrary evidence. First, it seems so commonsensical. After all, the reasoning goes, such massive amounts of viewing/listening/reading must engender massive effects. After all, smart people would not expend so much effort to get on television or in the newspaper if it were not important. After all, advertisers and politicians would not spend all that money on advertising if it did not work. Second, maintaining the myth serves the interests of media friends and media foes alike. Buyers and sellers of media time are unlikely to admit to little or no payoff; media critics hesitate to admit to tilting at windmills. A third reason can be added: People tend to notice figure, not ground—change, not stability. That is, we note and remember "consequences" that do occur, not what does not happen. Thus, we attend to the relatively few youngsters who adopt leather and lace in imitation of Madonna, but not to the many who stick with skirts and sweaters; we remember the hundreds who fled Welles's Martians, but forget the millions who sat back and enjoyed the show; we discuss, dissect, and condemn the few who reenacted the Rodney King beating on a hapless truck driver in South-Central Los Angeles, but ignore the tens of thousands who engaged in no beating, no looting, no taking to the streets. In short, we focus on "obvious consequences," regardless of their magnitude, and we ignore "nonconsequences," regardless of their magnitude.

Ultimately, it is unproductive to search for massive media effects. First, such a focus confuses massive with "important." Large numbers need not be implicated to make an effect important, as when a few voters change the outcome of an election. More crucial, particularly when focusing on adolescents, a focus on massive effects ignores differences among audience members, differences that are key to understanding how and why mass media affect people.

CONDITIONAL EFFECTS

Much current media research conceptualizes individual interpretations of, hence responses to, media and messages as essentially constructivist acts. Media supply material out of which individuals construct meanings. Effects depend at least as much on the receiver's attributes as on the form and content of media messages per se. Individuals interpret and respond to messages differently depending on abilities, interests, social relationships, immediate and long-term needs, and expectations about message intent. Thus, rather than examining large, undifferentiated samples of the mass audience and basing inferences about effects on changes in some small portion of the total (e.g., what proportion of viewers used a "hot-line" number to respond to a Planned Parenthood public service announcement broadcast on network television?), recent work attempts to specify sets of attributes or conditions that define theoretically important subgroups, groups that should be particularly responsive to a given medium or message (e.g., what proportion of sexually active teenagers, currently engaged in establishing independence from parental authority, responded to a particular kind of Planned Parenthood PSA broadcast on MTV?).

This conditional approach, with its assumption that individuals respond to messages in terms of a variety of social, psychological, and physical factors, is particularly appropriate in the examination of adolescents and media.[6] If what individuals take from mass media depends significantly on the perspectives, needs, concerns, and abilities each brings to the media, then the evidence of numerous patterns in which different youngsters negotiate adolescent developmental tasks, combined with the way in which each task seems to capture adolescent information seeking and processing, points to the importance of looking for mass-media effects on subgroups of adolescents. The challenge of such a conditional approach is to identify, *a priori*, theoretically interesting conditions and attributes that will locate differential responses within important adolescent subpopulations.[7] Clearly, one important defining dimension of those subgroups consists of the particular developmental task individual youngsters face at any given time.

AN EXAMPLE

Information relevant to most adolescent tasks is readily available in the mass media, often within a single message—small wonder that media engender a multitude of effects, but usually no single, overriding outcome. Several examples, both hypothetical and empirical, illustrate how the needs, concerns, and experiences of different subgroups of adolescents lead them to respond quite differently to the same media message.

Consider *Beverly Hills 90210*, currently one of the most popular television shows among U.S. teens. The central plot of a recent episode focuses on an evolving romantic relationship between a high school boy and girl and their struggle with the girl's parents, who have forbidden them to see each other. Subplots include portrayals of various peer interactions (How do peers relate? Should friends lie for each other?), examination of what holding a job entails, and at least one discussion of the implications and ramifications of the Los Angeles riots. In other words, the episode touches on such adolescent issues as developing cross-gender relationships, establishing independence from parents, peer relationships, occupational roles, civic roles, and more. It is not difficult to imagine how the program can affect different teenagers quite differently, depending on, among other things, the developmental task the viewer currently faces. Adolescents in the throes of establishing independence from parents might interpret the episode in terms of the portrayed parent-child interactions. Others, more involved in exploring cross-gender relationships and perhaps their own sexuality, will respond primarily in terms of how to behave with the opposite sex. Still others may use the program for its advice on how to establish and maintain peer relationships. Clearly, the overall meaning of the show, or the scenes and themes deemed most important, or both, depend on concerns adolescent viewers bring to the screen.

Examinations of responses to Madonna's controversial video "Papa Don't Preach" illustrate similar subgroup differences in responses to a media message. The video portrays a young girl's love affair resulting in pregnancy, and her consequent difficulties telling her father that she plans to keep the baby. "Adult" interpretations range from Ellen Goodman's "a commercial for teenage pregnancy" to a pro-life group's characterization of it as "advocating alternatives to abortion." White college students saw the video as being about the difficulties of teenage pregnancy. African-American students, however, especially females, interpreted "Papa Don't Preach" as primarily concerning male-female and father-daughter relationships, the "focus of the Black viewers . . . on the boy/girl and father/daughter relationships [possibly reflecting] the currently more problematic nature of establishing cross-sex relationships in Black society."[8]

With high school students, the video had more impact among females. Both the nature of their family relationships and their prior pregnancy experiences located clear subgroup differences in responses. Girls whose fathers stressed social harmony in interpersonal relations made significantly more personal connections between the narrative and themselves than did girls whose fathers stressed the importance of exploring ideas at the possible expense of social harmony. Girls who reported they had been pregnant, had experienced a pregnancy scare, or had a friend who had been pregnant were more likely than others to connect the narrative to their own lives.[9]

The issue, then, is not whether mass-media messages affect adolescents. Of course they do. But quite clearly, different adolescents focus on different message elements, interpret messages differently, and ultimately respond in many different ways. Although we may argue about size and importance of any particular effects, the evidence demonstrates that most humans learn from—and sometimes base their behavior on—information obtained from mass media. The appropriate questions, then, do not ask whether mass media affect adolescents; rather, they ask which messages (or parts of messages), under which conditions, affect which perceptions, beliefs, and behaviors among which adolescents.

CONCERN WITH SEX AND VIOLENCE

Although mass media present information relevant to most adolescent developmental tasks, many of which have received at least some research attention, most public concern focuses on the degree to which media messages contribute to negative or antisocial behaviors, particularly in the realms of sex and violence. Given a media system that daily reports or portrays seductions in the hundreds and body-counts in the thousands, and growing public awareness that a significant proportion of our adolescent population daily risks unwanted pregnancy, sexually transmitted diseases, and bodily harm, such concern is not surprising.

There is some irony, however, in both the form and the substance of the ongoing debate about these two issues. In spite of four decades of research producing literally hundreds of empirical studies pointing to a link between media violence and agressive behavior, scholars, politicians, and representatives of the mass media still debate whether there is any *causal* relation between the two. In spite of four decades of questions and debate about the influence of mass media on teenagers' sexual behavior, fewer than a dozen empirical studies directly address the issue (excluding studies of responses to pornography, not generally considered typical media fare). It speaks volumes about American culture that we hesitate to accept indications of a causal linkage between media violence and adolescent aggression, and will not gather the data necessary to examine a linkage between media portrayals of sex and adolescent sexual behavior.

MEDIA AND VIOLENCE

Most media representatives and a few scholars criticize the research on media violence and aggressive behavior, contending that most studies are methodologically flawed in one way or another, and that no studies find that even a substantial plurality of youngsters engage in "real-life" aggression as a result of exposure to media violence. The contention that most studies of media violence suffer from methodological flaws is correct because it characterizes *all* behavioral research. The perfect behavioral study simply does not exist. However, research on effects of media violence is atypical in that there are so many studies using so many different approaches, designs, materials, measures, and even empirical paradigms. The result: The flaws in one study are usually corrected in another. Thus, we can safely say that methodological flaws are not generally replicated across the hundreds of extant studies—but the finding that media violence contributes to adolescent aggressiveness replicates quite consistently.[10]

The second criticism, of course, assumes that *massive* effects must be demonstrated before causal claims are to be taken seriously. However, as we have seen, there exist good theoretical reasons *not* to expect most individuals within a given audience to respond similarly to any particular media content. Moreover, effects that implicate relatively few individuals can be very important. For example, if violence-viewing were shown to increase aggressive behavior in only .1 percent of the almost 30 million adolescents in the United States, we might call such an effect "small," but few would deny its "importance."

Comstock and Paik's *Television and the American Child* examines thirty years of empirical research on the influence of television and film portrayals of violence on adolescent perceptions and behavior.[11] Their argument dovetails nicely with much of the preceding. First, they present evidence that mass media affect behavior by influencing the development of individuals' cognitive scripts, scenaria that roughly guide actions depending on cues operating in some subsequent situation. For example, frequent viewing of police drama may help shape viewer conceptions of how to respond when approached by a real police officer, depending on available cues operating when one is approached. Second, they demonstrate that "susceptibility" to a given message varies dramatically as a function of individual interests, needs, concerns. Third, they document various message characteristics that affect individual interpretations, including the degree to which a behavior is portrayed as efficacious (e.g., is explicitly rewarded or punished), normative (e.g., is justified, congruent with accepted social norms), and pertinent (e.g., is familiar or useful, implicates conditions similar to those of the viewer, addresses issues important to the viewer). Any such message characteristic may influence the likelihood of learning and action depending, of course, on individual differences. Finally, they also argue that effect size, in this case amount of aggressive and antisocial behavior, need not be large in order to qualify for social significance.

Comstock and Paik's conclusions are both convincing and chilling. Taken together, the literally hundreds of relevant studies, with their different approaches, different weaknesses and strengths, and different findings, offer compelling evidence that viewing mass-media portrayals of violence is causally linked to a small but socially significant amount of adolescent aggression. Moreover, the causal linkage pertains at least as strongly to seriously delinquent behavior (e.g., violent assault) as to milder aggressive acts (e.g., verbal abuse, questionnaire responses). Finally, many characteristics of typical media portrayals, from the formulae of straight news reporting to the dramatic conventions by which good guys defeat bad guys in much narrative fiction, facilitate acquisition of precisely the kinds of antisocial behavior about which we are most concerned. In short, although media portrayals of violence are only one among many contributors to aggressive behavior among adolescents, there is solid evidence that for some adolescents under some conditions, viewing violence plays a significant causal role.

MEDIA AND SEX

Inferences about mass-media effects on adolescent sexual beliefs and behaviors require more caution simply because so few studies directly address the issue. Nevertheless, the conditional approach to media effects described above, plus the few studies that do exist and some of the work on young adults' responses to pornography, point to a similar conclusion.

Evidence exists that mass media do influence adolescent and young adult beliefs about sex and sexual behavior. Some years ago, teenagers who lacked alternative sources of information reported turning to mass media for information about the norms of dating behavior, presumably to learn how to interact with the opposite sex.[12] More recent work demonstrates a relationship between exposure to typical television programming and beliefs and expectations concerning sexual behavior within the larger society. College students who frequently view soap operas (with their incessant sexual themes) give higher estimates of real-life love affairs, out-of-wedlock children, and divorces.[13] For some individuals, media messages may affect personal perceptions and expectations regarding their own sexual behavior. High school and college students attributing great sexual proficiency and satisfaction to television characters tended to report *less* satisfaction with their own first experiences of coitus than did students not making such attributions.[14] Finally, experimental research on pornography shows that viewing sexually explicit depictions portraying women as indiscriminately promiscuous and euphoric in response to any sexual stimulation increases callousness toward women among college males—and even some females. Consequences range from increased disrespect for women to the trivialization of reactions to rape.[15]

An additional condition operates when considering media influences on adolescent sexual beliefs in the United States. Information from the mass media about most developmental issues usually competes with information from many other powerful sources. Parents, teachers, churches, all have something to add to the ongoing discourse about adolescents' independence, occupational and educational choices, racial and ethnic stereotypes, consumer behavior, body image, and so forth. When it comes to sexual socialization, however, the influence of many of the traditional "socializers" wanes. Although we may currently be more comfortable discussing some of the biological and health dimensions of sex than we were thirty years ago (adolescents do report learning about such things as the origins of babies and menstruation from parents and schools), parents and/or teachers play a lesser role informing teenagers about petting, masturbation, prostitution, intercourse, and so forth. Apparently such topics are too embarrassing, too difficult to address. The resulting absence of competing information (peers do talk, but often perpetuate ignorance) lends the mass media additional influence. To the extent that media operate as the dominant source of information (in some instances, perhaps the only source) about precisely those sexual issues that most interest adolescents, to that extent the likelihood that mass media affect sexual beliefs and behavior increases dramatically.

Ultimately, the same variations in individual susceptibility and in message characteristics that mediate responses to media violence also operate in relation to media portrayals of male/female interactions (and, for that matter, in relation to most other kinds of media content). The potential for media influence in this arena is somewhat increased, however, by virtue of the lack of competing messages on issues of sexual behavior. To reiterate, under some conditions, some adolescents model some sexual expectations and behaviors on their interpretations of media content. The degree to which this is of social concern, of course, depends on the nature of that content and the nature of what society is willing to label acceptable.[16]

THE PROBLEM OF CONTROLS

What does such a conditional approach to mass media effects imply about the current furor over "negative" media messages? Should we worry about the violent rap lyrics, or displays of sexuality common to many music videos, or violence and gore in films, or implicit worship of the trappings of wealth that have characterized so much of prime-time television from *Leave It to Beaver* to *Beverly Hills 90210*? Do parents, or schools, or governmental agencies need to step in? If so, how? Unfortunately, there is no simple answer to such questions.

As noted above, the evidence indicates it is unlikely that particular media messages move *large numbers* of adolescents to become more aggressive, more sexually active, more likely to experiment with alcohol and drugs, or more obsessed with pursuing increased wealth. In spite of the thousands of hours of television and film violence most adolescents have consumed by the time they finish high school, far fewer of them have engaged assaultive behavior than have not. On the other hand, the evidence also indicates that mass media do affect smaller numbers of adolescents in important ways. Indeed, a given message may "cause" a multiplicity of different behaviors among different youngsters, including some of the negative actions that generate most public concern (e.g., the research tells us that viewing television violence has engendered greater aggressiveness among at least some adolescents).

Exactly what constitutes "socially significant negative effects" depends both on who is making the value judgement (e.g., one person's friendly kiss is another's seductive embrace) and on conditions external to particular media content. Several years ago Arnold Schwarzenegger, a powerful icon among adolescents, "terminated" policemen by the dozens in the highly popular and graphic *Terminator* films, but there was no public outcry for boycotts of the movie, and no one lectured the film industry. Currently, however, Ice-T raps: "I got my 12-gauge sawed off / I got my headlights turned off / I'm 'bout to bust some shots off / I'm 'bout to dust some cops off," and law-enforcement organizations demonstrate, politicians pontificate, mass media present numerous "examinations" of the effect of rap music on teenagers, Time-Warner reconsiders its policies regarding record releases, and untold numbers of rock performers wallow in new-found devotion to the First Amendment (while Ice-T, no doubt, makes a few more trips to the bank). One suspects that such factors as temporal proximity to the Los Angeles riots, race of the performer, and the relatively recent development of music video (enabling adults to see what they previously had been unable to hear, which, in turn, gave rise to numerous calls for controls on popular music) all played a role in the outcry engendered by "Cop Killer," independent of what the lyrics say.

From this perspective, the issue is not whether mass media affect adolescent perceptions, beliefs, behaviors. Rather, it is one of society's judging how many adolescents need to be put at risk, in what way, before various corrective actions are viewed as necessary and justified. Such judgments tend to vary depending on who makes them. If mass media cause a few teenagers to increase the frequency with which they get into scuffles in the school yard, perhaps something like classroom instruction about media and violence is needed. If, on the other hand, media violence influences significant numbers to engage in criminal behavior, more draconian corrective strategies, up to and including possible legal controls on media content, might merit consideration. The problem, given the value Americans place on free expression and First Amendment guarantees, is obtaining agreement on what constitutes a "socially significant" number (and, to some extent, what constitutes criminal behavior). For some, very few violent incidents tied to media content are enough to warrant legislative controls; for others it requires numerous instances for which the connection between media and violence can be established; and for still others no amount of any kind of effect justifies legal constraints. Unfortunately, the sensitivity of the issues (violence, sex, drugs, suicide, and an understandable desire to protect youth at risk versus a presumed inalienable right to unfettered free expression) often leads to extreme positions, making the debate more notable for sound and slogan than substance and sense.

A MIDDLE GROUND

There is a middle ground. It entails compromises on the part of advocates both of censorship and of unfettered free expression. It requires recognition that a society in which significant numbers of adolescents are significantly at risk (of violence, crime, AIDS, other sexually transmitted diseases, out-of-wedlock pregnancies, drugs, depression, suicide, and more) is intolerable. It also requires recognition that a society that abrogates freedom of expression is equally intolerable. Clearly, all of our institutions—parents, churches, schools, social and professional organizations, government, and the mass media—are responsible for addressing the problem.

In one of the more interesting attempts to explore the middle ground, the Carnegie Council on Adolescent Development has sponsored a series of "linkage seminars." These are small gatherings at which one or two child advocates and behavioral researchers "link-up" with a dozen or so film and television writers and producers, people directly responsible for creating media messages, to discuss ways the media can help address some of the problems confronting adolescents. The seminars are designed to minimize defensiveness and facilitate sharing of information, concerns, doubts, and goals. Discussion avoids focusing on "what the media are doing wrong." (In the past, such gatherings often became confrontations, each side telling the other what not to do: for example, "Quit showing sex and violence!" met "Don't trample my right to unfettered free expression!" and little was resolved.) Rather, the seminars, following the advice of even the most elementary texts on group dynamics, take a more positive approach. They assume that the same principles that operate to influence youngsters' acquisition of negative beliefs and behavior from media messages can also engender positive beliefs and behaviors.

Typically, a seminar begins by presenting the real-life social dimensions of some adolescent realities (e.g., in 1989, 67 percent of all teen births occurred outside marriage; homicide is the second leading cause of death for all fifteen- to twenty-four-year-olds in the United States),[17] and considering the social implications of such facts. Participants are then asked to suggest ways in which the mass media might help. The ensuing discussion tends to be lively and exciting. When asked to assume the offensive rather than being put on the defensive, writers and producers have offered some strikingly creative ideas.

Although it is difficult to document empirically, some of the ideas and suggestions generated at these linkage seminars appear to have lodged in the thinking of at least some of the active producers in the industry. A few seem to have made their way into an occasional episode of one or another show. And it seems quite likely that some of them, under some conditions, have positively influenced at least some adolescent viewers.

WHAT IS A TEACHER TO DO?

Finally, teachers (and parents) can take direct action by discussing media messages with students. At first glance, such a suggestion may sound obvious and/or simplistic. However, such talk is far from the norm, particularly in schools—particularly regarding television.

Guided discussion can lead students to more elaborated, thoughtful consideration of the meaning of media messages. Evidence indicates that verbal processing requires more such cognitive effort than does pictorial processing, and leads to more abstract, generic thinking, probably because it facilitates conceptual as opposed to perceptual elaboration of the message or model.[18] It follows that asking youngsters to discuss media messages in ways that encourage them to move beyond the perceptual surface of typical television portrayals can lead them to recognize implications and meanings that, typically, they seldom consider critically or deeply. For example, left to their own devices, adolescents probably think about something like Madonna's "Papa Don't Preach" in terms of its specific concrete narrative (e.g., "Gee, it was nice the way her father finally hugged her"). But when asked to discuss the pregnant girl's future, these same adolescents can be encouraged to confront more conceptual issues: child support, limiting future opportunities, the general problem of teenage pregnancy, and so forth. In short, the kind of guided discussion that teachers can encourage has tremendous potential to lead youngsters to develop new perspectives and/or insights about whatever media message serves as the stimulus for discussion.

Unfortunately, a norm against serious discussion of "entertainment" content exists in many, if not most, classrooms. Although a number of "critical viewing" curricula exist, most focus on the nature of the television medium rather than on content.[19] Moreover, they are more notable for their absence from the day-to-day context of most schools than for any significant role in training students how to bring critical faculties to bear on television. (Recall that less than a decade ago Senator William Proxmire gave a "Golden Fleece" award to the developers of such curricula, ridiculing the idea of teaching children how to watch television.) Of course, many teachers will protest that they do, in fact, talk with their students about television. More often than not, however, such discussion concerns a news or documentary program, or educational television, or a "docu-drama" with obvious "formal-curriculum" relevance (e.g., "Roots" or "JFK"). Seldom do situation comedies, prime-time soaps, or music videos serve as a focus of classroom examination.

Several factors inhibit such classroom discussions. First, entertainment content is perceived to be irrelevant to formal schooling. A recent examination of television and children in Australia describes how teachers and students differ in attitudes toward and use of television, and how schools tend to enculturate children to equate school work with "not-television" and television with "not-schoolwork."[20] It is as if teachers and students implicitly negotiate a position defining entertainment television as "nonserious," therefore to be ignored, if not actively discouraged. Second, many teachers view just those television topics most in need of discussion as simply too hot to handle. That is, they believe (with some validity) that the people who so vocally attack the media for purveying objectionable messages to children and adolescents will be just as quick to criticize teachers for attempting to address such issues in the classroom, even though attempting to moderate media impact. Consider, for example, a recent episode of "Hollywood 90210" which concerned accusations (ultimately unfounded) of a sexual relationship between a teacher and a student. In most public high schools, it would require a brave teacher to use that program to discuss any of the several themes in the show (e.g., sex, teacher/student relationships, rumor, due process). Yet, given that particular program's appeal and relevance to the adolescent audience, and most youngster's eagerness to talk about their favorite programs, that particular episode might serve as the perfect starting point for serious discussion of any of those issues.

Discretion being the better part of valor, it is probably unwise for teachers concerned with moderating presumed negative impacts of media content to focus initial class discussions on issues such as sex or drugs. Nevertheless, teachers occupy a unique position and have a unique opportunity to make a difference in the way media content influences students' conceptions of the world. They need to watch what their students watch (everything has its cost), then to initiate the kind of dialogue that will help reveal if they see what their students see. Simply the exchange of different interpretations of media messages can help both adolescents and adults develop deeper, more elaborated conceptions of any of the issues potentially prevent in media content.

Notes

1 Vision Videos, *Rising to the Challenge* (Arlington, Va.: Parents Music Resource Center, 1988), videorecording.

2 Steven Starker, *Evil Influences: Crusades against the Mass Media* (New Brunswick, N.J.: Transaction Publishers, 1989).

3 For several general reviews of empirical research on the effects of mass media on children and adolescents, see Peter G. Christenson and Donald F. Roberts, "Popular Music in Early Adolescence" (Working paper for the Carnegie Council on Adolescent Development, Washington, D.C., January 1990); George Comstock et al., *Television and Human Behavior* (New York: Columbia University Press, 1978); George Comstock with Haejung Paik, *Television and the American Child* (San Diego, Calif.: Academic Press, 1991); and Donald F. Roberts and Nathan Maccoby, "Effects of Mass Communication," in *The Handbook of Social Psychology*, Vol. II, ed. Gardner Lindzey and Elliot Aronson (New York: Random House, 1985), pp. 539-98.

4 S. Shirley Feldman and Glen R. Elliott, eds., *At the Threshold: The Developing Adolescent* (Cambridge: Harvard University Press, 1990).

5 William J. McGuire, "The Myth of Massive Media Impact: Savagings and Salvagings," in *Public Communication and Behavior*, Vol. I, ed. George Comstock (Orlando, Fla.: Academic Press, 1986), pp. 178-207.

6 For more complete discussions of the conditional approach, see Jack M. McLeod and Byron Reeves, "On the Nature of Media Effects," in *Television and Social Behavior: Beyond Violence and Children*, ed. Stephen B. Withey and Ronald P. Ables (Hillsdale, N.J.: Lawrence Erlbaum Associates, 1980), pp. 17-54; and Roberts and Maccoby, "Effects of Mass Communication," pp. 540-42.

7 McLeod and Reeves, "On the Nature of Media Effects," pp. 19-24.

8 Jane D. Brown and Laurie Schultz, "The Effects of Fandom, Race and Gender on Interpretations of Music Videos," *Journal of Communication* 40 (Spring 1990): 88-102.

9 Margaret Thompson et al., "Long-term Norms and Cognitive Structures as Shapers of Television Viewer Activity," *Journal of Broadcasting and Electronic Media* 35 (Summer 1991): 319-34.

10 See especially Comstock and Paik, *Television and the American Child*, pp. 234-85. See also Comstock et al., *Television and Human Behavior*, p. 250.

11 Comstock and Paik, *Television and the American Child*, pp. 234-85.

12 W. M. Gerson, "Mass Media and Socialization Behavior: Negro-White Differences," *Social Forces* 45 (1966): 40-50.

13 Nancy L. Buerkel-Rothfuss with Sandra Mayes, "Soap Opera Viewing: The Cultivation Effect," *Journal of Communication* 31 (Summer 1981): 108-15.

14 Stanley J. Baran, "How TV and Film Portrayals Affect Sexual Satisfaction in College Students," *Journalism Quarterly* 53 (Autumn 1976): 468-73; and Stanley J. Baran, "Sex on TV and Adolescent Sexual Image," *Journal of Broadcasting* 20 (Winter 1976): 61-88.

15 For reviews of research on responses to pornographic films, see Neil M. Malamuth and Victoria Billings, "The Functions and Effects of Pornography: Sexual Communications versus the Feminist Model in Light of Research Findings," in *Perspectives on Media Effects*, ed. Jennings Bryant and Dolf Zillman (Hillsdale, N.J.: Lawrence Erlbaum Associates, 1986), pp. 83-108; and James Weaver, "Responding to Erotica: Perceptual Processes and Dispositional Implications," in *Responding to the Screen: Reception and Reaction Processes*, ed. Jennings Bryant and Dolf Zillman (Hillsdale, N.J.: Lawrence Erlbaum Associates, 1991), pp. 329-54.

16 For a general discussion of the role of mass media in sexual socialization, see Kimberly K. Massey and Stanley J. Baran, "Mass Media and Sexual Socialization: A Tale of Scientific Neglect," *Journal of Communication and Media Arts* 1 (Spring 1992): 17-34.

17 Fred M. Hechinger, *Fateful Choices: Healthy Youth for the 21st Century, Executive Summary* (Washington, D.C.: Carnegie Council on Adolescent Development, April 1992); and U.S. Congress, House of Representatives, Select Committee on Children, Youth, and Families, "Youth and Violence: The Current Crisis—A Fact Sheet" (Washington, D.C.: Government Printing Office, n.d.).

18 For a more complete summary of cognitive effort and message elaboration, see Albert Bandura, *Social Foundations of Thought and Action: A Social Cognitive Theory* (Englewood Cliffs, N.J.: Prentice-Hall, 1986), especially pp. 70-74. Also see Gavriel Salomon, *Interaction of Media, Cognition, and Learning: An Exploration of How Symbolic Forms Cultivate Mental Skills and Affect Knowledge Acquisition* (San Francisco: Jossey-Bass, 1979).

19 James A. Brown, *Television "Critical Viewing Skills" Education: Major Media Literacy Projects in the United States and Selected Countries* (Hillsdale, N.J.: Lawrence Erlbaum Associates, 1991).

20 Bob Hodge and David Tripp, *Children and Television: A Semiotic Approach* (Stanford: Stanford University Press, 1986).

AT THE CROSSROADS:
Voices from the Carnegie Conference on Adolescent Health

The Need for a Core, Interdisciplinary, Life-Sciences Curriculum in the Middle Grades

H. CRAIG HELLER
Stanford University

Any campaign to improve adolescent health must involve the schools to be successful. Why should we assume that schools have to be a major player? Remember the retort of Willy Sutton when he was asked why he robbed banks? He replied, matter of factly, "Because that's where they keep the money." We have the broadest access to young people in the schools. In addition, the schools have an enormous infrastructure with a professional staff that gives us the opportunity, at least for some of the time, to isolate youth from harmful, stressful, social environments. Through the schools we have the best chance to present useful knowledge to adolescents to help them make meaningful and wise life decisions. Schools also provide opportunities for adolescents to encounter positive role models and to develop productive relationships with peers.

The importance of the schools in the promotion of adolescent health and well-being and in the production of fully functional adults is emphasized by consideration of the costs and consequences incurred when schools fail. Studies published by the Children's Defense Fund show that currently one out of seven students drops out of school. The demand for unskilled, poorly educated laborers in our society is declining. A dropout is twice as likely to be unemployed, and seven-and-a-half times more likely throughout his or her lifetime to be on welfare. A male dropout earns about $300,000 less in his lifetime, and pays about $80,000 less in taxes in his lifetime. Simply from

The following chapters are edited versions of speeches presented at "Crossroads: Critical Choices for the Development of Healthy Adolescents," a conference sponsored by the Carnegie Corporation of New York and the Carnegie Council on Adolescent Development, Washington, D.C., April 12–14, 1992.

the standpoint of costs of lost productivity, the grand total—the cost to the nation of one year's class of dropouts—is about $300 billion.

Because the unemployed frequently do not have health insurance, the additional financial burden of health-care costs increases the $300 billion figure. On the whole, the lower socioeconomic levels of our population have less health insurance and greater health problems. It can be argued that the roots of these costly problems are, to a large extent, in our failure to educate our adolescents. In this age group in particular, less education results in development of less healthy life-styles and greater prevalence of problems with drugs, violence, and, of course, unplanned pregnancy.

Teen pregnancy is a special case in point. We currently spend over $20 billion a year on welfare to families started by teens. Teens are much more likely to have low-birth-weight babies, and the health-care costs of a low-birth-weight baby during its first year can be on the order of $400,000 to $500,000. On a cost basis alone, ignoring the social, emotional, and personal tragedies of poor adolescent health, we must keep students in school and use the educational system to promote healthy lives and choices.

Efforts to solve these enormous problems must have a prime focus in the middle grades. Students come into the middle grades (grades six through nine) somewhat naive, somewhat malleable. They still seek adult attention and guidance. Their learning curves are steep; they are capable of a lot. In general, they are capable of much more than we currently expect of them and inspire in them. Yet it has to be recognized that adolescence may be a time of turmoil. This is amply documented in Fred Hechinger's *Fateful Choices*.[1] Adolescents are going through the travails of puberty and experiencing the dominant influence of peer pressure in their lives. They are exposed to increased opportunities for high-risk behaviors. Because their needs are not understood or addressed by the educational system and available support systems, they become progressively alienated from school and more likely to become tuned-out and turned-off as they enter high school. The cost of salvaging an alienated individual in high school is great, and the probability of success is very low. The situation is summarized concisely by a quote from the Carnegie Council on Adolescent Development's report *Turning Points*: "Middle grade schools—junior high, intermediate, and middle schools—are potentially society's most powerful force to recapture millions of youth adrift, and help every young person thrive during adolescence. Yet all too often these schools exacerbate the problems of young adolescents."[2]

Why are we doing poorly? One reason is school organization. To a large extent, middle-grade schools, especially junior high schools, remain organized along the lines of high schools. They are assembly lines for the efficient delivery of education in discipline-bound packets. At fifty-minute intervals students shuffle down hallways to individual classrooms where different teachers attempt to add discretely different pieces to the product. Unlike the well-designed factory, however, insufficient attention has been paid to how well the parts fit together, how durable they are, and how firmly they are attached. All too often, the product that comes off the middle-grades assembly line is a dysfunctional collection of parts with no engine and an erratic steering mechanism.

The assembly-line organization of middle-grades schools balkanizes knowledge and destroys the interconnectedness that young people are trying to find. They are asking for the relevance of information, one body to another, and to themselves. The very structure of the schools obscures interconnectedness and relevance. Organization of curriculum along strict disciplinary lines sets some students up for failure. If a student does not do well in one discipline, that student sinks or swims in that one classroom with that one teacher. When information is connected through interdisciplinary presentation, a student can always excel in one area and the resulting positive reinforcement helps him or her to improve in other areas as well. Interdisciplinary organization of schools creates networks of caring adults that are more effective in helping students succeed than individual teachers working alone can ever be.

The assembly-line model is also not optimal for dealing with the behavioral problems of this age group. Peer pressure and role models are highly significant influences on adolescents. Too often the school organization precludes meaningful contact with teachers and the establishment of positive peer groups working on school-related issues. The structure of the schools is something that is not working in our favor.

Fortunately, there are significant ongoing efforts to improve school structure for the middle grades. Over the past decade a strong middle-school movement has developed that seeks to reorganize the middle grades using the middle-school philosophy, which promotes core curricula, team planning and teaching, and active engagement by the learner.

Another serious barrier to improving the educational experiences for adolescents is the inadequacy of existing curricular materials. You may ask, "How can it be claimed that our school materials are poor? Just look at the books we have in the middle grades. They're beautiful, full color, glossy books. These are the best that money can buy." But, when you look inside many of these glossy, beautiful books, a different perspective emerges. In the life sciences, they tend to be well-illustrated vocabulary lists presenting watered down high school–level materials. The interesting relevant material is omitted, leaving behind the vocabulary words enmeshed in vapid text.

Problem-solving skills are not emphasized. Most importantly, the materials covered are not relevant to adolescent experience. Important but sensitive information is left out. Students view these texts as dull. A vicious cycle is created. Students are not necessarily interested in life cycles of liverworts and mosses. Therefore, they do not learn about the life cycles of liverworts and mosses, and as a result do poorly on tests. The tendency is to assume that students cannot learn such difficult concepts so the texts are watered down even more. Adolescents are capable of more complex learning and higher-order thinking skills than we expect but we have to get them interested and "turned on."

An extremely important issue is that current curricular materials on health-related information are minimized and marginalized. Since this subject is not integrated into the mainstream of science or social science curricula, it is trivialized for consideration by young people.

Adolescents face increasing opportunities for and pressures to engage in high-risk behaviors. They are forming attitudes toward life-styles that will have enormous impact on their health and well-being for the rest of their lives. Many will not receive more life-science education beyond the middle-grades level. It is frightening to think that adolescents are making life-determining and life-threatening decisions armed with the level of information they currently receive in middle-grades curricula. The materials now available in the schools to deal with the serious health and behavioral problems of adolescents are grossly inadequate. *Fateful Choices* presents the results of a survey of teachers showing that a high percentage think that sexually related topics should be presented in the middle grades, but only a small percentage of schools in this country do so.[3]

At Stanford University, we have mounted an enormous effort with support from the Carnegie Corporation of New York and the National Science Foundation to create a two-year, interdisciplinary, core, middle-grades curriculum in human biology. The purposes of the Hum Bio curriculum (as we call it) are to combat disaffection and alienation from science by making science interesting to adolescents, while at the same time using science to build a relevant knowledge base—information that young people can use even if they never take another course in biology in their lives. Health and safety issues are integrated with the science, and studying human behavior helps the student to build decision-making skills. The human organism and the adolescent in particular is the focus of study and the vehicle for teaching the various aspects of life sciences. Does our focus on the human and on the adolescent and our inclusion of behavioral sciences mean that we teach less science than a standard life science curriculum? We believe the opposite is true. We can teach more biology, not less; we can challenge the students more once we capture their interest and their commitment. A committed, engaged student can be expected to learn and retain more. It is not necessary to teach genetics by starting with Mendel's pea plants. You can start with human genetics and get the students interested in sex determination and genetic diseases they have heard about such as cystic fibrosis and sickle-cell anemia. It is important to lead with topics that adolescents find interesting and relevant. You do not have to teach about life cycles by starting with mosses and liverworts. Biology does not have to begin by tiptoeing through the phyla. Adolescents are interested in themselves. We can capitalize on that simple fact to get their attention and get them tuned in and turned on to school.

An extremely important aspect of the Hum Bio curriculum is the integration of information on behavioral sciences, biological sciences, and safety and health. These topics are not simply brought together between the same two covers, but the interconnections are emphasized in *each* unit. For example, when we teach the nervous system, we teach about drugs. When we teach about heart and circulation, we teach the effects of fatty foods, cholesterol, and stress. One unit in the Hum Bio curriculum is "Your Changing Body." It begins with the descriptive information of what happens during puberty. Then information on hormones and their roles in puberty is presented, including the menstrual cycle. Lastly the unit deals with the conscious experience of going through puberty, including feelings about body changes, gender, and attractiveness. Dieting, anorexia, and steroid abuse are discussed. The important point is that the focus is on issues of great concern to adolescents and through responding to that concern we are able to convey a great deal of information about the biology of hormones as well as important information about relevant behavioral and health issues.

The Hum Bio curricular materials are highly interactive and oriented around activities. Every page of text asks for student response. These are not simply fill-in-the-blank questions, but mini-activities. Calculate how much blood your heart pumps per hour; find the blind spots in your field of vision; create a scenario in which an adolescent's wish for independence conflicts with parents' or guardians' standards. Each response requires engagement with the materials. Every unit has a core of essential activities, but many more activities are available as supplements to the student text. For example, Table I presents the unit organization for "Nervous System: Mission Control." This text, designed for a three- to four-week period of time, is organized around the key ideas listed on the left. Class activities separate from the text are listed for each part of the text. Those in boldface are considered essential to the unit and the others are recommended, giving the teacher a rich selection. None requires sophisticated equipment. Some activities are designed as complex instruction modules for those teachers who like to use this mode of learning. Suggestions are made for in-depth projects.

The activities in Table I illustrate that even though Hum Bio is primarily a life-sciences curriculum, it builds connections to other areas as well. Mathematics and physical sciences are abundantly represented in the nervous system unit activities. In other units, language arts and social studies are incorporated extensively. Our goal is to create maximum opportunity for creation of diverse teacher teams and a set of materials around which a core curriculum can grow.

Table 1. Nervous System: Mission Control Unit Organization

Key Ideas	*Activities*			*Projects*
	Name	*Instructional Activities*	*Complex Instruction Activities*	
A. Organization of the Nervous System Using a roadmap to explore the organization and structure of the nervous system	**A.1 Blood Brain Barrier**	✓		1. Research Questions
	A.2 Model of Nervous System: "Brain On A Stick"	✓		2. The Mind and Body
	A.3 Model of Brain Regions: "Thinking Cap"	✓		
	A.4 A Map of the Nervous System	✓		3. Sleep and Dreams
B. Reflexes—How the Nervous System Works Learning how the nervous system works through reflexes controlled by your brain	**B.1 Building a Neuron**	✓		
	B.2 Simulation Of A Reflex Arc	✓		4. What Is Intelligence?
	B.3 How Fast Is Your Reaction Time?	✓		5. Information Received by the Brain—Amount and Range
C. Sensory Communication Becoming familiar with sensory receptors as vehicles of communication	**C.1 What is Light?**	✓	*	
	C.2 What is Refraction?	✓	*	
	C.3 The Way Lenses Work	✓	*	
	C.4 Colors-Where Do They Come From?	✓	*	

Table 1. Nervous System: Mission Control Unit Organization (Continued)

Key Ideas	*Activities*			*Projects*
	Name	*Instructional Activities*	*Complex Instruction Activities*	
C. Sensory Communication Becoming familiar with sensory receptors as vehicles of communication (continued)	C.5 The Eye: Exploring a Mammalian Eye (Dissection)	✓		1. Research Questions
	C.6 Designing/Building a Model of the Eye	✓	*	2. The Mind and Body
	C.7 Optical Illusions	✓		
	C.7-C.17 C.I Activities for Vision		✓	3. Sleep and Dreams
	C.18 Catch a Wave	✓	*	
	C.19 Sound in a Vacuum	✓	*	4. What Is Intelligence?
	C.20 Singing Glasses	✓	*	
	C.21 How Do You Hear?	✓		5. Information Received by the Brain—Amount and Range
	C.22-33 CI Activities for Hearing		✓	
	C.34 Balance and Equilibrium	✓		
D. Brain Regions and Functions Exploring the brain as it coordinates the systems of the body.	**D.1 Brain Functions**	✓		
	D.2 Thinking Fast	✓		
	D.3 Learning and Reasoning	✓		
	D.4 Exploring Your Memory	✓		

The unit outline for the nervous system does not seem to reflect the claim made above that the best way to teach about drugs is to integrate that information with learning about the brain. In fact, embedded throughout the unit, wherever appropriate, are references to the actions and effects of drugs. This coverage is then extended in a companion unit, "The Effects of Drugs and Alcohol."

In the Hum Bio curriculum we bring biology together with issues of health and wellness and also issues of behavior. Our effort has been to capture the interest of adolescents and to address their concerns. Through hands-on problem-solving approaches we hope to enhance learning and strengthen decision-making skills. The outcome of an improved, relevant information base and more highly developed decision-making skills should be that adolescents will make wiser choices about their lives. It is hoped that the Hum Bio curriculum will contribute to decreasing alienation from school in general and science in particular. The challenges ahead are great, however. To implement this curriculum will be an enormous job. Teachers must get excited about the possibilities; they will have to receive new and additional education. They will have to learn to cooperate with each other and to team effectively in an interdisciplinary approach. We are confident that teachers will respond well to these challenges. Teachers have been integrally involved in all stages of the development and testing of the Hum Bio curriculum, so we are confident the materials are responsive to their needs and will be "user-friendly."

My sense is that teachers recognize the need for new materials such as the Hum Bio curriculum, but greater barriers will be administrators, school boards, and state policymaking bodies. Getting the broad base of support necessary for implementation will be a challenge because the Hum Bio curriculum is quite different from traditional fare. Some units will be viewed as controversial, but they are needed. Most units will require major changes in the way schools and teachers currently work. The time will come when we will need the help of many diverse individuals and organizations to get Hum Bio into the schools. But we absolutely must change life-sciences education in the middle grades in this country, because it is our best hope for improving adolescent health and well-being.

Notes

1 Fred M. Hechinger, *Fateful Choices: Healthy Youth for the 21st Century* (New York: Hill and Wang, 1992).

2 Task Force on Education of Young Adolescents, *Turning Points: Preparing American Youth for the 21st Century* (Washington, D.C.: Carnegie Council on Adolescent Development, 1989), p. 8.

3 Hechinger, *Fateful Choices*.

Linking Health and Education in the Middle Grades

GORDON M. AMBACH
Council of Chief State School Officers, Washington, D.C.

One of the critical roles of the chief state school officer and of state education agencies is vigorous cheerleading. It is being out there in the front and advocating that it is absolutely essential to see health and education joined together. You cannot have good health without good education, and you cannot have good education without good health. People have to continue to say this over and over again, and then carry that simple message into their dealings with legislators, governors, Congress, and the president. It may seem simple, but it is the kind of thing we must do to pull our efforts together.

Focused around the first national education goal—readiness for school—there has been an interesting turning of heads toward linking health and education. If you were to sit in on the deliberations of the National Education Goals Panel, where they are struggling with the question of how one measures "readiness for school," you would hear more than debate about whether children should go to pre-kindergarten or start pre-kindergarten at the age of three or four. You would hear discussion about what measures there should be with respect to the availability of prenatal care and nutrition, what measures of health services and child care from birth until pre-kindergarten.

The debate about joining health and education goes on in many places. The principal issue must be the penetration of a concern for good health throughout the schools. By penetration, I mean that the message becomes a commitment for each and every person who is working with children. I am not slighting the experts, the health educators or those who are expert in health care who are working in the schools. But, as you and I look now at cutbacks in education and health, and as we look at the difficulty in making certain that every child is healthy and well educated, we realize this is a task for everyone, not just experts. We have to keep pounding away at prevention. That means working with all personnel in the schools.

The schools must provide reliable and persuasive information about health to overcome the misinformation of the streets. The schools must provide a special relationship for each student with at least one caring adult. The caring adult should be someone familiar enough with the student to serve as a mentor, coach, or confidant; someone who can enable the student to get to the right point of information and expert service when needed.

The relationship of each student to a caring adult is particularly important in our middle schools. There we must overcome the impersonal environment and facelessness of the student body. The condition of student anonymity is caused in large part by population mobility and large school size, which impede efforts toward genuine caring connections. The schools must make a special effort to provide caring relationships. They must provide examples of the kinds of personal relationships we expect as the behaviors we intend students to exhibit when they are adults. The way that happens is for all those persons who are in the schools to live and work that way in their schools.

The scope of the challenge before us is immense. The more anyone thinks about the penetration of responsibility throughout the entire school personnel population—2½ million individuals—the greater seems the task. It requires substantial commitment to staff development for the adults who must have this caring relationship.

If I were selecting one strategy to push across our country to improve the health and education of students at the middle-grades level, it would be to assure a caring relationship between each student and at least one adult in school and at least one adult outside of school, and, furthermore, to assure these three individuals know each other well. If we could make that happen, it would be a very significant gain.

Let me conclude with one thought about the importance of public officials' connecting funding streams in health and education at the local, state, and federal levels. This is the prime task to which policymakers must give attention. We can approach connections of services by way of spinning up new organizational arrangements, coordinating councils, and other devices. Sometimes they are important, but they are not nearly as important as having responsible officials at federal, state, and local levels think through the problems at the point-of-service contact and ask the question, "How can I change the flow of our agency funds to connect them with other sources and make something more effective happen?" That is collaboration. That is really connecting health and education.

Transforming Schools into Powerful Communities

DEBORAH MEIER
Central Park East Secondary School, New York

Our schools represent a lesson in creating a powerful community. In both the elementary schools and the high school, we have made possible strong relationships between and among people. There is no point in labeling these relationships cognitive or affective. They are relationships around issues, around life, around things that matter to young people.

A community embodies the hopes of human beings. You cannot learn to play tennis if you have never seen it played. You cannot teach children the power of wonderful ideas if they have not been immersed in a community that cares about wonderful ideas, that believes in them, that explores them, and that puts them into practice.

Intellectually and morally, we are a serious and respectful community. Despite the fact that I speak as an expert on middle schools, I started out as a pre-kindergarten and kindergarten teacher. I have come to believe that there is nothing children need in the middle grades that they do not also need for the rest of their lives. Children may need some things more than others at different ages. Every age I have worked with, however, seems to me to be critical. I have come to the conclusion that children, and human beings in general, need and deserve a decent environment at every single age. Whether they are six or sixty, people are more amazingly alike than they are different.

We finally did an in-depth study of the first seven graduating classes of Central Park East (CPE) Elementary School graduates—students who had completed sixth grade between 1978 and 1985. It took a lot of work to track down all those youngsters, but we did it. Of the first 135 we reached 119. We managed to have phone conversations with most of them, and long face-to-face interviews with about 40, plus conversations with many of their families. It turns out that even though they left our school following sixth grade, before the onslaught of adolescence, and most went on to pretty terrible schools, schools that do not graduate most of their incoming ninth graders, the CPE students survived. In fact, 90 percent managed to earn high school diplomas, and another 6 percent received general education diplomas. We did not have any direct relationship with them after they were twelve years old—nevertheless, contrary to the usual proportions in high schools, two-thirds went on to college.

Reading the interviews is a reminder of what counts. It is a reminder that a powerful community can have a transformative impact on other human beings at any age. People who care, who have access to young people for an extended period of time and who create a community around them, for them and their families, have an enormous effect. The impact of a good school is evident not only among children nor only in the acquisition of academic skills; it has an effect on the entire constellation of family and student beliefs in their powers and their ability to handle the world around them.

I saw a television program some years ago that remains a metaphor for what I am talking about. The interviewer asked some high school dropouts, seventeen or eighteen years old, whether they knew anyone who had ever graduated from college. These three dropouts said no. I thought, what an odd thing to say. They had been in school for almost twelve years, and had had somewhere between twelve and fifty teachers, all of whom had graduated from college. On the other hand, this was not a strange statement at all. The youth did not include any of those teachers among the people they knew because they did not know their teachers. The fundamental fact in our school, and in schools like ours, is that at times the children may be angry with us, they may hate us, they may love us, they may be disgusted with us, they may want us "out of their faces"—but they include us among the world of people they know. We are part of their universe. We are part of the web of influences in their lives.

Curiosity is one of the things that keeps us alive. We wonder why. We wonder what tomorrow will bring. Our intellectual curiosity about the world around us, our interest in it, our noticing that this or that is an amazing fact, an amazing idea—this is what makes each day memorable. Pursuing our interests develops habits of mind that give us hope, that sustain us through pain. It is fundamental to our health. Immersing children in a culture in which such habits are valued is health-promoting, more health-promoting than any health-ed course or program ever invented.

Children go to institutions called high schools, created for a variety of reasons a century ago, which fail to sustain their curiosity. Instead they drive young people mad. Students develop ways of adjusting, techniques for handling madness, which we then attribute to their hormones. None of us, at any stage in our life cycle, would survive well in such institutions. No other institution we know of, even the army or prison, is organized so mindlessly. In no other institution do we change supervisors and peer groups every forty-five minutes, or engage in a totally different activity every time the bell rings, without any particular sequential order.

This kind of high school could not conceivably be an institution intentionally created to give our minds good exercise and to help us develop intellectually serious habits, not to mention intellectually serious connections with people. Young people go to schools in which adults are allowed no time to act as serious mentors. Teachers are not models of people who engage in serious discussion because students never see teachers engage in a serious discussion, serious debates, or an argument about something that we teachers want them to argue about.

The typical high school is a setting in which the adults and the students are not members of the same community. Instead, they exist in two unconnected communities inhabiting the same building. We have abandoned them in adolescence to a community in which there are no adults to have an influence on them. Then we decry the fact that they create a peer culture that does not have the values we as adults want them to have. This is insanity. We commit a crime in spending our resources to create institutions that foster habits so adverse to the physical and emotional health of young people.

In our school we decided to reverse all of that. We have created a high school that is essentially like a good kindergarten. All we really did was to adopt the practices that I knew worked in pre-kindergarten and kindergarten and keep them going through elementary school, through middle school, and all the way up through twelfth grade. We should not be surprised to find that this works. If we look at universities like Oxford and Cambridge or other elite universities we find that they are informed by the same ideas.

Students at Oxford, for example, have a central tutor, someone who knows them well and who helps to orchestrate a powerful learning community around them. The assumption is that novices learn from experts. Students are surrounded by and immersed in a community of people who are more expert than they are. That is what we did in our high school and our middle school. Youngsters stay with the same small cluster of teachers for at least two years. Each child has a principal adviser who knows him or her and his or her family well. I am an adviser myself.

The culture of the schools includes an understanding that young people need to learn from their families. We believe all families have things to teach their young. A school that implies to young people that the adults in their life outside of school are not worth respecting has lost an important ally. We find many ways to tell the children's families that they are important.

If the parents' first contact with school, their first conference with a teacher or administrator, makes them feel more powerful, more useful, more knowledgeable, and better able to help their youngster, they are likely to come back for more. If, however, coming to school is only a political act, to show the school you care, then parents with busy lives, who feel tired and defeated, find it difficult to visit the school—and each time it gets harder. All this just to show teachers you care? Parents need some strength and hope that they *can* do well for their children.

School size is a major drawback to creating sane and healthy learning environments. The size of the school should be based on the number of teachers who can gather around a table together. That means no more than

250 or 300 students, or 15 to 20 adults. I do not mean that this is the right size for a "program" or a "house." It is the ideal size for an ongoing, life-giving, healthy school.

No matter how many good programs there are, or how brilliantly conceived, because of their context they often turn into a charade. It is the *culture* of the school, not its programs, that counts. To create a culture is not easy; it takes a lot of face-to-face encounters. We built big buildings because we had some other idea in mind—factory-style efficiency—and because of the cost of space in large urban areas. But the buildings exist. What we want to do is use them to house small communities, each with sufficient autonomy to create for young people a living model of what it is like to be in control of one's environment, to have strong, stable, and continuous relationships.

Big buildings need not be our enemy. They can contain small schools. The building of which I am the official principal has over a thousand pupils. It houses, however, three separate schools, each with its own parent association, its own school head, its own operating life.

We need not put only children between the ages of eleven and fifteen together. There are different strengths and weaknesses at different ages; mix them up. It is a wonderful fact of life in our building that our adolescents see four-year-olds and seven-year-olds and that the young children see older adolescents, and look up to them as models. This reminds us of the basic idea that learning takes place when we have contact with people who are more expert than we are, when our community is composed of various stages of expertise.

Finally, we need to see our buildings as places that can house services other than education. Instead of assuming that the school, the board of education, and the principal must run all the services that children need, why not share these buildings with others? Let the building house health services, and family services, and after-school services. For school people to pretend to take on all the tasks only exhausts us, drowns us, makes us ineffective. Let us create a school culture that acknowledges its limits, and collaborate with other experts whose services children need. The power of the school is not a matter of bricks and mortar, but of the human relationships we create that give young people the courage and ability to create other healthy relationships on their own. We should help them to establish such relationships beyond the boundary of our school but we should not pretend to be more than we are.

The Potential Effects of Community Organizations on the Future of our Youth

JAMES P. COMER
Yale University School of Medicine

For the past twenty-five years, I have worked in the New Haven schools and now across the country. In these years we have really come to understand that changes in the nature of our economy and in community life have led to great social stress on families, resulting in the underdevelopment of many young people.

Children go off to school unable to meet the expectations of the school, and the schools have failed to adjust in ways that would make it possible for these young people to achieve. These underachieving young people interact in school in a way that causes underachievement on the part of staffs, students, parents, and everyone involved. Poor performance eventually leads to problem behavior and dropping out. A number of school interventions, ours and others, have been helpful, sometimes dramatically helpful, but it always occurred to me as we were working that the school alone was not enough.

The school needs support from the surrounding community, yet the community that existed in the pre-1940s in small towns, rural areas, or collections of small towns in big cities, a community that was so supportive of young people, no longer exists. Communities are still very much needed because no matter how much the society changes and science and technology improve, children's needs are still the same. Children need the support of meaningful, important people.

I always look to the community organizations, particularly those organizations serving young people, as places where we must recreate community or create elements of it that would meet the continuing needs of young people. Serving on the Carnegie Council on Adolescent Development's Task Force on Youth Development and Community Programs has been an important opportunity for me to explore with my colleagues some of the ways we can think about and restructure these organizations so that they can meet the essential developmental needs of adolescents. What we found in looking at a wide variety of organizations was that many are working, often in very exciting ways, to promote good physical and mental health among our young people.

They are working in many different ways, including health education, fitness and nutrition, health screening programs, on-site services, direct services to young people, and cooperative relationships with community health providers. On the mental-health side, we found programs in stress management, life-skills training, coping skills, discussion groups, counseling in the areas of sexuality and conflict management, and many, many others. Then there were the programs that had positive mental-health outcomes, even though they were not labeled mental-health programs, such as the educational programs like our own that address the developmental needs of children by creating a climate and experiences that support their development and effective functioning. There are other approaches that involve cooperative learning, peer-group leadership activities, and the like, simply a wide and rich variety of programs designed to support the needs of young people.

Many of the organizations involved are doing a very good job with very dedicated people working very hard, and often working hard under very difficult circumstances. Frequently the preparation of the people involved is limited for lack of funds to support their training. These people are often paid very little for their important work.

For the most part, the programs are not comprehensive, coordinated, or integrated over the life span of young people. There are too few programs and many, many young people in need. There are barriers to participation in these programs, and there are too few young people involved as a result. A natural question is why we need comprehensive, coordinated, integrated programs with continuity over the lifetime of young people. To consider that question, I would like to review briefly some of the critical aspects of the development of adolescents and then think about a model program that represents a way all of the programs serving youth can and must function.

Let us think about adolescent development—the critical aspects of it—for a moment. Adolescents have developed from a position of total dependency at birth to a point where they are considering being involved in what is a complex real world around them. They have many options, which will lead in positive or negative directions. Ultimately we hope that they will be able to meet all of their adult tasks and responsibilities. To be able to do this, they need support from important adults, from their parents and the other people who come into their lives.

They form emotional bonds to all of these adults, particularly to their parents. These adults help them channel the aggressive energy they are born with, important but at times destructive, into the energy of learning, work, and play. They help them to grow along developmental pathways in constructive ways. These young people and caretakers are part of an essential social network of friends and institutions. All of these people and institutions transmit attitudes and values about learning and health to the young people with whom they are involved.

Around preadolescence (age ten or eleven) and early adolescence (age twelve or thirteen), young people depend less on the adults and caretakers around them and begin to modify these relationships. There is a tremendous thrust for independence, a sense of personal adequacy, and for personal identity. It is then that peers and the peer-group culture become extremely influential.

Those who are experiencing success in school and see the possibility of life success are more likely to be pulled into positive peer-group cultures with positive physical and mental attitudes, values, and ways. Those who are experiencing school failure with less chance of life success have a greater possibility of involvement in negative peer-group cultures with negative physical and mental attitudes, values, and ways. Yet all young people in this day and age are vulnerable because of the complexity of the society and the nature of adolescence. Adolescents have enormous amounts of energy and ability, without the needed judgment and experience to make decisions that are good and useful for themselves and others.

At the point of their greatest need, we abandon our children and adolescents. Let me use a personal experience to make this point. When our youngsters were in elementary school, we lived in a suburban community just outside of New Haven where people greatly valued education. When we went off to the Parent-Teacher Association meetings or the open house every year, we had to go very early in order to find a parking place. It was just packed. When we went to middle school, we did not have to go early because there were plenty of spaces. When we went to the open house in high school, the parking lot was almost empty.

We abandon the young people at adolescence during a time when the negative peer-group cultures are beginning to pull in ways that can be very troublesome. During this time, young people do tell us to go away, but they do not mean far away. They mean right around the corner so that they can call us.

I believe that community organizations, across the board, while they have been doing very important work and are a very important resource, can be even more effective if we develop a way to make these programs more comprehensive and accessible. They need to organize with an eye toward child and adolescent development and behavioral principles. They could be much more systematic and deliver the services over time, because we cannot do it at an early age and expect it to act as a vaccination forever. From the earliest period possible through the time young people enter the adult world of work and total participation, they need the support of meaningful, important adults.

Now there is the question of cost. We always worry about cost, and, yes, it is expensive. But it is less expensive than spending on jails. It is less expensive than spending on people with poor health, especially preventable poor health. And it is less expensive than spending on unwanted children who ultimately have large numbers of problems.

While I recognize that we can do much now, at the same time we should not forget that there are structural problems that must be addressed in the larger society if we are to address the problems of our young people. There are economic forces at play that have disrupted and traumatized families and communities and made it difficult for parents and others to carry out their traditional supportive child-rearing functions. Parents and communities functioning successfully are the least expensive and the most effective way to rear children and prepare them to be successful adult citizens of the society. We have to pay attention to the cost of destroying communities and making it impossible for people to have the kinds of jobs and opportunities needed so that their families can function well.

Community organizations of all kinds are an important resource that can help us recreate the critical aspects of community that made it possible for all of us to grow up and participate in the mainstream of society. They can make it possible for many more young people in future generations to have the same opportunity.

Annotated Bibliography of Selected Publications on the Adolescent Years

LINDA L. SCHOFF
Carnegie Council on Adolescent Development, Washington, D.C.

Archer, Elayne, and Michele Cahill. *Building Life Options: School-Community Collaborations for Pregnancy Prevention in the Middle Grades*. Washington, D.C.: Academy for Educational Development, 1991.

This handbook for school administrators, educators, community youth workers, and those concerned about the high American teen birth rate is based on the assumption that effective pregnancy-prevention programs must target young adolescents in the middle grades. Drawing on the experiences of pregnancy-prevention programs throughout the country, concrete guidelines for creating developmentally appropriate, school-community collaborative programs that introduce young adolescents to life options and decision making are described. (Adapted from publication.)

Beyth-Marom, Ruth, et al. "Teaching Decision Making to Adolescents: A Critical Review." Working paper commissioned by the Carnegie Council on Adolescent Development, Washington, D.C., March 1989.

The report evaluates adolescent decision-making programs and their curricula. Programs are evaluated on how adequately they teach normatively prescribed steps of decision making and how effectively and accurately they incorporate research about adolescent decision making into program design. (Adapted from abstract.)

Brindis, Claire D. *Adolescent Pregnancy Prevention: A Guidebook for Communities*. Stanford, Calif.: Health Promotion Resource Center, 1991.

The urgent need to prevent teenage pregnancy transcends race, economic status, religion, and other community characteristics. The goal of this manual is to help communities develop fully integrated, communitywide programs of education and prevention. By following the manual's program guidelines and methods for assessing needs, communities can create appropriate pregnancy- and risk-prevention strategies at the local level. (Adapted from publication.)

Children's Defense Fund. *The State of America's Children 1991*. Washington, D.C.: Children's Defense Fund, 1991.

This report looks at the future of American children and, ultimately, the future of our nation. How such trends as deteriorating family life, increased levels of poverty, inadequate health care, and rising numbers of violent crimes affect children is examined. The report provides recommendations for federal, state, and local governments and the private sector ranging from legislation and increased funding for pregnancy and AIDS prevention to the formation of family-school-community partnership programs to reverse the negative trends. (Adapted from publication.)

Children's Safety Network. *A Data Book of Child and Adolescent Injury*. Washington, D.C.: National Center for Education in Maternal and Child Health, 1991.

This source book on child and adolescent injury can assist those involved in injury-prevention efforts. The primary presentations are charts and graphs on injuries (automobile accidents, burns, rape, homicide, etc.) and related influences. According to the report, the United States needs more concentrated injury-prevention efforts and education. (Adapted from publication.)

Christenson, Peter G., and Donald F. Roberts. "Popular Music in Early Adolescence." Working paper commissioned by the Carnegie Council on Adolescent Development. Washington, D.C., January 1990.

The paper describes the developmental changes of early adolescence and the role that popular music plays in that development. Current research on adolescents' exposure to music, how they interpret its messages, what types of music they prefer, and how music affects mood and behavior is described. The implications of research on the use of music media to promote health-enhancing behavior among adolescents are discussed. The paper identifies potential opportunities for future study. (Adapted from publication.)

Cohen, Stu, and Renee Wilson-Brewer. "Violence Prevention for Young Adolescents: The State of the Art of Program Evaluation." A paper prepared by the Education Development Center (EDC), Inc., for the conference "Violence Prevention for Young Adolescents," held in Washington, D.C., July 12–13, 1990, supported by Carnegie Corporation of New York. Washington, D.C., September 1991.

As part of a nationwide survey of violence-prevention initiatives, EDC asked programs to describe evaluation tools they used to determine their own program effectiveness and success, and to identify barriers to evaluation. Ways to improve evaluation and expand successful programs are discussed. (Adapted from publication.)

Dryfoos, Joy G. *Adolescents at Risk.* New York: Oxford University Press, 1990.

One in four adolescents age ten to seventeen in the United States is at high risk for experiencing serious family, social, or educational problems. Dryfoos discusses the prevalence of adolescent delinquency, substance abuse, pregnancy, and dropping out of school, and the overlap of these high-risk behaviors. Successful interventions in each of these areas are discussed, and general concepts that are essential to the creation of effective programs are identified. (Adapted from publication.)

Feldman, S. Shirley, and Glen R. Elliott, eds. *At the Threshold: The Developing Adolescent.* Cambridge: Harvard University Press, 1990.

This edited volume synthesizes the most current knowledge about and research approaches to the study of normal early adolescent development. Researchers from psychology, biology, education, sociology, and other disciplines summarize advances made toward understanding the principles that shape this often misunderstood stage of life. The physiological and psychological changes of puberty, the social and environmental contexts in which these changes occur, and some of the uniquely adolescent behavioral, health-related, and coping processes are discussed. This volume highlights an interdisciplinary approach in the study of early adolescence and suggests opportunities for future research. (Adapted from publication.)

Flora, June A. "Strategies for Enhancing Adolescents' Health through Music Media." Commentary prepared in connection with the commissioned paper "Popular Music in Early Adolescence" by Peter G. Christenson and

Donald F. Roberts for the Carnegie Council on Adolescent Development, Washington, D.C., February 1990.

The commentary expands on the commissioned paper "Popular Music in Early Adolescence" by suggesting media strategies ranging from educational exchanges between media professionals and health educators to saturation of the media with tailored, health-promoting messages to enhance positive health behaviors in adolescents and their family members. A successful approach designed to increase the "healthfulness" of media requires a combination of strategies aimed at the media, advertisers, policymakers, and educators. Future areas for research and communication strategies are suggested. (Adapted from publication.)

Gans, Janet E., et al. *AMA Profiles of Adolescent Health Volume 1: America's Adolescents: How Healthy Are They?* Chicago: American Medical Association, 1990.

Approximately 25 percent of adolescents lead "high-risk" lives. Adolescents are experiencing health problems at earlier ages and are engaging in multiple unhealthy behaviors. The report presents trends in mortality, abuse and neglect, substance use, sexual activity, depression, and other risks among adolescents. The impact of race, ethnic group, poverty, age, and gender on adolescent life-styles and health is considered. Many of the debilitating health problems of adolescence rise from social and behavioral sources versus being biomedical in nature. (Adapted from publication.)

Gans, Janet E., Margaret A. McManus, and Paul W. Newacheck. *AMA Profiles of Adolescent Health Volume 2: Adolescent Health Care; Use, Costs, and Problems of Access.* Chicago: American Medical Association, 1991.

Fifteen percent of the nation's adolescents are uninsured according to this second volume in AMA's series on adolescent health. Volume 2 assesses how well the nation's health-care system meets the needs of adolescents. Some of the questions addressed are: Who among the adolescent population uses health-care services and for what reasons; how much adolescent health problems cost and who pays for them; what kinds of nonfinancial barriers are faced in the delivery of health care; and what steps should be taken to reduce financial barriers and also to make adequate health care accessible to all adolescents. (Adapted from publication.)

Gittler, Josephine, Mary Quigley-Rick, and Michael J. Saks. "Adolescent Health Care Decision Making: The Law and Public Policy." Paper prepared with the support of Carnegie Corporation of New York as a background paper for United States Congress Office of Technology Assessment's Adolescent Health Project. Washington, D.C., June 1990.

The paper provides a basic overview of the allocation of legal authority in adolescent health-care decision making among adolescents, their parents, health-care providers, and the state. Issues of parental consent and notification and an adolescent's right to confidentiality are covered. The authors also consider research and findings about the competency of adolescents to make decisions about their own health care. (Adapted from publication.)

Hamburg, David A. *Today's Children.* New York: Times Books, 1992.

Early childhood and early adolescence are two of the most crucial developmental periods for children. The author looks at both stages of development from a multidisciplinary perspective. How such trends as poor prenatal care, changes in family structure, substance abuse, inadequate child care, and high rates of poverty affect our youngest population and their opportunities to lead healthy, productive lives is analyzed. The author discusses specific interventions in education, health, and social environment to prevent damage to infants and young adolescents during these critical times in their lives. Examples of promising, innovative programs that are making a difference in young peoples' lives are described. (Adapted from publication.)

Hechinger, Fred M. *Fateful Choices: Healthy Youth for the 21st Century.* New York: Hill and Wang, 1992.

Young adolescents between the ages of ten and fifteen are at a crossroads, characterized by high risks and high hopes. Whether they grow up to be healthy, productive members of their community or follow a path toward permanent physical and psychological damage is society's choice and responsibility. Many risks, including pregnancy, sexually transmitted diseases, substance abuse, violence, and poor nutrition, touch the lives of all adolescents, regardless of socioeconomic status, and jeopardize their ability to learn and excel in school. The author recommends specific, fundamental changes in the way we educate our young adolescents about health, responsibility, and conflict resolution; in the way we provide health care to this population; in the way parents, teachers, and other adult role models involve themselves in the lives of teenagers, and in the way we deal with the health-threatening social trends in poverty, substance abuse, and violence. (Adapted from publication.)

Hendee, William R., ed. *The Health of Adolescents*. Chicago: American Medical Association, 1991.

This edited volume provides a comprehensive, interdisciplinary overview of adolescent health and development for professionals involved in adolescent health promotion. Healthy physical and psychological adolescent development is defined and contrasted with aspects of unhealthy behavior, including substance abuse, sexually transmitted disease, pregnancy, injury, and depression. The social factors that influence the kinds of decisions adolescents make about their health, problems and barriers to access and delivery of adequate health care, and ways to better meet the health-care needs of adolescents are discussed by researchers from a variety of disciplines. (Adapted from publication.)

Jones, Reginald L., ed. *Black Adolescents*. Berkeley, Calif.: Cobb and Henry, 1989.

Adolescence is a complicated process all young people go through. The contributors to this volume illustrate how environmental and social circumstance heighen the complexity of this period and create many unique challenges for black adolescents. What it means to be a black adolescent from psychological, sociological, medical, historical, and other perspectives is described. Many of the problems that all adolescents face—pregnancy, substance abuse, violence—have reached epidemic proportions in the black community. Race relations, urban stress, teenage parenting, and delinquency are some of the issues addressed from black perspectives. (Adapted from publication.)

National Commission on the Role of the School and the Community in Improving Adolescent Health. *Code Blue: Uniting for Healthier Youth*. Alexandria, Va.: National Association of State Boards of Education, 1990.

"For the first time in the history of this country, young people are *less* healthy and *less* prepared to take their places in society than were their parents." The unprecedented changes in society, community, and family have robbed young adolescents of the stability they need to grow up healthy, able to learn, and ready to participate in the world of work and community. To reverse the crisis facing our nation's youth, the National Commission has put forth a strategy based on making affordable, accessible, comprehensive health care a guaranteed right for all children and youth. The commission also recommends that an aggressive, coordinated battle for adolescent health be fought in the local communities and neighborhoods; that we organize health-care services to meet the needs of the people rather than the needs of the providers; and that we place a greater responsibility on schools to set high standards for healthy behavior. (Adapted from publication.)

National Guidelines Task Force. *Guidelines for Comprehensive Sexuality Education*. New York: Sex Education and Information Council of the U.S., 1991.

This guide provides a framework for sexuality education from kindergarten through twelfth grade. A suggested curriculum is provided to assist educators in creating comprehensive, developmentally appropriate programs that address the biological, psychological, cultural, and spiritual aspects of sexuality. The goals are to provide accurate information, to allow young people to explore their own sexual attitudes and values, to help them develop interpersonal and decision-making skills, and to encourage youth to develop and exercise sexual responsibility. The premise is that providing accurate information and the opportunity for honest dialogue about sexuality gives young people the insight to make health-enhancing, responsible decisions. (Adapted from publication.)

Prothrow-Stith, Deborah, and Michaele Weissman. *Deadly Consequences: How Violence Is Destroying Our Teenage Population and a Plan to Begin Solving the Problem*. New York: HarperCollins Publishers, 1991.

The authors approach the epidemic of violence within our teenage population from a public-health perspective. They explore the social contexts in which violence occurs, with emphasis on the impact of poverty in urban areas. Just as a network of preventive strategies successfully contributed to reductions in smoking and drunk driving, so too a consolidated effort to teach peaceful conflict resolution and ways of coping with anger could reduce violence on the streets and save lives. Prothrow-Stith recommends strong efforts to change behavior by deglamorizing violence in media and advertising, providing adult role models at home and in the school as guides and mentors for youth, and working with the family, school, and community to implement effective, targeted interventions. A state-by-state list of violence prevention programs is provided. (Adapted from publication.)

Task Force on Education of Young Adolescents. *Turning Points: Preparing American Youth for the 21st Century.* Washington, D.C.: Carnegie Council on Adolescent Development, June 1989.

"Middle grade schools . . . are potentially society's most powerful force to recapture millions of youth adrift, and help every young person thrive during early adolescence." The report of the Task Force recommends the transformation of middle-grade schools to better meet the needs of a generation of young adolescents faced with changing families and lack of community support. Intervention in the middle grades will benefit all adolescents, and especially those at high-risk for later problems. The Task Force recommends creating small, supportive learning communities where teachers provide close guidance and students engage in cooperative learning, placing a strong emphasis in the school on health-promoting behavior and fitness, and creating family and community partnerships with schools to enhance education and health-care support and opportunities. Concrete ways for educators, families, health promoters, legislators, and all concerned groups and individuals to implement Task Force recommendations are discussed. (Adapted from publication.)

U.S. Congress, Office of Technology Assessment. *Adolescent Health Volume 1: Summary and Policy Options*, OTA-H-468. Washington, D.C.: U.S. Government Printing Office, April 1991.

At the request of Congress, the Office of Technology Assessment (OTA) conducted an extensive review of the physical, emotional, and behavioral health status of the nation's 31 million adolescents. OTA found that one out of five adolescents has at least one serious health problem. *Volume I* of the three-volume report is the executive summary and considers the impact of race/ethnicity, gender, and poverty levels on adolescent health. Barriers to health care that are unique to adolescents, such as legal and confidentiality issues, are identified. *Volume I* also presents major policy options and specific strategies at the federal level to improve adolescent access to health care; strengthen and refocus federal efforts in data collection, basic research, and program evaluation; and foster positive environmental changes for our nation's adolescents. (Adapted from publication.)

U.S. Congress, Office of Technology Assessment. *Adolescent Health Volume II: Background and the Effectiveness of Selected Prevention and Treatment Services*, OTA-H-466. Washington, D.C.: U.S. Government Printing Office, November 1991.

Volume II defines adolescent health and takes an in-depth look at what it means to be an adolescent in terms of unique physical and mental health problems, emotional issues, and the impact of family and peer relationships on adolescent well-being. Current research findings and data, prevention programs, and treatment services for specific adolescent health problems—including sexually transmitted diseases, nutrition, pregnancy, and drug abuse—are presented. Gaps in research, legislation, and social services are identified. (Adapted from publication.)

U.S. Congress, Office of Technology Assessment. *Adolescent Health Volume III: Crosscutting Issues in the Delivery of Health and Related Services*, OTA-H-467. Washington, D.C.: U.S. Government Printing Office, June 1991.

Volume III focuses on the accessibility of adequate health care and the challenges and barriers adolescents face in obtaining services. The urgent need to bring health-care services to adolescents through school-linked and community-based health clinics, staffed by professionals trained to work with adolescents, is addressed. OTA also tackles the complex financial problems of health insurance, Medicaid funding, and benefit packages and the legal problems of parental consent and notification of treatment. Barriers to health care that affect selected groups of poor and minority adolescents are identified and discussed. (Adapted from publication.)

Wilson, Modena H., et al. *Saving Children: A Guide to Injury Prevention*. New York: Oxford University Press, 1991.

This guide for childhood injury prevention covers injuries on the highways, in the home, and in school and recreation environments. Injuries and accidents are discussed from a developmental perspective and those most prevalent for young adolescents are identified. Strategies for intervention, prevention, and education are addressed. (Adapted from publication.)

CONTRIBUTORS

GORDON M. AMBACH is executive director of the Council of Chief State School Officers, Washington, D.C.

MADALYN CIOCI is a doctoral student in organizational psychology at the University of Michigan.

JAMES P. COMER is the Maurice Falk Professor of Child Psychiatry at the Yale Child Study Center, associate dean of the Yale School of Medicine, and director of the school development program, Yale University.

JOY G. DRYFOOS is a researcher, writer, and lecturer supported by the Carnegie Corporation. She is author of *Adolescents-at-Risk: Prevalence and Prevention* (Oxford University Press, 1990).

JACQUELYNNE S. ECCLES is professor of psychology and chair of the Combined Program in Education and Psychology at the University of Michigan. She is author of "Development during Adolescence: The Impact of Stage/Environment Fit," *American Psychologist*, February 1993.

ROBERT W. GLOVER is a research scientist at the Center for the Study of Human Resources, the Lyndon B. Johnson School of Public Affairs, the University of Texas at Austin.

DAVID A. HAMBURG is president of the Carnegie Corporation of New York. He is author of *Today's Children: Creating a Future for a Generation in Crisis* (Times Books, Random House, 1992).

RENA D. HAROLD is associate professor in the School of Social Work at Michigan State University, and an adjunct associate research scientist at the Institute for Social Research at the University of Michigan. She is coauthor, with Allan Wigfield, of "Teacher Beliefs and Student's Achievement Self-Perceptions: A Developmental Perspective," in *Students' Perceptions in the Classroom: Causes and Consequences*, ed. D. H. Schunk and J. L. Meece (Lawrence Erlbaum, 1992).

FRED M. HECHINGER is senior advisor to Carnegie Corporation of New York. He is former education editor and editorial board member of the *New York Times*, and is author of *Fateful Choices: Healthy Youth for the 21st Century* (Hill and Wang, 1992).

H. CRAIG HELLER is the Bing Professor of Human Biology and Biological Sciences at Stanford University. He is coauthor of *LIFE: The Science of Biology* (published jointly by Freeman and Sinauer Associates, 1992).

KLAUS HURRELMANN is professor of sociology and education and director of the Research Center Prevention and Intervention in Childhood and Adolescence, University of Bielefeld, Germany. He is coeditor, with Friedrich Losel, of *Health Hazards of Adolescents* (De Gruyter, 1991).

NANCY LEFFERT is research associate in the Adolescent Mental Health Project, University of Minnesota.

RAY MARSHALL, who was Secretary of Labor under President Carter, holds the Audre and Bernard Rapoport Centennial Chair in Economics and Public Affairs at the University of Texas-Austin. He is coauthor, with Marc Tucker, of *Thinking for a Living: Education and the Wealth of Nations* (Basic Books, 1992).

DEBORAH W. MEIER is founder-principal of Central Park East Secondary School, a New York City public high school.

ELENA O. NIGHTINGALE is special advisor to the president of Carnegie Corporation of New York, adjunct professor of pediatrics at Georgetown University, and a lecturer in social medicine and health policy at Harvard University. She is author of "Children and Childhoods: Hidden Casualties of War and Civil Unrest," *JAMA*, August 1992.

ANNE C. PETERSEN is professor of adolescent development and pediatrics, vice president for research, and dean of the graduate school, University of Minnesota, Minneapolis. She is coauthor, with Jeylan Mortimer, of *Youth Unemployment and Society* (Cambridge University Press, forthcoming).

WENDY PENNER is a doctoral student in organizational psychology at the University of Michigan.

RICHARD PRICE is professor of organizational psychology at the University of Michigan. He is author of *Fourteen Ounces of Prevention* (American Psychological Association, 1988).

DONALD F. ROBERTS is Thomas More Stroke professor in the department of communications at Stanford University. He is coauthor, with Gary A. Fine and Jeylan T. Mortimer, of "Leisure, Work, and the Mass Media," in *At the Threshold: The Developing Adolescent*, ed. S. Shirley Feldman and Glen R. Elliott (Harvard University Press, 1990).

LINDA L. SCHOFF is administrative assistant to the Carnegie Council on Adolescent Development, Washington, D.C.

RUBY TAKANISHI is executive director of the Carnegie Council on Adolescent Development, Washington, D.C., an operating program of Carnegie Corporation of New York. She is author of "An Agenda for the Integration of Research and Policy during Early Adolescence," in *Early Adolescence: Perspectives on Research, Policy, and Intervention*, ed. Richard Lerner (Lawrence Erlbaum, forthcoming).

BARBARA TRAUTLEIN is a doctoral student in organizational psychology at the University of Michigan.

LISA WOLVERTON is a Ph.D. candidate in medieval studies at the University of Notre Dame and is currently pursuing dissertation research in Prague on a Fulbright Scholarship.

Index